LIVES OF
WOMEN PUBLIC
SCHOOLTEACHERS

WOMEN'S HISTORY AND CULTURE
VOLUME 8
GARLAND REFERENCE LIBRARY OF SOCIAL SCIENCE
VOLUME 833

WOMEN'S HISTORY AND CULTURE

LIVES OF WOMEN PUBLIC SCHOOLTEACHERS

SCENES FROM AMERICAN EDUCATIONAL HISTORY

MADELYN HOLMES
BEVERLY J. WEISS

GARLAND PUBLISHING, INC.
NEW YORK AND LONDON
1995

Library of Congress Cataloging-in-Publication Data

Holmes, Madelyn, 1945–
    Lives of women public schoolteachers : scenes from American educational
        history / Madelyn Holmes, Beverly J. Weiss.
            p.   cm. — (Women's history and culture ; vol. 8) (Garland refer-
    ence library of social science ; vol. 833)
        Includes bibliographical references and index.
        ISBN 0-8153-0838-8 (acid-free paper)
        1. Women teachers—United States—Biography.   2. Public schools—
    United States—History.   3. Women teachers—United States—Social con-
    ditions.   I. Weiss, Beverly J.   II. Title.   III. Title: Lives of women public
    schoolteachers.   IV. Series: Women's history and culture ; 8.   V. Series:
    Garland reference library of social science ; v. 833.
    LA2311.H58   1995
    371.1'0082—dc20
    [B]   95-3112
                                                                                       CIP

Printed on acid-free, 250-year-life paper
Manufactured in the United States of America

CONTENTS

PREFACE

In the early 1980s we were drawn to the burgeoning field of women's history and were struck by how women historians had by and large neglected the story of what women have actually done. Although they uncovered pioneers—the lonely women who led the way into medicine, politics, and science—historians have given short shrift to women who worked in the so-called women's professions: teaching, nursing, and fiction writing. Nancy Hoffman's pathbreaking documentary history of teachers, *Woman's "True" Profession,* which came out in 1981, was not followed by a chain of other books. We became convinced of the need to write about the lives of women schoolteachers.

Our book focuses on the careers of twelve women who taught in the public schools in the United States. Each of us had begun our research on teachers in Massachusetts before we met. Madelyn Holmes, an historian, had worked for two years at the Salem Maritime National Historic Site. She published an article in the *Essex Institute Historical Collections* in 1986 on women teachers in Salem before the Civil War. Beverly Weiss was a psychology professor at Framingham State College, the direct descendant of the first public normal school in the United States, where she participated in preservice and in-service teacher programs. In 1989 she edited *Pioneers in Education: A History of Framingham State College* on the occasion of its sesquicentennial celebration.

When we met in the mid-1980s, we began to discuss our mutual interest in public schoolteachers' narratives and decided to collaborate in writing a book that would supplement the traditional accounts of educational movements with research documenting how teachers actually taught and lived. It was also our observation that the role of normal schools had been largely neglected in the literature on the development of higher education for women in the nineteenth century. Finally, we wished to counteract the stereotypical profiles of early teachers and normal-school graduates that have commonly appeared in historical books and articles.

We chose the particular women in this book because we found their lives and work meaningful to us, and their narratives were consistent with our goals. While we do not contend that these women were representative of all teachers in the United States, the stories of their lives relate genuine chapters in educational history, and in some essential respects their careers mirror those of countless other forgotten women teachers. From our original focus on Massachusetts teachers in the nineteenth century, we gradually expanded to include both nineteenth- and twentieth-century teachers in the South, Midwest, and West. Our collaboration brings together profiles of Framingham-trained teachers with profiles of East and West Coast women schoolteachers and principals from the 1830s through the 1960s.

Madelyn Holmes selected teachers in Salem, Massachusetts, as examples of the first generation of women public schoolteachers. Although the two teachers profiled left scanty historical records, their long careers at the city's grammar schools for girls could nonetheless be traced amid the vast archive of historical data in Salem.

Beverly Weiss had begun to compile a series of narratives about the Normal School and its graduates, drawing on records that Marilyn Foley, the executive secretary of the Alumni Association, had made available to her at the Framingham State College Alumni House. Archivist Sally Phillips assisted in locating additional materials in the college's Whittemore Library. For this book, Beverly Weiss chose to write about Electa Lincoln Walton and Ellen Hyde because those two women exerted an enormous influence on the teaching at the Normal School throughout the nineteenth century.

Electa Lincoln Walton was associated with the Normal School during its early days in Lexington, Massachusetts, first as a student and then as a teacher and as acting principal. She remained in close contact with the Normal School throughout the century and was its historian and spokeswoman. Ellen Hyde, the principal of the Normal School from 1875 to 1898, was deeply conscious of the philosophy and ideals of the founders of the Normal School, and she had the knowledge and the administrative skills not only to implement them but also to refresh and professionalize them.

The remaining three Normal School graduates were chosen because they brought the best that the Normal School had to offer to other states. The life of Catherine Tilden Avery provided an opportunity to study a city school system in Ohio. There are many connections between Massachusetts and Ohio through its early colleges and schools, as well as through abolitionist activities; this biography provided an opportunity to trace a few of them. Marion P. Shadd was particularly intriguing because of the era in which she lived. She was a student in Washington, D.C., during Reconstruction and returned there to teach in the early days of the organization of the public schools in that city. Moreover, she is one of the few women of color identified as a graduate of the Normal School. Lelia Patridge left a substantial heritage in the form of two books about teaching. Unlike the other teachers whose stories are told here, her long career took her to several different states and school systems in Pennsylvania, Illinois, Florida, and Kentucky. Each experience made its own distinctive contribution to our narrative.

Madelyn Holmes chose rural teachers in Massachusetts and California so that she could compare women's lives on the East and West coasts. She focused on the rural community of Stow, Massachusetts, because the residents had shown an interest in their school history by restoring their 1825 one-room schoolhouse and making it a public museum. Living in the neighborhood of Stow for five years, she was able to uncover long-buried school documents and to interview an elderly niece of the schoolteacher she profiled. From a research base in Los Angeles, she was able to make contact with a still-existing rural school community in Santa Paula, California. The teacher profiled there was the longest-serving teacher at the one-room country school. She conducted interviews with farmers who had been students at the school during the 1930s, and she assembled local historical data generously supplied by Santa Paulan historian Mary Alice Orcutt Henderson.

For the chapter on twentieth-century urban schoolteachers, Madelyn Holmes selected a teacher in Cambridge, Massachusetts, and another in Los Angeles, California. She conducted research on the Cambridge public-school system while teaching at Harvard University; she chose to profile the sister of Tip O'Neill, the former speaker of the U.S. House of Representatives. Mary O'Neill Mulcahy's teaching career, which spanned more than forty years, included tenure as one of the first principals of a K–8 Cambridge public school. For her West Coast teacher profile, Madelyn Holmes selected Lucy Arline Jenson, who served as elementary-school teacher and principal in Los Angeles contemporaneously with Mary Mulcahy. Lucy Jenson had been principal of the West Los Angeles school that Madelyn Holmes attended, as well as teacher at the elementary school that her mother had attended in East Los Angeles.

Selecting a teacher from the South, Madelyn Holmes coordinated her choice to complement the African American teacher in Washington, D.C., whom Beverly Weiss had chosen to profile. Cora Webster Kelly, a white teacher from Alexandria, Virginia, taught during the late nineteenth and early twentieth centuries, contemporaneously with Marion Shadd. Both teachers were honored by the cities in which they taught, and their names now adorn elementary-school buildings. Madelyn Holmes carried out archival research at Lloyd House, a history library in Alexandria, and is indebted to Miriam Wiener, long-time resident of Alexandria and local historian, for assisting with interviews.

Many people have assisted us and encouraged us in our work. We wish to thank the following: Dr. Virginia Brereton of Tufts University; Margaret Coughlan of the Children's Literature Center of the Library of Congress; Robert Dudley of Santa Paula, California; Professor Christine Evans of Lesley College; Thelma Fletcher of Stow, Massachusetts; Professor Lois Gibson of Coker College; Mrs. A. Benay Glymph, principal at the Marion P. Shadd School in Washington, D.C.; Gail Grieb, archivist at Stetson University; Charles C. Hay III, archivist at Eastern Kentucky University; Judy Haven of the Gutman Library, Harvard Graduate School of Education; Dr. Milbry Jones of the U.S. Department of Education Library; Fritz Malval, archivist at Hampton University; Mrs. Ruth Metcalf, principal of the Santa Clara School; Professor Margaret Nelson of Middlebury College; Mrs. Jody Newman of the Stow Historical Society; Elizabeth Norris of the National YWCA; Professor Mary Jane Oates of Regis College; Mrs. Connie Schwarzkopf of West School Society in Stow, Massachusetts; Ann Sindelar of Western Reserve Historical Society; Mrs. Brenda Edmonds Wallace, a member of the Shadd family; and Mona Wei, archivist at Chicago State University.

We would also like to thank all of the people who shared their memories with us in interviews, many of whom we have quoted from and listed in endnotes. In addition, both of our families have helped us in manifold ways. Madelyn Holmes would like to thank her aunts Laura Sapp and Edith Steelman and uncle Bernard Steelman of Los Angeles, California, for assistance with her West Coast research. Beverly Weiss gratefully acknowledges the assistance and support of her colleagues at Framingham State College and particularly the Ellen Hyde Group.

To Lewis Holmes and Jerry Weiss

Practice School at Framingham Normal School, 1893.
Teacher, Miss Nellie Dale.

I INTRODUCTION

The end has come, as come it must
To all things; in these sweet June days
The teacher and the scholar trust
Their parting feet to separate ways.

They part: but in the years to be
Shall pleasant memories cling to each,
As shells bear inland from the sea
The murmur of the rhythmic beach. . . .

And one shall never quite forget
The voice that called from dream and play,
The firm but kindly hand that set
Her feet in learning's pleasant way. . . .

And, when the world shall link your names
With gracious lives and manners fine,
The teacher shall assert her claims,
And proudly whisper, "These were mine!"
                                    —John Greenleaf Whittier,
                        "'At School-Close' Bowdoin Street, Boston, 1877"[1]

There are almost forty-four million teachers in the world today, making "education the single largest modern wage-sector employer."[2] In the United States alone, nearly 2.4 million people teach in public schools.[3] Yet although books enumerating problems with schools are plentiful, books about successful schoolteachers are rare.

This is a book about the women teachers in various regions of the

United States who have made a difference in the lives of millions of Americans since the early 1800s. It relates a series of stories about women who have taught successfully in one-room classrooms, in multicultural city schools, in temporary bungalows, in traditional gender-segregated schools, in progressive schools, in racially segregated schools, in elementary and high schools, and in teacher training schools. Using historical documents, journals, oral histories and archival materials, we have placed these women in the context within which they spun out their careers and lived their lives.

These profiles focus attention on the successes of classroom teachers. The words of Ellen Hyde to the graduating class of the Framingham Normal School in 1886 still today capture the motivation of dedicated teachers: "To hear lessons and control restless children six hours a day through thirty-six weeks in the year is wretched drudgery, but to train and develop human minds and characters is the most inspiring work in the world."[4]

This book is about the practice of teaching; it describes what teachers have done and continue to do to work effectively with children. None of these women achieved prominence in her lifetime outside her local community. Today their accomplishments are largely unknown, even though, in a few cases, their names adorn buildings in the communities where they lived and worked.

Yet each teacher had a significant impact. She influenced her society, her community, sometimes more than one generation of young people, and— probably most significantly to each teacher—she changed a few individual lives through the students she nurtured and taught. These teachers continue to offer us, their students too, a window on the past, models of professional women who developed strategies for themselves based on their own values and gifts. Although some readers may be struck by the constraints under which they labored, these women, themselves aware of the demands and the difficulties of their work, did not fret about constraints. They were consumed by what they could and did accomplish in the field of public education.

We have chosen to write about women teachers because they have dominated the teaching workforce in the United States since the 1860s. By 1890, when nearly 400,000 teachers taught in public schools, women comprised 66 percent of the total. The proportion of women public schoolteachers peaked in 1920, at which time they represented 86 percent of a total of 719,188 teachers.[5] In the modern era following World War II, the size of the teaching force has more than doubled, increasing from 1,045,125 in 1950 to 2,398,000 in 1991. Women constituted 79 percent of all teachers in 1950 and 72.1 percent in 1991.[6]

Women have been connected so closely with the profession that teaching, especially of young children, has been viewed as a woman's job, "an extension of the female role at home."[7] Women, however, also have outnumbered men as secondary schoolteachers. "By 1880, women were already 60 percent of high-school teachers—and a similar proportion of their students."[8]

It took women a longer time to enter administrative positions in public schools. Not until 1909, when Ella Flagg Young was appointed superintendent of schools in Chicago, were women deemed qualified to head metropolitan school systems. Nevertheless, in rural counties throughout the Midwest and West, the job of county superintendent of schools was frequently filled by a woman by the beginning of the twentieth century. On the state level, Georgia Lee Witt Lusk pioneered as superintendent of public instruction in New Mexico from 1930 to 1959, and the position of elementary-school principal had become a woman's job by 1940.[9]

Because women have long dominated the profession of schoolteaching in the United States, this book will document "what women actually did on their jobs," describing characteristics "such as income and status, hours and demands and occupational culture."[10] Teachers have most often taught in isolated classrooms, and many still do today despite trends toward team teaching, peer coaching, and other collaborative techniques. They use materials in their unique ways, supplementing them with projects and constructions of their own, and they develop relationships with children given into their care, often igniting a spark that will last a lifetime. But they and their successes may be invisible except to those who were their students.

Former Under Secretary General of the United Nations Ralph Bunche remembered Emma Belle Sweet, teacher at Fourth Ward Elementary School in Albuquerque, New Mexico, who awakened him to his potential.[11] Political writer Theodore White wrote about his "marvelous" sixth-grade teacher, Miss Fuller, at the Christopher Gibson School in Boston. She made him realize how important history was, "driving home the point that history connected to now, to us."[12]

It has always been difficult to define what combination of qualities creates a good teacher. According to Irving Howe: "In my own experience as a teacher, I came to believe there was something mysterious in the art of good teaching—some mixture of intellectual seriousness and natural rapport."[13] Writer and education critic Neil Postman tried to pinpoint what makes for good teaching and ended up with a similar conclusion: "There are as many methods of good teaching as there are ways by which teachers communicate a love of learning, a respect for facts, a fascination for an idea."[14]

However elusive the qualities of a good teacher may be, each of us remembers one or two special teachers who made learning important to us and made us feel able to learn. We agree with Tracy Kidder, author of *Among School Children*, a book about contemporary teacher Christine Zajac, when he says, "A lot of what you read about education strays into the general. . . . I learned that education is what happens in these little rooms."[15] The lives and working conditions detailed in our book could be replicated by the thousands or even millions of forgotten women whose histories lie buried in local communities. Women teachers might say with William Pickens, a former slave, that their stories should be written, not because they were outstanding examples but because there were so many of them.[16]

Our narratives about teachers will permit us to highlight some of the pivotal changes in public education and to trace some of the recurring issues and debates among educators and citizens who, in the end, must support the system with their taxes. We can identify educational philosophies and practices as they have changed and recurred over the years.

Historians have analyzed educational history by examining institutional growth, changes in pedagogical theory and practices, and even political and social change as reflected in school systems. Rarely, however, have historians written about the people who have done the educating, the schoolteachers. But the stories of their lives constitute an important record, not only because they document the professionalism of teaching, but also because they tell of the development of roles for women outside the home.

Systems of public education had their origins in the nineteenth century. Although there were schools, many of them receiving public support, in the seventeenth, eighteenth, and early nineteenth centuries, they were not the organized, graded, structured systems that emerged in the late nineteenth century.[17] Moreover, in the new republic, education for girls had not been treated with the same urgency as education for boys. Education for boys antedated education for girls by two centuries. It was not until the end of the eighteenth century that public schools began to open to girls, and often then only at times when the boys were not using them. When coeducation in the common schools did begin to emerge, early in the nineteenth century, it was gradual and often dictated by economic considerations: that is, when a community could not afford separate schools. Around 1800, one teacher in ten was a woman,[18] and the surge toward education for girls and women had begun.

During the first decades of the nineteenth century, academies and seminaries for women were established. Emma Hart Willard founded Troy Female Seminary in Troy, New York, in 1821, and Catharine Beecher started Hartford Female Seminary in Hartford, Connecticut, in 1823. In Massachusetts, Bradford Academy, coeducational at the beginning, opened in 1803. The first academy incorporated for girls alone was at Pittsfield in 1807, followed by Joseph Emerson's Ladies Seminary at Byfield (1818) and Saugus (1824). George B. Emerson, later a proponent of the normal schools and for many years a member of the Massachusetts Board of Education, opened a private secondary school for girls in Boston in 1823, and Mt. Holyoke Seminary was incorporated in 1837.[19] This list, not an exhaustive one, illustrates the growing concern for education for girls and women and the rapidity with which young women who had the economic means embraced the opportunities for acquiring an education, limited though it was. Young women who did not have access to private academies had very little choice, for in 1837 there were fewer than twenty public high schools in Massachusetts.[20]

The academies and seminaries accomplished several important purposes. First, they demonstrated that "sex differences were not of as much importance in education as had been supposed."[21] In time, they contributed to creating a pool of young women who were educated well enough to make it feasible to open colleges exclusively for women. The first private women's colleges in Massachusetts, however, were still a long way off in 1839 when the first normal school began its work in Lexington. The normal schools, institutions established to train teachers, were the forerunners of many of the institutions we call state colleges today. Their histories followed similar patterns in that most of them became teachers' colleges around 1930 and made the transition to liberal arts colleges about 1960. The first public normal school was established in Lexington, Massachusetts, in 1839, moved to West Newton in 1844, and to Framingham in 1853. In 1932 it was designated Framingham State Teachers College, and in 1960 it became a liberal arts college, Framingham State College.

The establishment of normal schools in Massachusetts has attracted the attention of historians interested in the development of public schools and of educators seeking the roots of concepts, issues, and practices still embedded in public schools today. The interest has centered on Massachusetts, because it was the first state to initiate and subsidize schools for the express and limited purpose of training teachers for the public schools. That was the centerpiece of a program to improve public education. For his role in this enterprise, Horace Mann, the first secretary of the Massachusetts Board of Education and an evangelist for the cause of school reform, has often been called the Father of Public Education.

The arguments about public education, then as now, were waged on philosophic grounds, over political considerations, and over religious issues.

But though the rhetoric still flows about the protagonists' intentions,[22] relatively little has been written about the actual lives and experiences of the students and teachers in the normal schools. Who were they? What did they teach, what did they learn, and how did they go about it? What did they think they were doing? What did they do when they graduated? The establishment of the normal schools was called "the great experiment," but it was those students and teachers who were the experiment. Had they not come to study at the normal schools or had many of them failed to teach well, "the experiment" would have been no more than a footnote in a chapter we cannot even imagine.

Analyses of the normal schools written in recent years tend to emphasize what the authors consider to have been the weaknesses of the normal schools in the nineteenth century.[23] They speak of the generally low educational level of the candidates, and the fact that many of them were young women who did not expect to make teaching a lifelong career. Quoting from the journal of Cyrus Peirce, the first teacher and principal at the Lexington Normal School, Jurgen Herbst cites Peirce's frustrations with his students.[24] Peirce was dissatisfied with many of his pupils' abilities and accomplishments. But as Arthur O. Norton points out in his introduction to Peirce's journal, "It [the journal] does not represent fairly the teacher who during these years was impressing upon his students—girls of sixteen, seventeen and eighteen years—lifelong habits, enthusiasms, and ideals, and a professional outlook as teachers."[25] Indeed, it is Mary Swift's journal that gives a "matter-of-fact, copious and systematic" account of the lessons, Peirce's methods of teaching, and the flow of life at the school.[26] It is, in part, through Mary Swift's pen that we come to understand the value of how and what Peirce taught. Nor does Peirce's account represent fairly the work of the young women who impressed distinguished visitors to the Normal School, such as Dr. Samuel Howe, Horace Mann, and George B. Emerson, as well as the school committees in the towns where the women went to teach.[27]

We have included in this book biographical sketches of women who were graduated from the Lexington/West Newton/Framingham Normal School because the influence of that Massachusetts school was so widespread. Many of them were intelligent, dedicated women who were well educated for their time and circumstances. They played a significant role in the development of the normal school, and they carried the ideals, philosophy, and educational practices to schools throughout the country and abroad. In these portraits, including that of an African American teacher, the reader will find documentation of the commitment and professionalism of normal-school graduates. Their lives counter the bleak characterization of normal-school graduates commonly found in critical analyses.

If the teachers shared some of the cultural prejudices of their times, and some of them obviously did, they also struggled to change the inequities they saw. Some, such as Electa Lincoln Walton, acted forthrightly; others, such as Marion P. Shadd, acted more circumspectly. As Ann Gordon has pointed out, women of the nineteenth century did not necessarily define themselves as powerless because they lacked the right to vote. Rather, they "acted upon a multiplicity of ideas about the common good and exercised power in myriad ways short of voting."[28] Our own values may shape how we perceive their efforts, but these women's lives can serve as catalysts for reflective examination of today's choices, goals, and strategies.

The profiles in this book focus on the working lives of teachers and administrators, featuring personal achievements. We describe each teacher's schooling and education, training for teaching, family background, and marital status. With these biographical details, we hope to illuminate portraits of genuine American schoolteachers. We subject stereotypical images of the schoolteacher to the scrutiny of historical study.

Although the details of individual stories are specific to the teachers and school systems described, many of the textbooks, classroom practices, school policies, and writings of school superintendents represent chapters in educational history. We look at how teaching methods as well as working conditions have varied over the two centuries. And we identify the special qualities that made each woman successful, describing how each reacted to the expectations of students, parents, and school committees. In this book we explore the lives of a number of teachers who taught America's children with dedication, skill, and compassion. Yet, in these pages, we are reminded again and again that "[t]he growth of American public education over the past two centuries owes much to the philanthropy of teachers, effort above and beyond what could reasonably be purchased either by their salaries or any intangible benefits that came their way."[29]

NOTES

1. John Greenleaf Whittier, *The Complete Poetical Works of John Greenleaf Whittier*, ed. Horace E. Scudder (Boston: Houghton Mifflin, Cambridge Edition, 1894), 234–35.

2. International Labour Organisation, *Teachers: Challenges of the 1990s* (Geneva: International Labour Office, 1991), 11.

3. National Center for Education Statistics, *Pocket Digest of Education Statistics 1992* (Washington, D.C.: U.S. Department of Education, 1993), 2.

4. Unpublished material. Framingham State College Alumni Association Archives.

5. Lawrence A. Cremin, *American Education, the Metropolitan Experience, 1876–1980* (New York: Harper & Row, 1988), 554.

6. National Center for Education Statistics, *Digest of Education Statistics 1992* (Washington, D.C.: U.S. Department of Education, 1993), 78.

7. Sari Knopp Biklen, "Women in American Elementary School Teaching: A Case Study," in *Women Educators: Employees of Schools in Western Countries*, ed. Patricia A. Schmuck (Albany: State University of New York Press, 1987), 226.

8. Geraldine Joncich Clifford, "Man/Woman/Teacher: Gender, Family and Career in American Educational History," in *American Teachers: Histories of a Profession at Work*, ed. Donald R. Warren (New York: Macmillan, 1989), 296.

9. Ibid., 328.

10. Biklen, 227.

11. James Haskins, *Ralph Bunche: A Most Reluctant Hero* (New York: Hawthorn Books, 1974), 17.

12. Theodore H. White, *In Search of History: A Personal Expedition* (New York: Harper & Row, 1978), 51.

13. Irving Howe, *New York Times Book Review* (May 20, 1990): 3.

14. Neil Postman, *Teaching as a Conserving Activity* (New York: Delacorte Press, 1979), 214.

15. Bruce McCabe, "The Soul of a Fifth-Grade Class," *Boston Globe*, 30 Aug. 1989.

16. William Pickens, *Bursting Bonds* (Boston: Jordan & More Press, 1923; reprint, Bloomington: Indiana University Press, 1991).

17. Michael J. Katz, *Reconstructing American Education* (Cambridge: Harvard University Press, 1987), 6.

18. Nancy Hoffman, *Woman's "True" Profession: Voices from the History of Teaching* (Old Westbury, N.Y.: Feminist Press, 1981), xv.

19. Thomas Woody, *A History of Women's Education in the United States*, vol. 1 (New York: Octagon Books, 1966), 341–43.

20. *Massachusetts Board of Education Report* (Boston, 1877), 39.

21. Edwin G. Dexter, *A History of Education in the United States* (New York: Macmillan, 1919), 433.

22. For example, see C. L. Glenn, Jr., *The Myth of the Common School* (Amherst: University of Massachusetts Press, 1988).

23. In addition to Glenn, see Jurgen Herbst, *And Sadly Teach: Teacher Education and Professionalism in American Culture* (Madison: University of Wisconsin Press, 1989), and J. Messerli, *Horace Mann: A Biography* (New York: Alfred A. Knopf, 1972).

24. Jurgen Herbst, "Teacher Preparation in the Nineteenth Century," in *American Teachers, Histories of a Profession at Work*, ed. Donald R. Warren (New York: Macmillan 1989), 219.

25. Arthur O. Norton, *The First State Normal School in America: The Journals of Cyrus Peirce and Mary Swift* (Cambridge: Harvard University Press, 1926), xx.

26. Ibid.

27. Samuel J. May, the second principal of the Normal School at Lexington, solicited information in 1844 about teachers who had studied at the school. A sampling of the eighty-three responses was published in the *Eighth Annual Report of the Massachusetts Board of Education* (1845); they indicated a high degree of satisfaction with these young women and their teaching.

28. Ann D. Gordon, "Writing the Lives of Women," *NWSA Journal* 1 (Winter 1988–89): 223.

29. Warren, *American Teachers*, 8.

WOMEN TEACHERS
IN NEW ENGLAND

Common, or public, schools in New England predated the establishment of the new republic, and there was a substantial increase in their number in the Commonwealth of Massachusetts after 1789 when laws were enacted requiring towns to support public education. Many of the newly created schools, however, faced problems and aroused public controversy: school buildings were often inadequate and unsanitary; books and instructional materials were in short supply; many teachers were incompetent; attendance was erratic; children were often not admitted until they could read and write; and support and supervision depended entirely on the local community.

By 1820 concerned citizens, such as James G. Carter, a young Harvard graduate, began to write pamphlets and newspaper articles calling attention to the deplorable conditions of the common schools. Carter mapped out a constructive policy to improve public education but met with strong opposition as well as support for his proposals. Some cities and towns in Massachusetts rejected any measures that would permit state interference in local affairs or that would centralize power in the hands of state officials. There were also citizens who wished to preserve the privileges of money and birth and who did not want to support public schools at all, favoring instead the private academies already available to those who could afford them.

A more general interest in popular education had sparked the establishment in Boston of the American Lyceum in 1826, and in 1830 a splinter group of professional educators and laymen interested in improving the common schools formed an organization called the American Institute of Instruction. Both the Lyceum and the Institute of Instruction sponsored lectures for the public on the improvement of education and the preparation of teachers.

Central to the discussions about how to improve public education was the issue of the competence of schoolteachers. Carter felt deeply about the issue of teacher preparation and tried unsuccessfully in 1827 to enact legislation to establish teacher-training schools. Critics feared that such schools would become regimented and that graduates of state normal schools, as they were called,[1] would have undue influence. Others argued that the ability to teach was inborn and that teaching pedagogy was impractical or worthless.

In the 1830s Lyceum lecturers described European models for teacher training to Americans, praising especially the Prussian state seminaries and the normal institutes in France. In Europe, those institutions trained young men, but in the United States voices had been heard advocating educational opportunities for women. In 1835 Catharine Beecher, who was a well-known speaker for the cause of the employment of female teachers, delivered an address to the American Lyceum supporting publicly funded schools for training teachers.

George B. Emerson, a prominent Boston educator, eloquently presented the arguments for establishing teacher training as a means of improving public education in a memorial (a position paper) conveyed to the legislature on behalf of the American Institute of Instruction in January 1837. The memorial was referred to the committee on education, presided over by James G. Carter, and it was he who drafted the law that created the Massachusetts Board of Education. On 20 June 1837 the board chose Horace Mann as its secretary, setting in motion his twelve years of active campaigning for the improvement of public education.

Mann supplemented the information supplied in annual town reports with his own observations from visits to schools throughout the commonwealth. Except in the largest cities, each school district employed two teachers each year. During a summer term of approximately four months the teacher was usually a young woman, seventeen or eighteen years of age. There was also a winter term of ten to twelve weeks, often taught by young men who were college students. In short, Mann estimated that although six thousand teachers were employed in the commonwealth each year, not more than two hundred of them regarded teaching as their vocation. Most teachers had no education beyond the basic reading, writing, and arithmetic they had learned in district schools, and many were deficient even in those areas.

Mann and the board of education concluded that the greatest single problem with free public schools was the lack of competent, committed teachers. In their first report to the legislature on 1 February 1838, the board urged the establishment of institutions for the training of teachers. It was the intention that the schools concentrate on the teaching of principles of pedagogy to avoid competition with the academies. Since there were fewer than twenty public high schools (some exclusively for men) in Massachusetts at that time, the challenge would lie also in finding suitably educated candidates for the normal schools.

The recommendation might still have met with indifference and delay except for the generosity of Edmund Dwight, a Boston merchant and member of the Massachusetts Board of Education. He offered $10,000 for the purpose of establishing "teachers seminaries," on the condition that the legislature appropriate an equal amount. The proposal was accepted and the legislature decided to establish three normal schools, one located in each of three regions of the state: northeastern (at Lexington/West Newton/Framingham), central (at Barre/Westfield), and southeastern (at Bridgewater).

The first normal school to open was the northeastern one, headed by principal Cyrus Peirce. On a rainy 3 July 1839 at a former academy building on the corner of the common in Lexington, Massachusetts, three young women (Hannah Damon, Sarah Hawkins, and Maria L. Smith) were examined for competence in the basic subjects by Horace Mann, Cyrus Peirce, George Putnam, Robert Rantoul, Jr. and Jared Sparks. They were admitted to the first state-supported teacher-training institution in the United States. The first normal school was established exclusively for women, and it was important not only because it was the first step in creating a corps of professional teachers (the majority of whom would be women) but also because it gave societal approval to new roles for women outside of the home.

The teachers profiled in this first section were participants in the evolving system of public education in the nineteenth century. Without the commitment and success of dedicated teachers such as these four women, there would have been little public school reform. Moreover, the stories of their teaching careers contribute to a fuller understanding of women's history. These women demonstrated the feasibility of placing women in charge of schools, and that it was possible as a schoolteacher in New England in the nineteenth century to have an impact on American society. They thereby widened women's sphere of influence and helped to create opportunities for their personal growth.

Mary Shepard and Mary Jane Fitz, teachers in Salem, were the first generation, starting out as untrained assistant teachers when they were teenagers and advancing to principalships of grammar schools for girls. Electa Lincoln Walton, portrayed in chapter 3, prepared herself to teach by attending the normal school. She then returned after a time to teach other prospective teachers and to serve as acting principal. Eventually, she broadened her educational activities, teaching elsewhere in Massachusetts, writing arithmetic textbooks with her husband, and organizing political movements in behalf of women and minorities.

The life of Ellen Hyde, portrayed in chapter 4, demonstrates the widening influence and sphere of opportunities open to the following generation of women teachers. She entered the Normal School, now located in Framingham, as a student in 1861, became a teacher there in 1863, and served as principal from 1875 to 1898. As principal of Framingham Normal School, she vigorously adhered to the original mission of the school: to prepare women to teach in elementary school. Ellen Hyde was the sole woman serving as a normal-school principal, and as such she commanded great respect within her community.

These four nineteenth-century women were dedicated and successful teachers; they left their imprint on their profession, their communities, and other women. Yet each of them worked within the educational system to bring about change; they were team players, not rebels or victims. The Salem grammar school principals managed large city schools, teaching young women to be upright, proud, American citizens. They taught the curricula the school committees mandated, using designated textbooks and examinations. At the Normal School, Electa Lincoln Walton and Ellen Hyde furthered the cause of professional teacher education. Both of them espoused the concepts, ideals, and practices of the founders of the school, particularly those of Cyrus Peirce and Horace Mann. They were also role models, independent and self-reliant women, actively involved in ameliorating the country's social problems.

NOTES

1. The designation "normal" was derived from the French *école normale*, or model school.

TEACHING IN SALEM, MASSACHUSETTS, 1830s–1860s: MARY LAKEMAN SHEPARD AND MARY JANE FITZ

Madelyn Holmes

Mary Lakeman Shepard, teacher from 1840 to 1869, had "her special gift for teaching and a manner all her own full of strong personal influence. She had the desire and power to make others see what she saw, know what she knew, feel what she felt, and to lift them above lower aims to the beauty of noble life. How interesting as a tale of romance, she made the lessons in history, geography or literature."[1]

Her contemporary, Mary Jane Fitz, who taught from 1836 to 1872, approached her job as principal of a Salem grammar school in an entirely different manner: "In the management of the school, no attempt is made at mere show, but the studies appropriate to each class are pursued with diligence, and a good degree of success; the principal judging, as we think wisely, that the essential, and solid matter of a good education should not give place to that of a more shallow and fanciful character."[2]

The careers and methods of teaching of these two women were intimately connected to the time in which they lived. During the decades in which they taught, Massachusetts (and specifically the city of Salem) was changing in several ways. Economically, the state had begun to assume an industrial profile, with railways and large textile factories in Lowell, Lawrence, and Salem. The formerly agricultural society became one of manufacturing centers populated by factory workers and Irish and French-Canadian immigrants.

Politically, the all-powerful Whigs saw their dominance erode during these years. The Democrats said they represented the groups left behind by the economic changes transforming the state. The Liberty Party focused on one issue—abolition of slavery—until 1848, when it expanded to include other reform issues and resurfaced as the Free Soil Party. The American Party, which in the 1850s became the Know Nothings, campaigned against new immigrants, specifically Catholics. Finally, in the years immediately preceding the Civil War, the Republican Party emerged as a unifying force in state politics until the end of the 1860s.

Social changes, however, touched the schoolteachers' lives most directly. Religious practice in Massachusetts became more varied by new strains of Protestantism and a growing Catholic population. At the same time, the established Christian denominations experienced upheavals in doctrine, affected by the growing influence of Unitarianism and transcendentalism. This was the age of the Lyceum lectures by Ralph Waldo Emerson, Henry Thoreau, and Salem's native son, Nathaniel Hawthorne. Women's participation in society was beginning to extend beyond the limits of the household, with the employment of female textile operators in Lowell, a burgeoning corps of women writers, and the expanding employment of women as schoolteachers.

The rapid increase in the proportion of female schoolteachers in the Salem school system elicited comment from the Salem school committee in 1846. "It will be seen that there are now but 8 Male Teachers constantly employed, while there are 48 Female Teachers, a large portion of whom perform the services for which but a few years since Males only were deemed competent."[3] This phenomenon was only a few years old, for it was in 1839 that the Massachusetts legislature enacted a law requiring the appointment of female assistant teachers at any school with more than one hundred students.

It was also during these years that public education in Massachusetts began to take shape as a state institution. Although there had been district schools and laws requiring towns to provide for public schooling as far back as the establishment of the republic in 1789, it was not until the 1830s that public-school education became organized into a system and in fact became a cultural and political cause. When Horace Mann was made secretary of the Massachusetts board of education in 1837, the reform of public schools became a moral crusade.

Mann's purpose and the underlying motivation for the reforms he undertook during the twelve years of his term have been the subject of controversy. Some twentieth-century critics have accused Mann and the board of education of leading a capitalist plot to reduce the lower classes to an obedient work force. Others have seen the systematization of the public schools as a means to combat street crime and juvenile delinquency. Still others have understood Mann's motive to have been the propagation of Unitarian religious beliefs. Perhaps all express an element of truth; the public schools of Massachusetts did impose both a philosophy and a method for educating the state's youth. Mary Shepard and Mary Jane Fitz played a role in that reform.

Mary Lakeman Shepard lived from 1824 to 1893 in the city of Salem. She was born on 30 May 1824, the daughter of Lydia Lakeman and Isaac Billings Shepard, a mariner. She became a grammar-school teacher in 1840 at the age of sixteen. She was employed as an assistant at the West School for Boys, later known as the Hacker School, until her appointment at the end of 1851 as principal of the Higginson School for girls. It was as principal of one of Salem's two public grammar schools for girls that she became well known and acclaimed both by students and the school committee. Her career as a teacher ended after twenty-nine years in 1869, when she was forty-five years old.

Mary Jane Fitz, two years older, was born on 19 January 1822, in the nearby town of Ipswich. Her parents were Mary Poland and Josiah Fitz, a carpenter. In 1836, at the age of fourteen, she was hired as an assistant teacher at the East School for Girls, and at sixteen she became teacher of the lower division. She remained in that position until 1845, when she was promoted to school principal, a job she held until her retirement in 1872.

The city of Salem, where the two women grew up, had already established a three-tier public school system, one of the earliest in the United States. The commonwealth of Massachusetts had from the beginning been a forerunner in public education, and Salem, as one of the first settlements, had participated fully in each new step taken to further education. Accordingly, Salem had opened a grammar school in 1637, only two years after the founding of Boston Latin School. In compliance with the Massachusetts school law of 1789, Salem had established primary schools for children from four to seven years of age and grammar schools for ages seven to fourteen. Salem was also among the earliest towns to institute secondary education in the form of the American high school.

Girls in Salem, however, had not been offered the same public education as boys. At a town meeting in February 1793 it had been voted that girls were to be instructed at the boys' writing schools for "two hours per day, one hour after the close of the morning session and one hour after the afternoon session."[4] But the Salem school committee reported in 1827 that in fact girls were not receiving any public-school instruction beyond the rudiments of a primary-school education.

The town meeting therefore authorized on 16 May 1827 the creation of two grammar schools for girls. In 1845, long after a town high school had been established in Salem, a high school for girls, the Saltonstall School, was instituted. Nonwhite children in Salem had also been excluded from the public school system. In 1807 the town opened a separate primary school for "colored children"; racially segregated education continued until 1843.

Although Salem was early in creating public schools, they competed with a strong private educational system. By the 1830s many more Salem children, particularly girls, received their primary-school education in private schools rather than in the eight public schools, taught exclusively by women. The primary schools were coeducational and accommodated from forty to fifty children.

Following success in the examinations, a Salem child of the 1830s could enter a grammar school—boys at age six, girls at nine. Regardless of their sex, children had to be able to read the Testaments and spell words of three syllables. The East School for Girls, where Mary Jane Fitz later became principal, educated 135 girls. It operated under a monitorial system, which meant that the older girls listened to the recitations of the younger ones. In 1836 Rufus Putnam, school principal, hired Miss Fitz as the second assistant at a salary of $30 per year. "As an additional inducement to these young ladies to remain in school, the master gave them private instruction, without charge, in some higher branches of study, as Latin, French, algebra, etc."[5] By 1838 Mary Jane Fitz was no longer a grammar school student but rather a full-time schoolteacher. She was soon promoted to teacher of the lower division of the school at an annual salary of $100. By 1842 the student body had increased to 212 girls and the principal employed three assistant teachers, including Miss Fitz, each paid $150. His salary was $700.

In 1845, the school committee voted to end male exclusiveness and gave two female teachers, Hannah Jelly and Mary Jane Fitz, authority to head the two girls' grammar schools. At that time the name of the school was changed to the Bentley School, in honor of the Reverend William Bentley. Mary Jane Fitz served as principal of the Bentley School for twenty-seven years, retiring at the age of fifty. The city of Salem praised her performance as principal: She served "in that capacity with great acceptance. The thoroughness and conscientiousness manifested in her work making her a valuable teacher."[6]

Mary Shepard probably attended the West School for Girls; her family's address was 22 North Street, in the west side of Salem. In the 1830s that grammar school enrolled 107 girls. Mary Shepard's teaching career began in 1840 with her appointment as an assistant teacher at the West School for Boys. Her salary was $150 per year. This grammar school, established in 1785, became known in 1845 as the Hacker School in memory of the school's first teacher, Isaac Hacker. The 140 Hacker School boys were taught by the principal and two other female assistants in addition to Mary. By 1850, however, the student body had decreased to 120 boys and only two assistants were still teaching.

The school offered instruction in a large number of subjects but the boys were examined in only four: arithmetic, reading, grammar (which included writing compositions), and geography. In addition, the boys studied drawing, vocal music, history, bookkeeping, and the elements of geometry and algebra.

During Mary Shepard's twelve years as assistant teacher at the Hacker School, "her special gift for teaching" became well known "on both sides of the Atlantic."[7] The Salem school committee appointed her principal of the Higginson School for Girls (formerly the West School for Girls) at the end of 1851, when she was twenty-seven years old. Writing in the school committee report of 1852 Henry Wheatland, a committee member, stated: "She has only had charge of the School for three months and from present indications we have no reason to regret the appointment."[8]

Female principals were paid less than half the salary of male grammar-school principals. Mary Shepard was hired at an annual salary of $300; male principals in Salem's grammar schools earned $700. Enrollment at the Higginson School was higher than at the Hacker School, approximately 160. The staff, consisting of three assistant female teachers in addition to Mary, taught the same subjects taught to boys. The only discernible difference was a policy established in 1848 to introduce "plain sewing as a branch of study into the female department of the grammar schools."[9]

During Mary Shepard's seventeen-year tenure at the Higginson School her special talent as a teacher was given full scope. As was most often noted, her prowess as a teacher of reading, composition writing, history, and geography revealed "her superior talents and acquirements." When she retired in 1869, the school committee minced no words in praise of her: "Few teachers have a higher ideal of their duty, or have striven more earnestly and successfully to make that ideal a fact."[10]

What Mary did in the classroom more than one hundred years ago remains good teaching today: "The scholars are practised here more in the exercise of their reasoning powers, and drawing inferences or conclusions from the subject contained in their lessons, than in the mere recitation drill of committing to memory the words of the respective authors."[11] Not only did she make her students think, but she effused an "unusual spirit and enthusiasm" that aroused in her students a genuine interest in learning.

The way she taught contemporary history —the Civil War—made the subject come alive for her students. Some afternoons were "devoted to scraping lint for the soldiers while her words, fired with patriotism, enforced the lessons of the war."[12] She successfully combined subjects, such as history and grammar. Some of her students wrote compositions, part of the grammar course, on topics "relating to the early history of this country, and described in a very felicitous style the peculiar characteristics of our pilgrim fathers."[13] The school committee praised her approach, for "it not only practices the pupils in this study but also incites to historical research."[14]

Even such a seemingly dry but important subject as geography was enlivened "by her freshness of manner and method."[15] During the three decades Mary Shepard spent in the classroom the teaching of geography underwent important changes, and many new textbooks were written. The underlying purpose and the hoped-for result, however, remained intact. It was through geography that a sense of patriotism was to be instilled. The most widely used means of accomplishing that goal was to praise local people and criticize everyone else.

One of the most blatant examples of that attitude is found in the earliest geography textbook written by an American, *Geography Made Easy*, by Episcopal minister Jedidiah Morse. Although published in 1784, the twenty-third edition of his *New System of Geography* (1822) was still widely used in Massachusetts schools in the 1830s. A critic of Morse's geography "accused the author of gross prejudice: . . . against the state of Rhode Island, the bulk of whose inhabitants had been dismissed as ignorant; against lawyers; against the inhabitants of Maryland, who had been described as negligent in dress, slothful, and ignorant; in short, against almost everyone and everything except the people and institutions of Connecticut."[16]

Reverend Morse was especially critical of Africans. In the description of the people of West Africa he wrote: "The inhabitants are negroes. They are a very degraded, and superstitious race. They believe in witchcraft, and offer sacrifices to devils."[17] Not content to relate only generalizations, he vividly recounted an example of manners and customs:

> The manners of the Abyssinians are characterized by a peculiar barbarism and brutality. They kill each other on very trifling occasions, and leave the dead bodies in the streets to be eaten by dogs. They eat the raw flesh of animals immediately after they are slain, while the blood is warm; and they sometimes cut steaks from living animals, and leave the wound to close up. Marriage in Abyssinia is a very slight connexion and dissolved at pleasure."[18]

In the 1820s Samuel Goodrich transformed geography textbooks, publishing his popular *Peter Parley's Method of Telling About Geography*. In the preface, he boldly asserts that he "has sought to give a work designed principally for the use of schools, the attractive qualities of books of amusement."[19] His book included many illustrations and was written in "a some-what colloquial manner" but presented the world in a similarly ethnocentric manner. For instance: "The six eastern States are often called New England. The people of the United States are very happy. They have a fine country, which produces beautiful trees, a plenty of grain, and delicious fruits."[20] In his thirty-seventh lesson on Africa, Goodrich refers to various groups of people as "barbarous," or "ignorant," or "uncivilized." He freely interjects his personal opinions, such as in this passage on the "ignorant and barbarous Hottentots": "Their climate is very warm, and the people can live with very little labour. They therefore become indolent and weak; I am inclined to think, however, that they are a better people than they have been generally represented to be. These people are exceedingly fond of ornaments."[21]

By the time Mary Shepard began teaching in the 1840s the Salem school system was using *Mitchell's Primary Geography*. The text was presented in eighty-three lessons, mainly as questions and answers, and was fully illustrated with 120 engravings and fourteen maps. S. Augustus Mitchell, the author, states explicitly in his preface that "wherever the subject has admitted of it, such observations have been made as tend to illustrate the excellence of the Christian religion, the advantages of correct moral principles, and the superiority of enlightened institutions."[22] Accordingly, in lesson 22, entitled "United States," he writes: "They are among the most intelligent, industrious, and enterprising people in the world."[23] Furthermore, he emphasized that "the people of New England are remarkable for their industry, good morals, and general intelligence."[24]

In the 1840s, in order to pass from primary school into grammar school, scholars in Salem had to answer oral exam questions in reading, spelling, arithmetic, and geography. The five geography questions were selected from the first forty pages of *Smith's First Book in Geography*. That book, similar in format to Mitchell's, was written by Roswell C. Smith, A.M., and included mostly straightforward physical geography, although the Bible is cited as the source of much of its information.

Smith also charts the political divisions of the world, beginning with the United States. He asks, "Why is our country often extolled as the best and happiest on earth?" The answer, "Because it is a free country," is italicized.[25] He discusses the presidents of the United States, devoting an entire lesson to the character of George Washington.

Moving beyond the United States, he divides the world into three zones: torrid, frigid, and temperate. For each zone he asks, "What is the character of the inhabitants?" The answer for the torrid zone: "They are dark-colored, passionate and indolent"; for the frigid zone: "They are dark-colored, ignorant and indolent"; for the temperate zone: "They are fair, robust, intelligent and industrious."[26]

By the time the scholars reached grammar school, they were greeted with *Smith's Geography on the Productive System*, "accompanied by a large and valuable atlas." This was a comprehensive description of world geography, with maps and lists of questions. The book's frontispiece illustrated the four areas of the world: barbarous, half-civilized, civilized, and enlightened. Because the book was written for older children the descriptions were not as blatant. For instance when Smith discusses Africa, "the least known, the least civilized and the least important . . . of the divisions of the globe," he begins with the nondescript phrase "the land of mystery."[27] Yet his bias was not much disguised. One of his explanations for why Africa remained mysterious was "the savage and forbidding manners of its inhabitants." In a period of U.S. history when Massachusetts was alive with outspoken opponents to slavery, Smith does not criticize "this traffic," but interjects an emotional adjective only to describe the African continent when he mentions the number of "negroes . . . yearly torn from this wretched country and sold as slaves." Nevertheless that population "has contributed 40 millions of vigorous men to the slave trade, and is yet any thing but depopulated."[28]

Mary Shepard earned the praise of the Salem School Committee in 1852 for the use of an innovative geography textbook. C. Pelton, A.M., came out in 1850 with a *Series of Outline Maps* that made use of musical verses to teach geography. As he described it, "The exhilarating effect of harmonious sounds will greatly facilitate the acquisition of this knowledge, and care has been taken that none but popular and approved airs be inserted in the work."[29] He starts out with a descriptive verse about the United States, sung to the air "Home, Sweet Home." Despite the innovative technique, the same theme of nationalism expressed with strong pro-American and anti-foreign bias reveals itself:

> Hail, land of Columbia! our dear native land,
> Where all that is lovely and all that is grand,
> By nature is blended in forest and plain,
> In lake and in river, and mountainous chain.
> Hail! hail! fair and free!
> There's no land like thee, there's no land like thee."[30]

In comparison with his glowing verses about the United States, his song about Palestine to the tune of "Auld Lang Syne" describes how "o'er the sacred region now the haughty Moslem reigns."[31] Even his air about

Europe emphasizes negative features:

> Parent and nurse of useful arts, of boundless wealth possess'd,
> Why is it that too frequently thy children are unbless'd!
> Extremes of wealth and poverty in every part we view,
> The wretched are the many there, the happy are the few.[32]

In the late 1850s the Salem School Committee introduced yet another geography textbook into the grammar schools, *Colton and Fitch's Modern School Geography*. Although it is more scientific in its maps and descriptions of the world, nevertheless in lesson XV, "Races and Conditions of Men," a bias toward Western values and specifically those of the United States is unmistakable. Written in question and answer form, the text asks, "What are the four principal states of society?" to which the correct answer is "Savage, barbarous, half-civilized, and civilized."[33] The page was illustrated with an engraving of "the savage state," portraying Indians in a canoe, bedecked with a bow and arrow. The text goes on to differentiate the four states of society:

What characterizes the Savage state?

A. The people in this state live chiefly by hunting, fishing and plunder; are generally at war; have no literature; and look upon their women as inferior beings.

How do men live in the Barbarous state?

A. Principally by pasturage and rude agriculture. People in this state usually live in tents, and wander from place to place with their herds.

What are the characteristics of Half-civilized nations?

A. They excel in many of the useful arts, have but little foreign commerce, are jealous of strangers, and make slow progress in literature and science.

For what are Civilized nations distinguished?

A. For rapid advances in science, literature, and the useful arts; superior social and religious advantages; and the general diffusion of knowledge.[34]

Finally, in the years following the Civil War, just before Mary Shepard's retirement from the school system in 1869, the Salem School Committee found a new method by Arnold Guyot for teaching geography. Guyot, who spent more than nine years addressing normal-school teachers in Massachusetts and New Jersey, was a self-proclaimed specialist teacher of geography from Switzerland. His plan centered on the use of classroom wall maps, "the base of all geographical instruction." The subject was presented in a series of three textbooks, representing the "three main stages" of the acquisition of knowledge: perceptive, analytic, and synthetic. "The simple power of perception through the senses predominates in the first; the analytic understanding in the second; the power of generalization in the third."[35] The three textbooks of *Guyot's Geographical Series* were actually written by Mrs. Mary Howe Smith, a teacher of geography at the Normal and Training School of Oswego, New York. As Guyot phrased it: "She consented to become my private pupil, and during over eighteen months which she spent under my roof, I readily yielded the pen to one so familiar with children's minds and language, and so thoroughly conversant with the habits and wants of the schoolroom."[36]

Mary Smith, in her preface to *Intermediate Geography,* described how the text "differs radically from all other works of the same grade." Her text "presents only the most fundamental and important ideas in each department of the subject, leaving all minor details to the future," in contrast to other texts "which present in the main details, without order."[37] The book was markedly more objective than the other nineteenth-century geography textbooks discussed. In her description of Africa, instead of criticizing African society, she states in a straightforward manner that "Africa has no great and powerful countries."[38] Similarly, instead of detailing bloodcurdling stories of barbarity, she asserts that "the interior of Africa is occupied by native kingdoms, the people of which are generally savages."[39] She expresses personal opinion sparingly, usually to praise rather than to condescend. For instance: "Brussels . . . is one of the handsomest towns of Europe," and Munich is "famous for the beauty of its public buildings."[40]

Nonetheless, her Western bias comes through in her description of the eastern and western coasts of Africa. "In these places companies of people from Europe or America have formed settlements, called colonies, and have taught the natives many things."[41]

Although Mary Shepard's attributes as a teacher of geography were appreciated by the Salem School Committee, the subject was closely tied to the teaching materials available for her use. As demonstrated, early and mid-nineteenth century geography textbooks were conscious vehicles for preparing proud Americans. Mary's creative contribution as a teacher, therefore, was circumscribed by the textbooks. She could help students learn, but she could not easily change the content of what they learned.

As a teacher of English, however, she had more scope for creativity, and it was as a teacher of literature and writing that she achieved her greatest triumphs. As an "authoress of considerable reputation,"[42] she appreciated fiction and poetry and was able to encourage her students to create noteworthy pieces of writing. In the 1855 school committee report there is considerable praise for the "original compositions" written by scholars from the Higginson School. "Many of the compositions indicated beauty and finish of style, as well as maturity of thought. We venture the opinion that few scholars of their age have attained a more clear and concise manner of expressing their thoughts in writing; this has been accomplished by the indefatigable exertions of the principal."[43]

Teaching English in Mary Shepard's era was closely tied to teaching morality, what we today call ethics. In her obituary we read how "the poems learned with her repeat themselves in times of need. There were afternoons when her reading took the place of recitations . . . no opportunity escaped her to point a moral, or adorn a tale."[44] Today, however, 150 years after Mary sat reading to her scholars, we can only speculate about the substance of the morality she taught.

We know that John Greenleaf Whittier's poetry was a favorite of hers, and we know that the *Grammar School Reader* by William D. Swan was required reading in Salem grammar schools in the 1840s. Swan, who was principal of the Mayhew Grammar School in Boston, was predictably opinionated about the proper method for teaching reading. He criticized the "method of requiring beginners to read familiar and easy words, instead of letters," whose "defect consists in neglecting to teach children the elementary sounds of letters."[45] That criticism is identical to the one made by Rudolf Flesch in 1955 in his bestselling book *Why Johnny Can't Read and What You Can Do About It.*

The methods Swan used to teach morality in his readers may appear old-fashioned today. Stories such as "Gratitude," "Importance of Early Rising," "Self-Denial," "Character of Washington," selections from the Psalms, the Book of Isaiah, and the New Testament would no longer be effective teaching instruments. In a chapter in the *Grammar School Reader* entitled "Anger," a boy is taught to control his anger when he sees a man beating a horse. Showing anger is counterproductive, the author preaches. Another story, "The Father," describes how happy a formerly rich family become when they lose their fortune and go to live a life on the land, poor and busy.

By the 1850s Salem teachers were given the option to switch to a series of readers by David B. Tower, and by 1858 the School Committee recommended "the valuable compilations of Hillard and Sargent," suggesting "that all other reading books, now in use, be discarded."[46] In contrast to Swan, George Stillman Hillard, author of *A Fourth Class Reader*, writes in his preface: "Young children are generally impatient of direct moral teaching, coming in the form of didactic precepts; and moral instruction, in order to be profitable, should be communicated indirectly, by narratives illustrating some heroic virtue, or fine affection, or by biographical sketches of men eminent for their greatness and goodness."[47]

The poetry, fiction, and biography in Hillard's readers were chosen with a purpose: to provide children with a moral basis for life. The poet Willis expresses some of the concepts succinctly in the *Fourth Class Reader:*

> If thy kind hand has aided distress
> And thou pity hast felt for wretchedness
> If thou hast forgiven a brother's offence,
> And grieved for thine own with penitence
> If every creature has won thy love,
> From the creeping worm to the brooding dove
> Then with joy and peace on the bed of rest
> Thou wilt sleep as on thy mother's breast.[48]

The readings in Hillard's series on the whole were more secular than earlier collections, including "descriptions of natural scenery and objects, sketches in natural history, [and] anecdotes of animals."[49] He also consciously aimed to expand the intellect of his readers by introducing a few poems that might be difficult for some scholars to comprehend. "But it does no harm to a boy or girl to read now and then a poem which somewhat tasks the faculties, and requires the mind, if one may so say, to stand on tiptoe to reach it."[50] Nevertheless, Hillard's overriding ambition was to "help to touch the heart, to kindle the mind, and train the moral sense of the coming generation."[51]

Although British writers such as Dickens, Scott, Wordsworth, and Tennyson, and early-nineteenth-century British women writers such as Jane Taylor, Mary Howitt, Mrs. Hemans, and Mrs. Barbauld, were well represented, Hillard also selected the works of many American authors. Alongside Massachusetts favorites Nathaniel Hawthorne and Henry Wadsworth Longfellow were a number of Massachusetts authors less well known today: Lydia Maria Child, Hannah Flagg Gould, and Catharine Sedgwick.

Hannah Gould, in 1856 a resident of Newburyport, was popular with young persons, according to Hillard, because her poems "are characterized by truth, and feeling and liveliness of expression."[52] The first few lines of "The Frost" illustrate her style of personifying nature:

The frost looked forth one still, clear night,
And whispered, "Now I shall be out of sight;
So through the valley, and over the height,
In silence I'll take my way."

Both Lydia Child and Catharine Sedgwick were familiar literary names in the nineteenth century. Each woman wrote a considerable number of books, the majority of which were not for children. Mrs. Child, who lived from 1802 to 1880, wrote outspokenly against slavery and for improving relations with the Indians. Her works included pamphlets, a multivolume history of religious ideas, and several novels. She also edited an abolitionist newspaper, and in 1826 founded the first American periodical for children, *Juvenile Miscellany*. Hillard chose several readings by Mrs. Child, including a short story entitled "The Dog-Churn" that teaches family solidarity, helpfulness to others, as well as respect for animals and the poor.

Nineteenth-century literary critics ranked Catharine Maria Sedgwick, who lived from 1789 to 1867, "with Washington Irving, James Fenimore Cooper and William Cullen Bryant as a founder of American literature."[53] By the twentieth century Sedgwick's "literary reputation suffered a sudden and dramatic decline,"[54] and "by the middle of the twentieth century, Sedgwick had become a footnote in the monumental *Literary History of the United States*."[55]

Catharine Sedgwick wrote six novels and countless short stories, always adhering to a moral purpose in her fiction. Hillard excerpted a story entitled "A Hasty Temper Corrected" from her book *Home* for the *Third Class Reader*. According to Hillard, the story teaches that "all discipline is turned to moral growth by the spirit of faith, and hope, and love."[56] Sedgwick's story describes a boy named Wallace whose passionate nature leads him into horrific acts of anger. His father doles out punishment, and finally Wallace proves to his father that he can control his temper. His father concludes with the moral to the story: "It is better to be virtuous than sinless—I mean, incapable of sin. If you subdue your temper, the exercise of the power to do this will give you a pleasure that you could not have had without it."[57]

Teaching morality was a specified facet of grammar-school education during the tenures of Mary Shepard and Mary Jane Fitz. Because these readers served as intrinsic elements of the English curriculum in Salem, we can presume that both women taught the same moral precepts. Their different styles of teaching, however, as well as their differing personalities elicited varying responses from their students. Because Miss Shepard was a writer herself, she was able to instill in her students an enthusiasm for writing. After she retired from teaching she lost her eyesight, but wrote three unpublished novels: Ruth Elliott's Dream, Pretty Lucy Merwin, and Faith's Festival. In contrast, the students of Mary Jane Fitz performed diligently, with "a good degree of success," as reported by the School Committee in 1851. After Miss Fitz retired from the Bentley School, she worked as a clerk at the registry of deeds.

Beyond the public and acknowledged appreciation of Mary Shepard's teaching, there remains a personal testimonial in the published journal of Charlotte L. Forten, an African American student from a prominent abolitionist family in Philadelphia, who came to the Higginson School in 1854. Mary Shepard was Charlotte's teacher for only nine months, between May 1854 and February 1855, but the bond formed between teacher and student lasted for many years.

Charlotte Forten was not a typical Higginson grammar-school student. She entered the last grade at the school when she was sixteen years old, somewhat older than her fellow students, and she was not from Salem. Previously, she had been educated by private tutors, because her father had refused to send her to segregated public schools in Philadelphia.

It may have been because of her special status that she was able to get to know her "dear, kind teacher," Miss Shepard, faster and more intimately than her fellow students. Her journal descriptions provide a unique glimpse into the personality, opinions, and everyday life of Mary Shepard. On several occasions, Charlotte's journal entries also offer insight into Miss Shepard's special ability as a teacher.

Charlotte's first mention of her teacher is on the third day of her journal, 26 May 1854: "Had a conversation with Miss Shepard about slavery; she is, as I thought, thoroughly opposed to it, but does not agree with me in thinking that the churches and ministers are generally supporters of the infamous system; I believe it firmly."[58] Opposition to slavery was an integral part of Charlotte's life in Salem, for she not only boarded with a black abolitionist family but she spent most of her weekends and evenings participating in antislavery demonstrations and meetings. On more than one occasion, she describes Mary Shepard's views on the subject. "Monday, June 5 . . . I fully appreciate her kindness, and sympathy with me; she wishes me to cultivate a Christian spirit in thinking of my enemies."⁵⁹ "Sunday, Oct. 29 . . . If she were better acquainted with the sentiments of the abolitionists, I do not think that she could regard any of them as unchristian; but she would see them as they are—truly christian, noble-hearted, devoted to the Right."⁶⁰

Her journal entries at the end of her Higginson School days, in February 1855, reveal the feelings of students and teachers:

> Thursday, Feb. 15. The day before examination, and a very busy day it is. The old school-room has been undergoing a thorough process of renovation, and looks really very bright and respectable. We had quite a dinner-party at the schoolhouse, with Miss Shepard for the presiding genius, and a merry, delightful party it was. Friday, Feb. 16. Evening—The dreaded examination day is over at last, and we feel very much relieved. The schoolroom was densely crowded. The girls did very well, and our teacher expressed herself much pleased. Everything passed off pleasantly, and everybody seemed very much delighted. I am extremely tired, but our dear teacher must be more so. I can scarcely bear to think how very soon I shall have to leave her. To me no one can ever supply her place.⁶¹

Charlotte Forten's references to Mary Shepard in her journal include many more of friendship and kindness than of awe or respect. They shared their thoughts and feelings. For instance: "Tuesday, August 8. This morning I took a delightful walk with her in Harmony Grove [the Salem Cemetery where Mary Shepard is now buried]. . . . My teacher talked to me of a beloved sister who is sleeping there. As she spoke, it almost seemed to me as if I had known her; one of those noble, gentle, warm-hearted spiritual beings, too pure and heavenly for this world."⁶² After graduation from the Higginson School, Charlotte, who went on to study at the State Normal School at Salem and then to teach at a Salem coeducational grammar school, stayed in close touch with Mary Shepard. At the end of 1856, Charlotte shared with her the excitement of receiving a letter from Whittier. "Saturday, Dec. 20. Spent the afternoon very delightfully with my dear friend Miss S. Showed her my precious letter, which I would show to no one else in Salem. She appreciates it thoroughly; and kindly pardons my presumption in writing to him,—the noblest poet, the noblest man of the age, with very few exceptions."⁶³

During the Civil War Charlotte volunteered to teach newly freed slaves in the Sea Islands, off Hilton Head in South Carolina. To celebrate

Christmas with her class at St. Helena's Island, she sent Whittier a personal request for a poem. Although he was in poor health in 1862, he composed a hymn for her class.

Mary Lakeman Shepard also wrote poetry. A collection of twenty-two poems, entitled *The Ships on the Sea,* was printed privately in Boston after her death. They are predominantly reflective poems about life and death. The final poem, entitled "home," was read at her request at her funeral at the Tabernacle Congregational Church in Salem in November 1893. She died at the age of sixty-nine, mourned by "friends near and far . . . [t]he world is changed for them now that her cordial greeting, her radiant presence and her words of courage and of comfort will come no more."[64] For Mary Shepard the poetess, however, death was "joy divine":

> Backward I look on earthly life,
> Its sin,
> its sorrow,
> and its strife.
> All, all now o'er!
> Serene,
> at rest,
> I serve my God, forever blest.[65]

Mary Jane Fitz died a few years later on 15 February 1897. She was seventy-five years old, and she also had been a member of the Tabernacle Orthodox Congregational Church in Salem. The headline of her obituary in the *Salem Evening News* read "Death of an Estimable School Teacher and Tabernacle Church member."[66]

Neither woman ever married; both lived at home in Salem with their fathers. Neither woman has been remembered in histories of education or in histories of the city in which they taught. Both women affected the lives of hundreds, perhaps thousands, of Salem citizens, teaching them how to be moral Americans.

NOTES

1. Obituary, *Salem Observer,* 2 December 1893.
2. Salem School Committee, *Annual Report of 1851,* 13.
3. Salem School Committee, *Annual Report of 1846,* 6.
4. Arthur L. Goodrich, *The Public Schools of Salem, Mass. 1626–1900* (unpublished manuscript, 1900), 28.
5. Salem School Committee, *Annual Report of 1853,* 43.
6. Ibid., 44.
7. Obituary, *Salem Observer,* 2 December 1893.

8. Salem School Committee, *Annual Report of 1852*, 27.
9. Salem School Committee, *Annual Report of 1848*, 16–18.
10. Salem School Committee, *Annual Report of 1870*, 12.
11. Salem School Committee, *Annual Report of 1854*, 30.
12. Obituary, *Salem Observer*, 2 December 1893.
13. Salem School Committee, *Annual Report of 1854*, 30.
14. Ibid.
15. Salem School Committee, *Annual Report of 1861*, 18.
16. Conrad Wright, *The Beginnings of Unitarianism in America* (Hamden, Conn.: Archon Books, 1976), 272.
17. Jedidiah Morse, *A New System of Geography* (Boston: Richardson & Lord, 1822), 270.
18. Ibid., 274.
19. Samuel Griswold Goodrich, *Peter Parley's Method of Telling About Geography* (New York: Collins & Hannay, 1832), preface.
20. Ibid., 37.
21. Ibid., 99–100.
22. S. Augustus Mitchell, *Mitchell's Primary Geography* (Philadelphia: Thomas, Cowperthwait & Co., 1843), iv.
23. Ibid., 37.
24. Ibid., 43.
25. Roswell C. Smith, *Smith's First Book in Geography* (Portland, Maine: Sanborn & Carter, 1846), 48.
26. Ibid., 57.
27. Roswell C. Smith, *Smith's Geography on the Productive System* (Hartford, Conn.: John Paine, 1842), 271.
28. Ibid.
29. C. Pelton, *Series of Outline Maps* (Philadelphia: C. Pelton, 1850), preface.
30. Ibid., 36.
31. Ibid., 98.
32. Ibid., 66.
33. George W. Fitch and George Woolworth Colton, *Colton and Fitch's Modern School Geography* (New York: Ivison, Phinney, Blakeman & Co., 1864), 11.
34. Ibid.
35. Arnold Henry Guyot, *Guyot's Geographical Series. Intermediate Geography* (New York: Charles Scribner & Co., 1869), preface.
36. Ibid., iv.
37. Ibid., preface by Mary Smith.
38. Ibid., 35.
39. Ibid.
40. Ibid., 47.
41. Ibid., 35.
42. Obituary, *Salem Observer*, 2 December 1893.
43. Salem School Committee, *Annual Report of 1855*, 26.
44. Obituary, *Salem Observer*, 2 December 1893.
45. William D. Swan, *The Primary School Reader. Part Second* (Philadelphia: Cowperthwait, Desilver and Butler, 1844), preface.
46. Salem School Committee, *Annual Report of 1858*, 12.
47. George Stillman Hillard, *A Fourth Class Reader* (Boston: Hickling, Swan and Brewer, 1857), iii.
48. Ibid., 53.
49. Hillard, *Second Class Reader*, v.
50. Hillard, *A Fourth Class Reader*, iv.
51. Hillard, *First Class Reader*, 4.

52. Hillard, *Second Class Reader,* 144.

53. Mary Kelley (ed.), introduction to Catharine Maria Sedgwick's *Hope Leslie,* xi.

54. Ibid., xiii.

55. Ibid., xii.

56. Hillard, *Third Class Reader,* 176.

57. Ibid., 181.

58. Charlotte L. Forten, *The Journal of Charlotte Forten: a Free Negro in the Slave Era,* ed. Ray Allen Billington (New York: W. W. Norton, 1981), 43–44.

59. Ibid., 47.

60. Ibid., 61.

61. Ibid., 70.

62. Ibid., 56.

63. Ibid., 86.

64. Obituary, *Salem Observer,* 2 December 1893.

65. Mary Lakeman Shepard, *Ships on the Sea* (Boston: Privately printed, 1894), 46.

66. Obituary, *Salem Evening News,* 15 February 1897.

3 STUDENT AND TEACHER AT THE FIRST STATE NORMAL SCHOOL IN THE UNITED STATES: ELECTA LINCOLN WALTON (1824–1908)

Beverly J. Weiss

Electa Lincoln Walton, circa 1900.

This is Electa Lincoln Walton's story, but it is also the story of the early days of America's first public normal school, established in Lexington, Massachusetts, in 1839, and of the young women who studied there. Nearly every account of public education in the United States refers to this normal school, but little has been written about the young women who studied there and then left to teach. These students and teachers are nearly unknown to us now, but some of them were well known and respected in their own time.

Electa Lincoln was one of the first graduates to serve as a teacher in the Normal School. Later she became the acting principal for more than six months, the first and only woman to hold that position during nearly two decades. In time she married and reared children, but she also found time to have a school of her own, write arithmetic texts with her husband, teach in the teacher institutes, serve on the Sanitary Commission during the Civil War, work for suffrage and equality for blacks, fight for school suffrage for women (voting on matters related to schools), lead the New England Women's Clubs, and write a history of the first fifty years of the Normal School. A woman for all seasons!

Electa Lincoln knew many of the young women from the first Normal School class and admired their adventurous spirit as well as their pioneering work. Electa maintained close ties to the Normal School throughout her life, and her history of its first fifty years was a reflection of her intimate knowledge of the school and the people who had shaped it.

THE FIRST NORMAL SCHOOL CLASS

Much has been made of the fact that when the school opened on 3 July 1839 in Lexington only three students presented themselves as candidates. But, over the course of the next few months, twenty-five young women entered the school.[1] Their commitment was for a year of study to be followed by a year of service in the public schools. All but three of the twenty-five students finished the course and honored their commitment. Eleven of them remained at the school for eighteen months. Five left to teach and returned for additional study, two of them completing three years of study as originally recommended by Horace Mann. At least fifteen of these young women taught for six years or more, and one of them, Adeline Ireson, completed fifty years of teaching in the Cambridge school system.[2]

Beginning at their tenth anniversary in 1850, the first class began to hold yearly meetings. Each year a member of the class was appointed to prepare an address for the next meeting. A record book was initiated, and the person giving the address copied it into the book along with an account of the yearly meeting. The Normalites' memories of their school days and an account of their later lives are recorded there.

The Normalites called themselves pioneers, which seems remarkable because they were very modest about their achievements. They never ceased to marvel at their experiences, or to treasure the close ties to each other and to Cyrus and Harriet Peirce (Cyrus Peirce was the first teacher and principal). There was also a lightheartedness about them, evident despite the quaintness of their language to our ears. For years they twitted each other about misdemeanors in the classroom or the boarding house, such as the time Hannah Damon, in retaliation for some unmentionable insult, tied Mary Stodder to her chair by her red tresses. She was rescued from her "durance vile" by Lydia Drew, who snipped off the hopelessly tangled locks with her scissors.

Nor were the distinguished gentlemen who came to visit spared. The girls were fond of impersonating their interrogators, re-creating the scene to suit themselves. As Mary Stodder said, "Horace Mann, Dr. Howe and Dr. Putnam might well be astonished at the words put into their mouths by saucy girls." She goes on, "But I merely mention these among ourselves. We can bear each other's laughter, for we have tried its power; but as we value our reputation, let not these stories come to the knowledge of our younger sisters, lest they feel justified in saying, as they have said, that they 'stand on giants' shoulders and see farther than the giants can'!"[3]

Over the years they gave voice to both the ideals and the conflicts of women of their time. In fact, during the period when many of them were caught up in activities related to the Civil War, they had little to say about the war in the record book. They did have a great deal to say about fulfilling their mission as women, expressing concern for those of their number who were not yet married. In time, all except four of them married and had children. It was a sensitive issue.

Most of these pioneer women had the satisfaction of succeeding at the difficult task they had undertaken in becoming teachers. They showed that teaching may be good preparation for motherhood and a great many other of life's missions as well. Mary Swift Lamson, for example, began by teaching blind and deaf children with Dr. Samuel Howe, served on the board of the first Girls' Industrial School at Lancaster, and helped to establish the Young Women's Christian Association (YWCA) in Boston.[4] She also took great satisfaction as a wife and mother. In short, she was the affirmation of Catharine Beecher's ideal woman. She expanded woman's sphere without repudiating any part of it.

On the other hand, Louisa Harris tried as delicately as possible to say that she was glad to have an alternative to marriage, and to have a respected position in the world in her own right. She told a humorous story about her attempts to cook dinner for the family with whom she boarded, at the climax of which she dropped the earthen pot of beans: "I told Mrs. W. on her return that my beans were so very delicious that the family had eaten the beanpot, too, and that was what had become of it. . . . Now will you wonder that with the smallest remnant of conscience I have never so far endangered my own peace or dignity, or so far imposed upon any son of Adam as to locate myself where similar duties would devolve upon me?"[5]

Louisa Harris never denigrated marriage and the family but seems to have chosen the single life. She taught for thirty-three years in public and private schools, and during that time she also had a literary career.

Most of these young women seem to have come from comfortable circumstances and had been well educated before coming to the Normal School (although often not well enough for Cyrus Peirce). Adeline Ireson may have been the exception. She was one of those who spent three years at the Normal School, and later accounts mention her diligence in supporting her mother. It is likely that her fifty years in the Cambridge schools were dictated by need. A public testimonial was held in her honor at Harvard's Sanders Theatre when she retired, and many of her famous pupils joined in the tribute to her, among them Governor William Russell and Mrs. Alice Freeman Palmer, president of Wellesley College. They praised her "quiet, self-respecting life" of service. She, in response, said that she had loved her work and that her only wish was that she were ten years younger so that she might continue.[6] For her, the Normal School made possible a dignified life filled with the satisfaction of service to others.

Rebecca Pennell followed another course. She taught in public schools for several years, then in the Normal School at West Newton and at Westfield (formerly Barre Normal School). She went to Antioch College in Yellow Springs, Ohio, while her uncle, Horace Mann, was president there. In 1853 she was appointed professor of physical geography, drawing, natural history, civil history and didactics, the longest title by far in the first Antioch catalogue. She was probably the first woman in the United States to hold the title of professor,[7] and she was certainly the first to demand a salary commensurate with her responsibilities.[8] Later she taught at Mary Institute in St. Louis, teaching in all about twenty-five years. She was married to Austin Dean in 1855 and, although she had no children of her own, adopted her deceased sister Eliza's young son.[9]

There were also antislavery workers among the early graduates. Lydia Stow Adams was an outspoken abolitionist, and she backed her words by maintaining a station for the Underground Railroad in Fall River.[10] These are examples of women from the first class at the Lexington Normal School. Not only did they teach in the common schools, some for many years, but they also used the knowledge, skills, and idealism fostered by the Normal School to advance social reforms of many different kinds.

First Normal School Building in Lexington, Massachusetts.

CYRUS PEIRCE AND THE MODEL SCHOOL

Electa Lincoln entered the Lexington Normal School in 1841 at the age of seventeen, still in time to be a part of all the excitement, adventure, and idealism of the new enterprise and to feel the threat of those who continued to attempt to dissolve the school. She began her studies under Principal Cyrus Peirce, the Harvard-educated minister whom Horace Mann had chosen because he had been so impressed with Peirce's philosophy and teaching methods.

Peirce was an experienced teacher with strong convictions about preparing young people to teach. Teachers in the common schools at that time relied heavily on textbooks and memorization because they themselves were often ill prepared to explain the subjects they were teaching. Peirce, however, expected his students to be well grounded in the subjects they were to teach; recitation was to be more than memorization and repetition.[11]

Peirce stressed the importance of having students give oral and written analyses in their own words, and he often asked students to present the ideas as they would to a class. He was also among the first to make use of the blackboard and of globes and maps. He avoided a single text in the study of geography, requiring students to search the available maps and books for information. At recitation, he might ask students to present the information they had found as a report on an imaginary journey. His emphasis was on the "exercise of the faculties" rather than memorization and repetition.

Peirce aimed to teach "precepts," or principles, and he asserted that there were "general principles to be recognized in education." The success of any principle or method, however, "must owe its power to the skill with which it is applied."[12] He taught in the Normal School by his own example, as he expected the students to teach in the Model School he had opened and afterwards in the public schools.[13]

As soon as the Normal School at Lexington had recruited its first students and had begun operations, Cyrus Peirce approached town officials with his plan for the Model School. He proposed that thirty children between six and ten years of age from local school districts be assigned. The children in the Model School would have the same course of study as those in the public schools, but they would be taught by students from the Normal School under the supervision of the Normal School principal. The proposal was favorably received and the Model School opened with twenty-one boys and twelve girls on 21 October 1839. The Normal School students assisted Peirce in preparing a classroom on the ground floor of the Normal School building, and Mary Swift, a student from Nantucket, was the first to be given responsibility for the school. Writing in his journal, Peirce freely admitted that the Model School would add greatly to his "labors and cares," but he also believed that it was an important addition, and "one on which [the Normal School's] success greatly depends."[14]

Why did Peirce consider the Model School so important? Peirce's instructional philosophy stressed the active participation of students, the use of demonstrations, and learning by doing. In the Model School, he demonstrated to student observers the pedagogical methods and materials he had developed by teaching the children himself. He asked his students to analyze the lessons and the behavior they observed; when he deemed them ready, his students applied what they had learned by teaching the children themselves. Peirce and his students observed in the Model classroom and criticized the lessons, both the teacher's grasp of the subject and the manner of presentation. Peirce also believed that it was important for teachers to learn about "juvenile development," and the Model School provided an opportunity for observing the children,[15] as psychologists today recommend.

The themes that Peirce conveyed to his Normal School students included learning by doing, the value of reasoning over memorization, the importance of observation and child study, discipline without punishment, and learning tied to common experiences.[16] To be sure they were embryonic concepts, then as now honored more in theory than in practice.

Peirce was not a man to tolerate mediocrity in himself or his students. He was demanding, difficult to satisfy, and given to recriminations. Nevertheless, he inspired many of these young women to become competent teachers, lifelong friends, and loyal supporters of the Normal School.

ELECTA LINCOLN

Electa Lincoln's early life had prepared her well for the career she was about to enter. She was born on 12 May 1824 in Watertown, New York. Her father, Martin Lincoln, was a Massachusetts man, and he brought his family back to Lancaster, Massachusetts, when Electa was two years old. Julia Ward Howe, who edited a book about New England women in 1904, notes that Martin Lincoln and President Abraham Lincoln were both great-great-grandsons of Jacob Lincoln. Martin Lincoln was a teacher by profession, and he taught in the public schools in Lancaster and at Lancaster Academy for several years. During that period he was Electa's first and only teacher. After some years the family moved to Roxbury and then to Boston, where Martin "kept a private school," and Electa attended the Thoreau sisters' school.[17] In 1841, she entered the Normal School at Lexington. She began her studies with Peirce, but he was forced by ill health to resign in 1842.

The Reverend Samuel J. May, an outspoken abolitionist, became the second principal, and Electa completed her studies under his guidance, graduating in 1843.[18] For the rest of her life she would be sensitive to the needs of African Americans, working for their suffrage and education and for the inclusion of black women in the women's action groups and clubs she led. It seems likely that she was strongly influenced by May's crusading activities, for he was so visible in the abolitionist movement that Mann felt obliged to admonish him about his public appearances and speeches.[19] Abolition was not universally embraced, even in Massachusetts, and Mann feared that May's activities might diminish public support for the normal schools.

There may have been an additional influence on the young Electa.

Although there is no indication in the school records, one of her classmates, Mary E. Miles, was a woman of color. Mary Miles and her husband, Henry Bibb, moved to Canada after the passage of the Fugitive Slave Law in 1850, the law requiring Northerners to assist in returning escaped slaves to their owners. Many African Americans, though free and living in the North, feared that they would be seized and sent south as slaves.[20] In Canada, Mary resumed her career as a teacher,[21] and it is likely that Electa was aware of her classmate's circumstances.

Electa went to teach at the Franklin School in Boston after her graduation, but within a short time Mr. May persuaded her to return to the Normal School at Lexington to teach. She was then nineteen and had a thirst for knowledge. She studied botany with Mrs. Peirce, French with Mrs. Mary Mann and other tutors, and elocution with the tragedian James Murdock and William Russell. She mastered the Pitman system of stenography and she studied higher mathematics. She was quite proficient at sketching and painting in oils.[22] Electa taught all of these subjects at the Normal School, and when Cyrus Peirce, restored to health, returned as principal in 1844, she continued to teach and to study privately. Peirce chose her as assistant principal in 1847. To Peirce she represented the ideal teacher, well educated in the "common branches," with advanced study in special fields, and trained in the art of teaching. She seemed always ready to learn more, and her energy was boundless.

Inasmuch as Peirce's practices were innovative, it is not difficult to understand why some of the most successful and best-educated graduates of the Normal School were asked to return as faculty. At Lexington they were all women, so that hiring graduates meant that these women had the opportunity to move into responsible positions. Both Mann and Peirce believed that women were capable of performing any intellectual task that men could, and they were dedicated to giving women the opportunity to try. For that reason, women served as assistants in Lexington during a period when other principals were adamantly refusing to hire women, even though the student bodies at the coeducational normal schools (Barre/Westfield and Bridgewater) were predominantly female. Another consequence of hiring graduates was that a continuous connection with the philosophy and methods of the founders was maintained. Therefore the importance of the Model School and experiential learning remained central concepts at the Lexington/Framingham Normal School, even though there appears to have been no general recognition in Massachusetts of their importance for several decades. Electa's extended association with the Peirces, the Manns, and other significant reformers of the period was important in giving continuity to the school and in maintaining the ideals of its founders.

THE MOVE TO WEST NEWTON

In 1844, the Normal School had grown to the point where it was in need of bigger facilities and more generous town support. The town of West Newton offered both of those, as well as easier access by means of the recently opened Boston and Worcester Railroad, and so the move was made.[23] Horace Mann and his wife, Mary Peabody Mann, whom he had married in 1843, built a home nearby, where the Normal students were always welcome. Mann himself spent much of his time away on lecture tours, initiating teacher institutes and fighting political battles, but the Normalites were welcomed by Mrs. Mann, who was an experienced teacher, by her sister, Elizabeth Peabody, most noted for her work in the kindergarten movement, and by Rebecca Pennell, Mann's niece and a graduate of the first class of the Normal School. The Manns also provided a home for Chloe Lee, an African American student (class of 1849) who was unable to find accommodations in the town.[24]

When the Normal School moved to West Newton in 1844, the Model School was again instituted through an agreement with the town. For the first few years, the Model School occupied one room in the West Newton Normal School.[25] A young man, George A. Walton, was placed in charge of the Model School in 1847, and, although he left the Model School after a year to become a principal in the Lawrence public schools, he had become an enduring part of Electa's life. As the number of children in the Model School increased from thirty-five to eighty, a new agreement was made with the town in 1848 for the grammar school across the street to serve as the Model School. A permanent teacher, Nathaniel T. Allen, approved by both the Normal School principal and the town's school committee, was given charge of the school, and the town assumed "a large portion" of the expense. A few months later, a primary school was also designated as a model school, and a recent Normal School graduate, Rebecca C. Lewis, was placed in charge.[26] These arrangements proved highly satisfactory to both the town and the Normal School for several years.

Electa Lincoln seems to have been involved in every activity of the Normal School. In a time when nearly everyone seemed to suffer from periodic illnesses, or to be in chronic "delicate health," Electa was robust and energetic. She wrote almost apologetically that she was never ill and even a headache was not a common experience. Her journal shows her to be a thoughtful and religious young woman, but her verve and energy may have irritated some who were less well endowed.

On 23 June 1848 Electa began a "private journal, a record of my heart's deepest desires." Foremost on her mind was George Walton. She found him "a queer specimen of humanity" but not a displeasing one, for "it excites my curiosity and I look to see what he will do next." Barely a week later she writes of returning from a social evening among friends with whom "social communion" is sweet, but "sweeter far are the moments spent by me in company with one friend and that friend G. I do dearly love him, he is so true, so good, so loving himself."[27] It was a love that lasted a lifetime, and the beginning of a professional partnership rare for the time. But courtship took time, and they both had work to accomplish before they married in 1850.

Later that summer Electa reflected on an address she had given at the Third Triennial Convention of the Normal School. The conventions were large public meetings that served to bring graduates of the school together and to create a forum for speeches by various educators. Invitations were circulated to the public and the attendance at this convention on 26 July 1848 was about two hundred people. According to Sara H. Page, who recorded the events of the day, "Electa N. Lincoln rose and delivered from the desk, in an easy and graceful style, a welcoming address."[28] She went on to speak about attacks that had been made against Peirce and the Normal School, and she urged the Normalites to show by their conduct as teachers that their "time here has been spent well."[29]

Electa analyzed her address, and wrote in her journal that she had done well, although she saw two points that she might have improved. The compliments "bestowed by responsible individuals" pleased her and humbled her:

> I see how little I deserve them. I think, not expecting so much from a lady as from a gentleman, they are particularly pleased with the intrinsic merit of the production. This makes me blush for my sex and makes me determined for one to endeavor to elevate that sex. They need elevation, Heaven knows, and they are not wholly to blame for their degradation; the men are as a general thing, directly or indirectly, a motive power to keep them down. Oh, it makes me sigh and blush and sigh again when I see the wide difference between woman as she is and woman as she should be.[30]

That is a rather startling feminist statement to have come from a young woman of ladylike demeanor with a responsible position in a very proper school in 1848. To be sure, it is a statement from a private journal and not a speech, but it does foreshadow the work of her later years.

One might wonder why she took such a prominent role on this occasion. Cyrus Peirce was present and had greeted the assembly, but he had left the longer address to her. Peirce's health was again failing, and he may not have felt up to the effort of making an address, or he may have wished to give Electa the opportunity to show her competence in representing the school. Others apparently thought that his time as principal might be drawing to a close, because he was presented with a silver vase filled with flowers. The brief presentation speech was a touching and affectionate tribute to him and his wife. At the end of the day, he brought the convention to a close with his familiar benediction, "Live to Truth,"[31] still today the motto of Framingham State College.

The following winter Peirce's health worsened, and in the middle of February 1849 he was forced to give up his post, leaving the management of the school to Lincoln. Electa wrote:

> Father Peirce is sick and has left school awhile, principally under my care and oh—how anxious I feel about that—all things may not go on right—and yet if I do my duty, what have I to fear? With God, the impartial judge, the question will not be 'what success has crowned thy labors?', but 'with what faithfulness were they performed?' Let me then earnestly strive, fearing nothing, hoping all things . . . [32]

Whatever qualms Electa may have had in private, she kept the school on course and running efficiently, to the complete satisfaction of Peirce, Mann, and the board of education. By April, it was clear that Cyrus Peirce would not return as principal. He resigned from the position, recommending that Miss Lincoln be named his successor. He felt that he had prepared her well for the post and that she was competent. But although the board respected Peirce's opinion, they were unwilling to appoint a woman to head one of the normal schools. They did, however, ask her to serve as acting principal until a suitable man could be found.

Electa, noting that Peirce had resigned, wrote, "I suppose I must take the lead till fall. Well two things I hope for; one is that I may satisfy the friends of the institution and another, that I may get Mr. Peirce's pay."[33] Her first hope was realized.

Although Electa had already been serving as principal for two months when the board asked her to take charge, she admitted to feeling some anxiety as she consented to serve, even though she felt it "would be the best arrangement." After a visit to Peirce, she wrote that she wished she might:

> catch some of his spirit—might imbibe some of his zeal, his willing-
> ness for self-sacrifice. I tremble when I think where I am
> standing . . . I'm inexperienced and ignorant of many things I should
> know while I stand here. I feel like one who has charge of a helm
> without having an acquaintance with the straits through which the
> ship is to be guided. . . . [34]

Electa's long association with Peirce, who had turned his hand to every chore at the school, provided a reassuring example for her. She went early
to the schoolroom, and, finding it in "good order," was nevertheless "obliged
to give it a little dusting, and the entry a little sweeping." When things were
"at rights" she settled herself to observe the children as they arrived.[35] The
new term began with a larger class, and Electa was not sorry—provided the
teaching could be done well:

> I wouldn't fail in this enterprise this term for a great deal. Many
> people think women can't do much. I'd like to show them that they
> can keep a Normal School and keep it well too, for one term at least.
> My motto shall be 'Succeed or Die' which was Mr. Peirce's motto and
> I rather think it'll be succeed. I have strong hope.[36]

Apparently, some of the debate over the merits of having a woman
in charge reached her ears, for she wrote:

> It has been said that women cannot do much in the way of conduct-
> ing a school like this and one man of thought and experience told me
> that I should find my situation here unpleasant from the feeling of
> others on this point. If there is such strong feeling in the community
> on the subject, I am all the more anxious to succeed. I will spare no
> pains—I will work diligently, faithfully. I leave no means I can com-
> mand untried, in order to bring and keep the School just where it
> should be. I will succeed. . . . I will never be pointed at as an example
> of the incompetency of woman to conduct a large establishment
> well.[37]

Electa had served as a teacher with Peirce and May through the difficult years when opponents had tried repeatedly to abolish the normal
schools and end the "great experiment." Now, nearly ten years after the

school's founding, she was concerned that the school continue to improve and grow, but she was even more concerned that the women who had seized these new opportunities not be found incapable. The Normal School was no hotbed of activists for women's rights, although there were several; many of the graduates had gone quietly and competently about the work they had chosen, often challenging long-held beliefs about women's abilities simply by succeeding. Electa had already shown herself to be more than equal to the task of teaching at this advanced level, and now she had the opportunity to show that the more complex administrative work was also within the scope of women's capabilities.

As the weeks passed, Electa wrote less of her insecurities and more of her philosophy and the work at hand. She noted that the classes were larger than ever in the new term. Large classes, she thought, were fine for students who were "determined to learn" and even were an advantage in that there were many more minds from which to learn. For the few who do only what they are "obliged to do," small classes are better so that the teacher can "watch them and lend a helping hand to bring them entirely up to the mark."[38]

Electa's way of expressing herself here is reflective of the philosophy of "perfectibility" of the reformers of the period. Imperfections, even those of motivation, were noted and appropriate education was offered as a means of improving the person's ability to move toward the ideal of self-sufficiency and independence. School policies were designed with this in mind. For example, Miss Lincoln issued a statement to the school on the observance of study hours. There was to be no communication during this period, and she made sure that everyone was "provided with materials as never to need to borrow, for perfect independence of all without ourselves, is a state invaluable. One who has learned to depend on herself has made a long, very long stride towards the attainments necessary for a teacher."[39]

Electa seems to have understood also that independence does not develop easily if one is expected to obey without question. She reported that "one young lady" had spoken to her "concerning something she didn't quite like in the conducting of the School. I was right glad she spoke so freely—I would have it so always."[40]

Miss Lincoln did succeed in her efforts to keep the Normal School on its course. There were no negative criticisms of her work, and the Massachusetts Board of Education and its official visitors were entirely satisfied with her administration. They were not, however, prepared to take the step of naming her principal. In September, Eben Stearns became principal, and Electa wrote many years later that he proved himself a "fit successor, devoted, earnest, exact, and gentlemanly." She enjoyed his "winsome humor" and found him a "delightful companion."[41] Her open, optimistic personality enabled her to recognize the best of his qualities, as she always seemed to do with her students, without the rancor one might expect under the circumstances.

One of the students, Emily Ward, described the events of that fall in her journal. She wrote that Mr. Stearns was inaugurated on Wednesday, 12 September 1849, noting that the Honorable Horace Mann, Barnas Sears, and George B. Emerson were present.[42] By that date, Mann had been elected to the U. S. Congress and Sears was the secretary of the Massachusetts Board of Education. Emily was very pleased that "Miss Lincoln, our dear teacher, is still with us and hope will be the whole year." A few days later she wrote of a pleasant visit with Miss Lincoln and commented, "Ah, what would this world be to us with all its beauty, if we had no true friends."[43]

Electa did remain for the year, assisting Stearns, filling in when he was ill, and generally continuing her teaching and supervising duties as she had always done. Stearns wrote that she "labored with untiring zeal and faithfulness, assisting him . . . as no other could have done, encouraging him by her example and cheerful spirit."[44] Apparently, these two young people found much to admire in each other's work, and they continued to hold high expectations for the students.

One of the students at the Normal School while it was under Electa's direction was Lucretia Crocker, who later received recognition as a science teacher and the first woman science supervisor in the Boston public schools. Although a classmate found her both lovely to look at and a competent student who easily took first place in the class, Lucretia Crocker said of herself that she was "so shy as to be afraid of the sound of her own voice."[45] She credited her training at the Normal School (elocution with Miss Lincoln, no doubt) with giving her the confidence to speak and teach effectively. Mann was present at her final oral examination in 1850 and was impressed with her grasp of mathematics and her lucid presentation. He remembered her when he became president of Antioch College, and he appointed her to a chair in mathematics and astronomy.[46] She was one of the first women to hold such a position and to teach a coeducational class for adult students.

Lucretia Crocker, along with another classmate, Georgiana Whittemore, remained at the Normal School as a teacher after her graduation in 1850. So when Electa Lincoln resigned in 1850 to marry George Walton, she left her role at the Normal School to three graduates who had also studied with Mr. Peirce. Mr. Stearns, too, proved subject to ill health, and he left the administration of the school to Crocker, Pennell, and

Whittemore for an extended period in 1851.[47] But there was much less comment about women being in charge, presumably because the school had clearly not suffered during the periods of Electa's guidance.

Outside the Normal School, the graduates during the ten years from 1840 to 1850 had begun to coalesce into a network of dedicated women who kept in touch with one another and who visited and supported the Normal School whenever possible. Electa maintained these ties throughout her life. Electa Lincoln Walton visited the Normal School, by that time in Framingham, in 1880 in the company of Lucretia Crocker and Abby May, the official visitor from the Massachusetts Board of Education. The principal was Ellen Hyde.[48] These were powerful models to stand before the Normal School students. All four of them were well known in 1880, the three visitors for their very visible roles in securing school suffrage for women, among other causes, and Miss Hyde because she was the only woman principal in the commonwealth and a frequent speaker at educational conferences. All except May were graduates of the Normal School, and they credited it with giving them the opportunity to live more productive lives than they could have done otherwise. Perhaps the school also provided a cause worth working for because, as Elizabeth Peabody somewhat enviously remarked, Miss Crocker attended the Normal School "from *taste,* not being obliged to earn her bread."[49] This was a reference to the fact that Lucretia Crocker's family was well to do and Lucretia did not need to support herself by teaching, although she did so for much of her life.

LIFE BEYOND THE NORMAL SCHOOL

Electa Lincoln married George Augustus Walton on 27 August 1850. He was a graduate of Harvard College and Bridgewater Normal School, and he held the Master of Arts degree from Williams College.[50] Cyrus Peirce regarded him very highly during the period when he had charge of the Model School in West Newton, and the two families maintained an intimate connection for a number of years. When the Walton's first child was born, she was given the name Harriet Peirce in honor of Cyrus's wife, who had been Electa's botany teacher.

At the time of their marriage and for several years afterward, George Walton was the principal of the Oliver Grammar School in Lawrence, Massachusetts, and they made their home in Lawrence for about eighteen years. During this period, five children were born to the Waltons, and Electa kept a small school for them and other local children during their early years. She and George also collaborated on writing arithmetic texts. To her dismay and anger, publishers refused at first to print her name as one of the authors.

The publishers asserted that the books would not sell with a woman's name attached to them, and so the first of the texts was published under George Walton's name alone.[51] In later books Electa's name was included, but the experience was a radicalizing one for her. She became an outspoken advocate for women's rights and suffrage. But women's rights were not her only cause. As might be expected for one with Electa's abolitionist sentiments, she turned her energies to the support of the Union Army. In 1861, the Sanitary Commission was formed to coordinate the activities of various groups of women who were working to send food, clothing, and medical supplies to camps and hospitals. Electa was an energetic volunteer, an adept organizer, and an effective fund-raiser.

It has been noted that Electa maintained close ties to the Normal School and to its graduates. It comes as no surprise, then, to find that she and Lucretia Crocker had been working with George N. Bigelow, Eben Stearn's successor as principal, to plan the "Quarter Centennial Celebration" of the founding of the normal schools.[52] The Normal School had once more outgrown its accommodations in West Newton and had moved to Framingham in 1853, and it was there that the celebration was to be held on 1 July 1864. Although Horace Mann and Cyrus Peirce had died, many others remained to recall the early struggles of the normal schools. Present and former members of the Massachusetts Board of Education were present, and the Honorable Josiah Quincy presided over the ceremonies. Samuel J. May returned to deliver the major oration, and Eben Stearns gave a historical sketch of the founding of the normal schools.[53] And beside them on the platform was Electa Lincoln Walton, who delivered the welcoming address on behalf of the Normal School:

> In a little book called "The Stars and the Earth," the author mathematically demonstrates, that by laws of light and motion, no action is ever lost. . . . This gathering of today is making a record which can never be effaced,—a record upon which we ourselves may gaze in coming years. And so now, could we recede, with disenthralled spirits, far away, millions of miles among the stars, turning to earth, we might see actually going on, the formation of the first Normal School in America.

> We might see its first principal, dear Father Peirce, as he left his island home for he knew not what arduous duties nor fiery trials, but with a unity of purpose and an iron will, ready to grapple with any difficulty that might beset his way, saying even then to his wife as he

neared our shore, "I would rather die than fail."

We might follow that leader to the quiet village of Lexington, enter with him the humble building dedicated to the then Normal experiment, where, on the third of July, 1839, some few friends of educational progress, with only three pioneer pupils, took the initiatory steps for the establishment of a Normal School, made the small beginning which has wrought untold effects; for the mustard seed has become a tree, the acorn a mighty oak.

... From a child whose life was so precarious that it would seem a breath might blow it away, and whose existence was looked upon by those who were ignorant of its true value, as an evil, not a blessing, it has become an Alma Mater,—our Alma Mater. And today she has made a feast, and called her children home. Her wide-spread arms would fain embrace all who have ever shared her life, or who have faithfully stood by her, and cheered and aided her. She bids you welcome! welcome to this crowning joy, linked with hallowed associations of twenty-five years. ... [54]

Her speech may sound oversentimental and flowery to our ears today, but there is no question that it was a very moving experience for the graduates in the audience and especially for the nine members of the first class and Mrs. Harriet Peirce, who sat among them.[55] It is impossible to know what they and Electa thought about the fact that it was now acceptable for her to speak in this public forum and to address this august assembly. Perhaps Louisa Stone Hopkins, class of 1853, spoke for them all when she read the poem she had written:

... So, young and full of courage, we looked the future through,
And thought—There's naught upon the earth we will not dare to do.
All holy work is Woman's work, unworthy she who scans
Each feebly-set partition that divides her work from Man's.[56]

Whatever Electa may have thought about the changing times, she continued to participate in a variety of educational and social activities. For a number of years, George Walton had been a frequent organizer and lecturer at the Teacher Institutes, which Mann had initiated in 1845 to supplement the work of the Normal Schools, since the three approved schools could not be expected to educate enough teachers for the entire state. As the population of Massachusetts grew and with it the number of schools, the secretary of the board found it increasingly difficult to visit them all, offer advice, and organize institutes as Mann had attempted to do. In 1868, an agent was authorized by the legislature to assist the secretary, and in 1871 George Walton was named Special Agent of the Massachusetts Board of Education for the "towns west of the Connecticut River."[57]

In his next report, the secretary of the board announced that George Walton's work was so satisfactory that his assignment had been "enlarged to embrace the whole of the four western counties."[58] The Waltons moved to Westfield and Electa continued to teach in the Normal School there as well as in teacher institutes throughout Massachusetts and New York. She also joined the Women's Christian Temperance Union (WCTU) and became president of the local organization.[59]

Electa also taught special courses for graduating seniors at Hampton Institute in Virginia, a school founded after the Civil War to educate African Americans and Native Americans. Both Lucretia Crocker, who worked with the New England Freedman's Society, and Electa turned their earlier abolitionist sentiments into the practical work of educating freedmen and in supporting the new institutions for blacks by helping to raise money among their affluent friends.

After a few years George Walton was named General Agent of the Board, and his activities took him throughout the state. The Waltons moved one last time to West Newton. George's reports to the Massachusetts Board of Education remain interesting documents for the modern reader, not only for the issues of the day (which seem to come around again and again), but also because of his careful language, which reflected his sensitivity to the women among whom he worked. At a time when teachers were consistently referred to as "he," George made careful distinctions using pronouns appropriate to the sex, or sometimes "he and she" when both were needed—common practice today, but arresting in that time. A sensitive man in his own right, he supported and shared Electa's attitudes toward women and their rights.

Electa, now approaching sixty years of age, renewed her friendships with women in West Newton and joined with them to organize the West Newton Educational Club. They devoted themselves to discussing educational questions of the day in order to vote intelligently on school issues. School suffrage for women in Massachusetts had recently been granted (1874), in some measure the result of the efforts of Abby May and Lucretia Crocker. The club was also active in raising money for Tuskegee Institute in Alabama, where another Framingham Normal School graduate, Olivia Davidson, was the "lady principal," chief assistant to Booker T. Washington and later Washington's wife.[60]

The list of organizations in which Electa served actively is long. She was a member of the West Newton Women's Society, the American Peace Society, the Society for the Prevention of Cruelty to Animals (opposing the killing of animals for sport or decoration), and the Wintergreen Club, a literary club. In 1883, the Waltons hosted a group that organized the Newton Suffrage League, of which she was president for some years.[61]

As late as 1902 she was actively involved in trying to mediate a dispute over the membership of women of color in the Women's Clubs. As one would surmise, she was "firmly opposed to the introduction of a race qualification for membership," and gave strong support to the clubs which had women of color as members.[62] She continued to be a popular speaker for public occasions and in private settings she gave literary readings and lectures on poets, her favorite being Whittier.

Somewhere in all of this busy life she found time to keep in touch with Harriet Peirce. Mrs. Peirce died in 1884 at the age of ninety, leaving a small bequest to the Normal School at Framingham to aid needy students.[63] Electa administered this fund for more than twenty years. Although Electa was a frequent and ubiquitous speaker, she left few articles or papers. But she did leave the history of the Normal School, which she wrote for the Fiftieth Anniversary (Semi-Centennial) Celebration in 1889. It is most interesting in that it contains information about the lives of many of the graduates and teachers of the Normal School in the first fifty years. She delivered the history as a speech to the distinguished company. These were her closing words: ". . . let those of us who teach be learners still, and may those who think they simply learn, fully realize that whenever their minds reach out to influence another, by just so much they are inevitably teachers."[64]

The address was published in the Massachusetts Board of Education Report for the year and so became part of the historical record.[65]

Electa Lincoln Walton died on 15 March 1908 at the age of eighty-four. George and three of their children survived her. Harriet Peirce Walton married a prominent lawyer and reared a family; Dr. George L. Walton was graduated from Harvard and became a neurologist; and Miss Alice Walton was graduated from Smith, earned a doctorate at Cornell, and became a professor of Latin and archeology at Wellesley College.[66]

One of her younger colleagues at the Normal School, a student during Miss Hyde's administration, wrote the following tribute to her:

Her life was so filled with good work that she had no fear of finding old age wearisome, and she never seemed weary; she grew old patiently and bravely; life was sweet to her and full of interest, and she opened her hands and her heart to all that was good and true and helpful, the same in the twilight of her life as in her younger days.[67]

Electa Lincoln Walton had come to the Normal School as a student at the age of seventeen in 1841. She was among the first women to teach at an advanced level, and the first to administer a state normal school. For more than sixty years she taught, wrote for teachers, inspired teachers, and worked with successive administrations at the Normal School. As a member of the first generation of normal school graduates, she had a significant impact on the careers of the next generation of teachers, some of whose stories follow in subsequent chapters. Electa never ceased learning, and expected the same of others who aspired to her profession. For her, the Normal School was the gateway to a useful and fulfilling life of advocacy in behalf of education, women's rights, and freedom and equality for people of color.

First Building Framingham Normal School in Framingham, Massachusetts, in 1853.

1. Mary Swift Lamson, ed., *Records of the First Class of the First State Normal School in America* (Boston: privately printed, 1903), 190.

2. Summary based on *Records of the First Class; Historical Sketches of the Framingham State Normal School* (Framingham: Alumnae Association, 1914), 99–103; and the *State Normal School Framingham, Massachusetts Catalogue of Teachers and Alumnae 1839–1900* (Boston: Wright & Potter, 1900).

3. *Records of the First Class*, 6.

4. Ibid., 197.

5. Ibid., 13.

6. Ibid., 204–6.

7. Madeline P. Stern, *We the Women: Career Firsts of Nineteenth Century America* (New York: Schulte, 1963), 158. Courtesy of the Antioch College archives.

8. Ibid., 166.

9. Ibid., 170.

10. *Historical Sketches*, 101.

11. Arthur O. Norton, *The First State Normal School in America* (Cambridge: Harvard University Press, 1926), 1.

12. Ibid., 280.

13. Ibid., 283.

14. Ibid., 11.

15. Ibid., 283.

16. These are themes which recur to the present day in the writings of educational reformists. Peirce speaks particularly of the folly of alphabet drills as a precursor to reading instruction (see Norton, *First State Normal School*, 282), and of the role of the senses in young children's learning (Norton, *First State Normal School*, 281). These themes were important to most of the teachers in this book, and are especially relevant to Lelia Patridge (chapter 6).

17. Julia Ward Howe, ed., *Representative Women of New England* (Boston: New England Historical Publishing, 1904), 247.

18. *State Normal School Catalogue*, 15.

19. Mary Mann, *Life of Horace Mann* (Boston: Walker, Fuller and Co., 1865), 168–72.

20. Samuel J. May was adamantly opposed to the Fugitive Slave Law. He pointed out that under the provisions of the law, the case against the alleged fugitive slave was reviewed by a commissioner or judge; the alleged fugitive's testimony, however, could not be admitted in evidence. A commissioner or judge who found that the accused had fled from bondage received $10, but a judge finding that the proof was not satisfactory received $5. "Thus, bribery was by this law superadded to every other device to enable the American slaveholder to recover his escaped slave, and return him or her to a still more cruel bondage." Samuel J. May *Some Recollections of Our Antislavery Conflict* (Boston: Fields, Osgood, 1869), 347. Courtesy Wayland Library Historical Collection, Wayland, Massachusetts.

21. Afua Cooper, "The Search for Mary Bibb, Black Woman Teacher in Nineteenth Century Canada West," *Ontario History* 83 (March 1991): 41.

22. *Historical Sketches*, 96; and "Mrs. Electa N. L. Walton: In Memoriam," *Woman's Journal* (Boston) 28 March 1908.

23. *First State Normal School in America: The State Teachers College at Framingham, Massachusetts* (Framingham: Alumnae Association), 4–5.

24. Ibid., 5.

25. Ibid., 55.

26. Ibid., 56.

27. Electa Lincoln Journal, 1848–49. Massachusetts Historical Society manuscript file.

28. "Proceedings of the Third Triennial Convention of the West Newton State

Normal School" (Boston: Leonard C. Bowles, 26 July 1848), 5. Framingham State College Alumni Association files.

29. Ibid.

30. Lincoln Journal, 18 August 1848.

31. "Proceedings Triennial Convention," 9.

32. Lincoln Journal, 18 February 1849.

33. Ibid., 12 April 1849.

34. Ibid.

35. Ibid.

36. Ibid.

37. Ibid., 18 April 1849.

38. Ibid., 13 April 1849.

39. Ibid.

40. Ibid., 18 April 1849.

41. Historical Sketches, 39.

42. Journal of Emily Ward, 12 September 1849. FSC Alumni Association files.

43. Ibid., 18 September 1849.

44. "Memorial of the Quarter-Centennial Celebration of the Establishment of Normal Schools in America, Held at Framingham, 1 July 1864" (Boston: C. C. P. Moody, 1866), 51. FSC Alumni Association files.

45. Cora Newton (class of 1877) letter reporting one of Crocker's visits to the Framingham Normal School. FSC Alumni Association document.

46. Ednah Dow Cheney, Memoirs of Lucretia Crocker and Abby W. May (Boston: Massachusetts School Suffrage Association, 1893), 7.

47. Historical Sketches, 39.

48. The Normal School Diary, Volume 5, 27 March 1880. This is a journal of events at the Normal School written by students and teachers over a period of many years. Some of the assigned scribes wrote detailed accounts of events, while others wrote little or missed significant events. Nevertheless, the diary does provide glimpses of school life not available from other sources. FSC Alumni Association files.

49. Document from the Peabody Collection, Olive Kettering Library, Antioch College, Yellow Springs, Ohio. Nina Myatt was most helpful to me during my visit to Antioch in 1987.

50. Howe, Representative Women of New England, 247.

51. Ibid., 248.

52. "Memorial of the Quarter-Centennial Celebration," 3.

53. Ibid.

54. Ibid., 5–10.

55. Records of the First Class, 99–100.

56. "Memorial of the Quarter-Centennial Celebration," 11.

57. Thirty-fifth Annual Report of the Massachusetts Board of Education (1872), 108.

58. Thirty-sixth Annual Report (1873), 167.

59. Howe, Representative Women of New England, 279.

60. Beverly J. Weiss, "Growth and Outreach," in Pioneers in Education (Framingham: Framingham State College), 25–28.

61. Howe, Representative Women of New England, 279.

62. History Committee of the Federation of Women's Clubs, From the Past to the Future: A History of the Massachusetts State Federation of Women's Clubs 1893–1988 (Canaan, New Hampshire: Phoenix Publications, 1988), 225. Women's Clubs Archive, Sudbury, Massachusetts.

63. Historical Sketches, 97.

64. Ibid., 53.

65. Fifty-third Annual Report (1890).

66. Howe, Representative Women, 279; and Historical Sketches, 98.

67. Historical Sketches, 97.

4 TEACHER AND PRINCIPAL AT THE FIRST STATE NORMAL SCHOOL: ELLEN HYDE (1838–1926)

Beverly J. Weiss

Ellen Hyde, circa 1862.

For the last quarter of the nineteenth century, the history of the Normal School at Framingham and the life of its principal, Ellen Hyde, were almost inseparable. There were many remarkable women who graduated from the Normal School, but there is no one who represents better the work and the spirit of the school, or who did more to advance it, than Ellen Hyde.

Ellen Hyde came to the Normal School as a twenty-three-year-old student in 1861, was graduated in 1862, entered the advanced program, and began teaching at the Normal School in 1863. She served as assistant principal under Annie Johnson, and succeeded her as principal in 1875. Over the next twenty-three years she guided the expansion of the Normal School, maintained its traditions, developed the practice school to a professional level, fostered the network of alumnae, reached out to women of color, and established cooperative, working relationships with the people of the town of Framingham.

The hopes and dreams of Horace Mann and of Cyrus Peirce, the first principal of the first normal school, were most fully realized at Framingham Normal School during Miss Hyde's administration. The reforms they espoused and the organization they set in motion were carried forward by many proponents across the commonwealth, but the Normal School at Framingham between 1875 and 1898 was in the hands of a true believer in the efficacy of well-prepared teachers and of an effective, well-educated administrator.

Ellen Hyde as Student and Teacher

Ellen Hyde was born in Rome, New York, in 1838. Orphaned at sixteen, she went to live with her uncle and guardian, J.B. Hyde, in New York. She attended the Neversink Seminary in Port Jervis, New York, and then continued her studies with private tutors.[1] Ellen Hyde was an admirable candidate for normal-school training because of the thoroughness of her education. The early proponents of the normal schools had envisaged students who would already be proficient in the common branches, particularly reading, writing, and arithmetic, so that the curriculum could be concentrated on the art and science of teaching. Thus, Ellen Hyde was considered an excellent candidate for the Normal School, and she was admitted with advanced standing by the principal, George Bigelow.

The course of study for the normal schools had been the subject of many debates. There was agreement that the main mission of the normal schools was to teach the art and science of pedagogy, but it was equally clear that a firm grasp of the subjects to be taught was also necessary. Politically, it would have been unwise to set up state-supported schools that would have been in competition with the academies and private schools. But the attempt by New York to subsidize academies and private schools to offer teacher training programs was not considered a success.[2] The Massachusetts Normal Schools, then, were to concentrate on the art and science of teaching, but they would conduct such reviews of the common branches as were necessary. That came to be policy for normal schools generally, although there were universal complaints that the candidates for the schools were not well enough educated.

D.P. Colburn of the Rhode Island Normal School, speaking to the first annual convention of the American Normal School Association in 1860, seemed to capture the sentiments of the normal-school teachers and administrators. After stating his belief that no one "can teach that which he does not know himself" and that those who are still learning the subject cannot give attention to methods of instruction, Colburn asserted: "There is not, however, a normal school in the country that can, at present, dispense with giving academical instruction. The question therefore is settled practically let the theory be as it may."[3]

The Framingham Normal School catalog for 1861, the year Ellen Hyde arrived as a student, stated that the course of study was one and a half years but that it might be completed in one year by well-qualified students. On the other hand, some students might need more than the usual time to complete the required course, which included the analysis of sounds, reading, writing, spelling, punctuation, grammar, critical analysis of Milton and other poets, the history and structure of the English language, composition, rhetoric, English literature, arithmetic, algebra, geometry, physical and political geography with map drawing, physiology, botany, zoology, geology, natural philosophy, astronomy, the history of civilization, mental and moral philosophy, school laws, the constitution of the United States, the theory and art of teaching, Latin, vocal music, and drawing. The advanced class required three years for completion during which time students continued the study of algebra and geometry and the sciences, as well as logic and higher mathematics, English literature, Latin, French, and German.

The school year was forty weeks in duration, divided into two terms. The first term ran from September through January, and the second term began in March following a four-week vacation and ended in July. Students were advised to furnish themselves with a Bible, a dictionary, a common atlas, and any other books they might have. The catalog did indicate, however, that the school had a "well-selected library" that was accessible to the students daily.[4]

The Normal School still comprised but one building, erected in 1853, at the top of Bare Hill in Framingham. A large assembly hall extended across the front of the first floor of the building, and it was there that the school day began with devotional exercises and Bible reading, a custom that continued well into the twentieth century. Frequently there were visitors or lecturers who addressed the entire school at that forum. It seems that interest in the Normal School had not abated, and members of the Massachusetts Board of Education took an active role in providing information, especially on the operation of state government, and in examining the young women on the subjects they were studying. Other prominent men, such as Bronson Alcott, father of Louisa May Alcott, presented lectures from time to time.

Principal George Bigelow had studied in Germany and was very familiar with the German schools that had served as models for the Massachusetts system. He was also a fine linguist, and the advanced class studied Latin, German, and French as part of their preparation for teaching in high schools. He was assisted by three young women, two of whom were graduates of the Normal School. The faculty also included a music teacher and a gymnastics teacher (Dr. Dio Lewis), and lecturers in mental philosophy, botany, and chemistry. It is interesting to note that most of the visiting instructors and lecturers had been educated as ministers or lawyers, although they were considered experts in other fields as well: the botany teacher was a minister, the chemistry teacher a lawyer.[5]

Because there were no dormitory accommodations at the time Ellen Hyde came to Framingham, those who were not able to live at home boarded with families in the town. Nevertheless, the school prescribed a schedule for rest, recreation, study, and sleep. There was a system of self-reporting, and the young women submitted slips weekly on which they were expected to report any infractions of the rules.[6] Board was available for $2.50 to $3.00 a week, often with an added charge for fuel and lights. Even though tuition was free to those intending to teach in the public schools of Massachusetts, the cost of board was an increasingly difficult problem for the Normal School students. By the end of the decade a dormitory was constructed adjacent to the original school building, in order to make the education more accessible to less affluent applicants.[7]

It is likely that Ellen Hyde kept a journal of her school days, but it has not survived. One of her contemporaries, however, did leave us her impression of Ellen Hyde as a student: "Ellen Hyde was a person no one could forget. She was the first girl to attract my attention after the school was in good running order, and I thought she was the most beautiful girl I had ever seen . . . and I never tired of the sound of her voice which was very musical."[8]

Ellen Hyde completed the basic course of study in July of 1862 and enrolled in the advanced class. After only one term George Bigelow invited her to join the faculty to fill an unexpected vacancy. She accepted the appointment and began her long career of service to the Normal School in March 1863.[9] Annie Johnson, who had been hired as an assistant to the principal in 1861, may have played a part in her selection.

ANNIE JOHNSON

Annie Johnson, born and educated in Maine, had begun teaching at the age of fifteen and had taught in private schools as well as public ones. Prior to coming to the Normal School, she had taught "every grade in Brunswick [Maine] from the primary to the high, and was principal of that."[10] Her father was a Presbyterian clergyman, and she had gained an excellent, if somewhat haphazard, education from various professors at Bowdoin College. She was particularly well versed in Latin but familiar enough with all the subjects of the curriculum to help young teachers. She was interested in architecture, botany, parliamentary law, and psychology.[11]

In 1866 when Bigelow resigned, the Massachusetts Board of Education appointed Miss Annie Johnson principal of the Normal School. There was an elaborate ceremony for her inauguration, presided over by Governor Bullock, who proclaimed a new "experiment"—a woman administrator. It was fitting, he thought, at a school where all of the students were women.[12] Despite Miss Johnson's obvious success and that of Miss Hyde who followed her, women were never appointed as principals at the coeducational normal schools.

Miss Johnson's first priority was to reestablish a model school. As an experienced teacher, she felt the lack of a model school most keenly. It had been an integral part of the Normal School during the Lexington and West Newton years, but in the move to Framingham in 1853 the Model School was not resumed. Stearns and Bigelow may have agreed with Mr. Dickinson, the principal at Westfield Normal School, when he declared: "We had a model school which is now given up, and I do not know that the Normal School is injured thereby."[13] He explained that the Model School he referred to was a public school and that the relations with the school authorities "were not entirely pleasant."[14]

Miss Johnson was well aware that there was little sentiment in favor of model schools at the time, nor had there been earlier. Peirce alone of the first principals had been convinced of their value, perhaps because he was the only one of them who was a teacher, and only at Lexington and West Newton under his direction had model schools been maintained for any extended period.[15] Although the Normal School was once again crowded, Miss Johnson contrived to set up a small classroom and made arrangements with parents in the town to have a few children come for demonstration classes. The 1868 Normal School catalog stated: "Connected with the School there is a children's class, to which the young ladies give oral lessons during the last year of the course."[16]

The Framingham School Committee report of 1869–70 indicated that at the request of the Massachusetts Board of Education a new school had been established at the Normal School building. Thirty children from the primary and intermediate schools were assigned to the Model School, along with a teacher appointed by the town. The report pointed out that the school would be under the charge of the superintending committee of the school board and Miss Johnson. The arrangements may have been facilitated by C.C. Esty, a member of both the Massachusetts Board of Education and the Framingham Superintending Committee, who thought highly of Annie Johnson's work. Miss Johnson apparently reciprocated, by involving herself in the affairs of the town; she was elected to the school committee in 1873, the first woman to sit on the Framingham Board.[17]

As Miss Johnson's assistant, Miss Hyde had participated in the work of the Model School, and when she was made principal it became one of her priorities. In 1875, Miss Johnson resigned to become principal of Bradford Academy. This time the board showed no reluctance in naming a woman as principal in Framingham: Ellen Hyde served in that capacity until 1898.

ELLEN HYDE AS PRINCIPAL

There are three recurring themes in the many letters written about Miss Hyde by the alumnae. The first is that the Practice School provided an unique and valuable experience, and the attractive, busy classrooms, guided by responsive teachers, were among their most vivid memories. Many also credit Miss Hyde with keeping before them the necessity to help the "Negro and the Indian" gain an education and to improve the conditions of their lives. Nearly all found Miss Hyde's life an example and an inspiration, of far more effect than her words, as eloquent as she was.

For much of the first seventy-five years of the Normal School, a diary or journal of each day's events was kept. In some years the records were lively and full of information, while for others they are missing or brief and dry. Nevertheless, the records complement the formal reports to the board of education and provide a glimpse of the day-to-day activities of the school. The transition to Ellen Hyde's administration seems to have gone smoothly.

The diary laments the loss of Annie Johnson but continues by saying: "Notwithstanding Miss Johnson's absence, school has seemed to go nearly as usual, for there have been no strange faces among us. Our teacher Miss Ellen Hyde has been our principal through the term, and all were heartily glad to know that she will continue to be for at least a part of next term."[18]

Although the board had been willing to appoint Ellen Hyde to the principalship, she was reluctant to accept because of chronic poor health. By March 1876, however, she had decided to undertake the charge and was duly appointed by the board. The Official Visitor, C.C. Esty, came to the school to make the announcement, and the students left no doubt about their reaction. They presented her with flowers as an expression of their pleasure, and spontaneously applauded a teacher who pledged the support of the faculty.[19]

Ellen Hyde seems to have begun at once to incorporate her own ideas into the administration of the school. She gave students more opportunities for self-governance and more choices about their activities. For example, the seniors and the advanced class were given flexibility in their study hours as long as they observed a ten o'clock bedtime. Students were free to organize clubs and societies consistent with their interests. In that spirit, the music club became a debating society considering such questions as "Should the Bible be abolished from the common schools?" and "Shall women vote?" (both questions were resolved in the negative). From time to time students planned an evening's entertainment that often included charades and community singing.[20]

Electa Walton noted this characteristic of Miss Hyde's administration in particular, referring to it as the "self-government of her pupils." She said, "Old time divisions such as one used often to see between teacher and pupils, are broken down, and instead great mutual confidence is established."[21] She spoke to critics, saying that the Normal School had no serious trouble from self-government, but that in any case "it is better to run the risk of an occasional irregularity than to subject students to the belittling effects of a great many rules."[22]

MODEL SCHOOL TO PRACTICE SCHOOL

In her first report to the board of education in 1877, Ellen Hyde wrote that there were thirty children in the Model School, all that could be accommodated.[23] A year later two rooms were being used for the Model School, with nearly sixty children attending. Two teachers, Ellen Williams and Augusta Barber, were in charge of the classrooms and the student teaching.[24] Miss Hyde called the work "invaluable and indispensable," providing an opportunity to learn and practice observation, write descriptions, and offer constructive criticism. She had ceased to refer to it as the Model School, preferring instead to call it the Practice School, "better indicating the purpose of the School and being less terrifying to those who were to teach in it."[25] Model school or practice school, Miss Hyde was virtually alone in advocating its inclusion as part of the Normal School curriculum.

The school catalog for 1877 emphasized the value of the Practice School to prospective applicants:

> This object [instruction in teaching] is kept in view from the first, but during the last year of the course is specially prominent, the pupils having constant opportunity to observe and criticize the teaching of others, and to practice teaching themselves, both as assistants in the school of practice (which includes pupils of all grades from primary to grammar) and as teachers of single classes of children, subject to the criticism of their classmates and teachers.[26]

Some letters remain from graduates of the Normal School relating their memories of the Practice School. The following words were written by a student who entered the Normal School in 1881 and graduated in 1883:

> The old building (Normal Hall) was not large and two of our recitation rooms, the North Room and the Geography Room were separated from the Model School by an ordinary partition and doors were sometimes left open between the rooms. Because of this proximity, we Normal students were often in contact with the Model School.

> In those days the Normal students dusted the entire building every morning supervised by the students in the advanced class. We were delighted to get in touch with the pupils in the Model School and were glad when our housekeeping duties took us to that part of the building. Those two school rooms seemed like a bit of paradise to those of us who had experienced the hard discipline in a district school of the "seventies."

> The Model School rooms were most attractive. There were plants in the windows, pictures on the walls, happy children moving about freely. There were low gentle voices of the teachers and an atmosphere of kindness and peace.[27]

Judging from this student's comment, the kindly attitude and freedom from punishment advocated by Peirce and practiced now for more than forty years in the Normal School had not yet become common in all of the schools of the commonwealth. This was not surprising, because the normal schools, now five in number (Framingham, Westfield, Bridgewater, Salem, and Worcester), were unable to supply as many trained teachers as were needed. In 1883, the board of education reported that "somewhat more than 30 percent of the teachers in the public schools of the Commonwealth have received more or less professional training in the normal schools."[28] The "more or less" refers to the fact that teachers might be hired after studying at a normal school or teachers institute without being graduated.

At Framingham, the work in the Practice School was becoming increasingly formalized and professional. In 1882, Ellen Williams, who had been the head teacher in the grammar department at the Practice School, was relieved of her teaching duties so that she could become the supervisor and critic for the Normal scholars. The Official Visitor, Abby May, reported on the success of the Practice School:

> The Model School under Miss William's care has become a flourishing and popular school, all of whose graduates, without exception, have taken a first rank in the high schools to which they have been admitted, in Marlborough, Southborough and Framingham, and have taken excellent rank in the Boys' Latin School and the Prince School of Boston. And this is not because they were selected scholars for our school. They were not better, probably, than the average; but under our care they have been admirably trained in the use of their faculties, and the school work has been made plain and pleasant to them, in spite of the fact that the course is not exceptionally easy, and is exceedingly thorough.[29]

A student in the Practice School wrote a letter to Miss Williams many years later describing his experience as a pupil:

> My love of nature was doubtless inborn, but the simple lessons in botany, mineralogy, and zoology at the Practice School showed me how to give it expression and direction. Those lessons were far ahead of anything in the public schools at that time, for they were based upon plants, minerals and animals, and not upon books. Even geometry was taught by what might be called the natural method. . . . In writing upon various subjects, I have found that illustrations drawn

from Nature are often of value—in fact, there is hardly any department of endeavor in which I do not note a greater efficiency because
of the scientific habit of thought which dates from my childhood days
at the Practice School at Framingham. Of no less value were the conscientious efforts of our teachers in applying what were then new
methods of instruction, and in arousing in the pupils that enthusiasm
without which any instruction is of little value.[30]

As the years passed, the old Normal Hall, built in 1853, became not
only too small for the burgeoning student body but also extremely uncomfortable. Even when new, the building was inadequately heated, and the
cracks at windows and doors made coats and hats the standard winter ap-
parel in the classroom. The official visitor to the school, Abby May, campaigned vigorously for an appropriation for a new building. When the approval finally came, Miss Hyde made certain that the plans included facilities for the Practice School.

May Hall, named for Abby May, who died before it was completed,
was dedicated in 1889. The Practice School occupied three large rooms, four
smaller recitation rooms and a principal's office on the east side of the first
floor of the new building. Writing retrospectively about the early 1890s, a
student recalled that there were fifty to sixty pupils and that it had the "character of a private school." Some Framingham parents sent their children to
the school because they believed their children would have a better educational experience. That opinion was by no means universal; some parents
distrusted "modern methods" or worried that their children would be used
as subjects for experiments.

Here is a description of practice teaching by one of the students:

> The lessons to the children were to be continuous each student tak-
> ing up where the other left off. These lessons were to be criticized by
> the teacher and the students. In a lesson of this kind all the young
> ladies in the class were to be prepared to teach a certain subject. When
> it came time for the lesson, a class of little children were brought in
> and one of the young ladies was called upon to teach. She then took
> charge of the class and taught the lesson. Her classmates listened with
> great interest occasionally jotting down a note. When she had finished
> the children filed out and the young ladies criticized the lesson that
> had just been taught. The points to be criticized were the prepara-
> tion and the development of the lesson and the manner of the
> teacher.[31]

In time, the town began to assist in defraying the expenses of the school, as it increasingly served the children of the town. Many graduates of the Normal School were hired for the local schools, and evaluations of the education offered at the Practice School changed in tone from cautious neutrality to positive appreciation. In 1896, the town of Framingham was divided into two school districts, and the Practice School in May Hall was designated the district school for that side of the town. Whatever air of exclusivity had hovered over the Practice School was soon dispelled: "The new district included some children from the underprivileged classes. The character of our school was changed. The classes were larger, new teachers were added to the training department, another school room was opened, and we were overcrowded."[32]

If the students at the Normal school had been spared, unrealistically, the problems of teaching immigrant children and those growing up in the poverty-stricken homes of factory workers, they no longer would be. In that same year students were sent for the first time for practice teaching in the city schools of Waltham. But Ellen Hyde's firmly held conviction that practice teaching be an integral part of the preparation of teachers was now gospel, and the state required all of the normal schools to provide that experience. What she alone had once defended for the Framingham students now became the standard for the state.[33]

OUTREACH

Earlier principals had concerned themselves with the cause of abolition, and Ellen Hyde took up the work of fostering educational opportunities for African Americans and Native Americans. It is difficult to document how many minority women studied at the Normal School, because the official records did not include that information. Sometimes stories or pictures gave some indication of race. Two women of color from the antebellum period, Mary E. Miles and Chloe Lee, have been identified. Marion P. Shadd was graduated in the class of 1875, spent two more years in the advanced class, and then went to Washington, D.C., to teach in the public schools. By 1887 she had become principal of the Lincoln School, and eventually she became the assistant superintendent for the system, the first woman to hold that position. An elementary school was named in her honor. Her story is detailed in chapter 9.

It appears that there were women of color as students continuously during Ellen Hyde's administration. One reason for that was the strong connection that existed with Hampton Institute in Virginia and Tuskegee Institute in Alabama. Hampton Institute was founded in 1868 by General Samuel

Framingham Normal School Class of 1890. Ellen Hyde, wearing a hat, is seated at top center. Annie Dawson, without hat, stands at her right.

Armstrong, who commanded a company of African American soldiers during the Civil War and whose family came from Massachusetts.[34] He was aided by the American Missionary Association, and he raised money from Boston philanthropists such as Miss Abby May and Mrs. Mary Hemenway, friends and associates of Lucretia Crocker, a graduate of 1850 and an officer in the New England Freedman's Society during Reconstruction.

In 1875 Elizabeth Hyde, a cousin of Ellen's, went to Hampton to teach. She began as a teacher in the Model School there and remained for thirty-seven years as teacher and administrator. Other graduates of the Normal School went to Hampton to teach for varying periods well into the twentieth century. Hampton students came to Framingham to study as well. One outstanding student from Hampton was Olivia Davidson. Olivia Davidson was born in Virginia in 1854. She moved with her family to Albany, Ohio, where she attended both public schools and a black-owned and -operated academy. After the Civil War, she began her teaching career with former slaves in Hernando, Mississippi, and in the rural schools of the state.

In 1878 Olivia enrolled in the senior class at Hampton Institute, hoping to gain a better education and to improve her teaching skills. She graduated with honors in 1879 and presented an essay at the commencement exercises. Mrs. Hemenway, who was in the audience, was very impressed with her presentation and decided at once to assist the talented young woman in continuing her studies.[35] Olivia's work at the Framingham Normal School sustained the high expectations for her, and she was graduated in 1881. For her graduation essay she chose the title "The Work of the Colored Teacher in the South." In the essay she asked her listeners who wanted to help her people to send books and teachers to the South, not food and clothing, "that are soon eaten or worn out, leaving the negro as poor as ever and as needy. . . ."[36]

Miss Davidson must be credited, certainly, with her own insight and wisdom, but it seems more than a coincidence that helping others to become independent was the philosophy of those associated with the Normal School. Electa Lincoln had written similar words in 1849, and at that very time, in 1881, Mary Swift Lamson from the first class, now on the board of the Young Women's Christian Association (YWCA), was espousing the same sentiments. That philosophy was at the base, also, of teaching the physically challenged, another contribution of women from the Normal School, who became teachers of the deaf and the blind.

Booker T. Washington was also in the audience at Hampton when Olivia Davidson gave her graduation essay. Soon after he went to Tuskegee to organize the new school in July 1881, he invited Olivia to be the first member of his staff. She proved an invaluable collaborator. She was experienced in teaching freedmen, and her training in the theory and practice of teaching at Framingham gave her a basis for planning curriculum and teaching effectively. Moreover, she took on the chore of raising funds for the new school, at first in the local community and eventually through her contacts in the North. She enlisted the help of the Framingham network and established connections for Tuskegee that survived well into the twentieth century.[37] Washington himself acknowledged that no one had done more "toward laying the foundation for Tuskegee Institute as to insure the successful work that has been done than Olivia Davidson."[38]

Olivia married the widowed Washington in 1886 and took over the care of his infant daughter, Portia. Two sons were born to them, in 1887 and in 1889, but she continued her work for the institute. In 1889 her long battle with consumption took her life.[39] Washington maintained the contacts with the Framingham Normal School, not only as a fund-raising activity but also as a school for his daughter. Miss Mary Moore, a graduate of the school and a teacher there, took his young daughter, Portia, to live with her so that she could attend the Practice School.

Another student from Hampton was Annie Dawson, born Spananadaka at Like-A-Fish-Hook-Village, Fort Berthold Indian Reservation, Dakota Territory, in 1868. When she was ten years old, she was sent to Hampton to be educated. Soon after, she was orphaned and left under the protection of the school. She was graduated from Hampton in 1885 and remained there as a teacher of young Native American boys for several years. In 1887, the decision was made to send her to the Normal School at Framingham. As her supervisor, it is likely that Elizabeth Hyde participated in the arrangements.[40] Correspondence between Ellen Hyde and Cora Folsom at Hampton Institute indicates that Annie Dawson had some difficulty meeting the standards, but Miss Hyde made the decision to accept her and to give her the extra attention necessary for her to succeed. She wrote, "She is a good child, studies hard, too hard sometimes, and is doing her best."[41]

Miss Dawson was graduated in 1890, and after a few years of teaching at Santee Normal School, a school for Native Americans in Nebraska, she returned to Fort Berthold to work as a field matron among her people. In 1902, she married Byron Wilde, who had studied at Bridgewater Normal School during her Framingham years. Annie Dawson Wilde died in 1968 at the age of one hundred, another woman educated by the Normal School for work she was uniquely qualified to perform.[42]

ELLEN HYDE AS MODEL

The graduates remembered Ellen Hyde for other reasons as well. She delighted in reading passages from great literature to the school at opening exercises, but she often read the day's news to them as well. Every event was an occasion for relating history, geography, and sometimes politics to their studies. When the Centennial Exposition opened in Philadelphia in 1876, the accounts of it were read from the newspapers, and the event was used to organize lectures, debates, and activities related to the curriculum: Governor Washburn visited and gave a series of lectures on government and on choosing a president, pointing out that it was an election year. Students debated the question "Were our forefathers justified in driving out the Indians from this district of the country?" Miss Hyde made them aware of history closer to home by reading from the journals of earlier students, which inspired one young woman to write descriptions of their own days for those who were yet to come. And the students sent a picture of their school and boarding house to the Centennial Exposition.[43]

Miss Hyde was a well-traveled woman and had made several lengthy trips abroad for study and for rest during her years at the Normal School. Her travels undoubtedly made her more aware of events in Europe as well as the influential work of German educators. The school journal shows that she regularly brought current events to the students' attention. For example, on 5 May 1877 she discussed the "war between Russia and Turkey," made all the more realistic because a Framingham graduate, Corinna Shattuck, was in Turkey as a missionary and sent home letters about her experiences that were read aloud in the classroom.[44]

The students made it quite clear that Ellen Hyde was a demanding teacher, but she spiced the work with a variety of activities. Spelling geographical terms became more challenging when the place had to be located as well. There were special programs, such as a lecture by Alexander Graham Bell on "visible speech" (an oral method of instruction for the hearing impaired) or a historical tour of all the statues displayed in the schoolroom. Students were dazzled by lectures about Yellowstone National Park, illustrated with a stereopticon and accompanied by a display of petrified grasshopper specimens.[45] And in good weather there were visits to nearby fields and woods to study botany.

No doubt Miss Hyde had health as well as learning on her mind in planning the outings. Never in robust health herself, she incorporated sports and active games into the school's activities whenever possible. She engaged Mary J. Studley in 1877 as resident physician and to instruct the young women in health and physiology.[46] Dr. Studley was an 1852 graduate of the Normal School, as well as a graduate of the Woman's Medical College of New York.[47] Her duties also extended to teaching the natural sciences after Maria Eaton (class of 1867), who had completed several years of study in Germany, resigned her position at the Normal School to teach chemistry at the new Wellesley College for women.[48]

Although Ellen Hyde must have been aware of the growing number of women's colleges, she continued to advocate an extended program for the Normal School and a high-school diploma as a condition for admission. The Normal School's advanced class had been offered since 1852, and since 1869 four years had been required for students to complete the regular school program and the advanced class combined.[49] While the Normal School had many students from families of limited means, it had always attracted a number of affluent young women whose families were unwilling to permit them to travel long distances to the coeducational colleges. As the women's colleges opened, the four-year program at the Normal School seemed no longer necessary to some and unwelcome competition to the private colleges to others. Pressure would mount over the next two decades to abolish the advanced program.

Miss Hyde, like Miss Lincoln before her, gently but firmly insisted that everyone do her best and come as close to perfection as possible. There were no grades or honors at the school. Ellen Hyde agreed with Mr. Peirce that learning should not depend on either rewards or punishments but rather on its own intrinsic pleasure and the student's self-discipline. Also, she had observed that students did differ in their abilities and gifts, and thought that each should be challenged to do her best. In that spirit, she had expected that Olivia Davidson would be an outstanding scholar, but she recognized that Annie Dawson needed more help and time to acquire the skills the school considered essential. She did not give up easily or allow others to do so. Antoinette Roof (class of 1886) recalled the struggles of a class trying to learn a complicated march and making the "same unthinking blunders" over and over again. Miss Hyde's voice "rang out clear and incisive, 'Young ladies, we will do this thing right if it takes all summer.'"[50]

Ellen Hyde was often called upon to speak to educators on "moral training." Discipline, she thought, "should rest on law, the golden rule, and it should give the greatest possible personal liberty." To the graduating class of 1886 she said, "To hear lessons and control restless children six hours a day through thirty-six weeks in the year is wretched drudgery, but to train and develop human minds and characters is the most inspiring work in the world." She urged them to look for the noble side of things, for "even the sun can be diminished by looking at it through the wrong end of your telescope."[51]

Miss Hyde had two other important messages for the class of 1886: "What you know is of vastly less importance than what you are; the best methods in the world are worthless tools without the true teacher's enthusiasm. . . . You are called and ordained to be good teachers but you had a prior call to be good women."[52]

Finally, she put into words what she had encouraged in the classroom by example and design:

> Cultivate a broad interest in the world's welfare. It is among the possibilities of the future to make yourselves felt (not necessarily heard or seen) in the adjustment of capital and labor, in prison reform, in justice to the Indian and the Chinaman, in the true elevation of your own sex, in wiser social relations, in a more Christ-like christianity. Life that offers such opportunities is good and sweet; it may be grand.[53]

Many years later, Lillian A. Ordway, a graduate of 1889, wrote about her memories of the Normal School and Ellen Hyde:

> Dignity and power emanated from Miss Hyde, our principal. . . .

These were the highlights of our days: Miss Hyde's Bible reading in the morning and her reading of poetry. Few can read as she could. To look at her was a pleasure, beautiful eyes, delicate, exquisite hands, a fine voice. . . . We delighted in the readings from the school diary of Father Peirce and his pupils and to hear of the graduates of the school who had accomplished great things, and all the time there grew in us an intense love, loyalty and pride in the school."[54]

That is a description of Miss Hyde at midlife, fourteen years into her administration of the Normal School. As the principal of the school she was required to make her residence in the dormitory. That she also made of the dormitory a home, and of its residents a family, was her choice. She herself had attended the Normal School at a time when there was no dormitory there, so that students either commuted or found accommodations in the town, a considerable problem for young women of limited resources who might be required to take on domestic chores in exchange for their board. In the residence hall as in the classroom, Ellen Hyde set an example for gracious and industrious behavior:

Miss Hyde read as we sewed, and although other authors were tried from time to time, Dickens was always the favorite, and we always returned to him. These evenings are among my pleasantest memories of school life. Then there were frequent "family meetings" in Miss Hyde's parlor, when the little happenings of the week furnished the text for short talks. The key-note of these talks was not "don't," but "do," not fault finding, but inspiration.[55]

The image of domestic tranquility evoked here conceals Ellen Hyde's struggle to find the money to maintain the aging residence in good condition. She and the students paid to have electricity installed in 1888, and it was not until 1890 that town water became available and solved the chronic water problem attendant upon living at the top of a hill.[56]

The year 1889 marked the fiftieth anniversary of the founding of the Massachusetts normal schools, the first state-supported teacher-training schools in the nation. Eight graduates of the first class attended the celebration, along with graduates from five decades.[57] A dazzled student marveled that the returning graduates formed a continuous line stretching down the hill from the Normal School and across the Framingham Common. But more important than the numbers was the unbroken, if less visible, line of Normal School students and teachers leading from Mann and Peirce to Ellen Hyde.

The town's decision to incorporate the Practice School into the public school system necessitated adjustments in the Normal School schedule. For the first time, in 1896, there were extended vacations at Christmas and during the summer. That also affected the residence hall, and Miss Hyde moved for the first time in many years, into a home of her own.

ELLEN HYDE RESIGNS

In the spring of 1898 Miss Hyde quietly submitted her resignation from the Normal School. The Massachusetts Board of Education reported the following resolution to the legislature:

> The Board of Education, in accepting the resignation of Miss Ellen Hyde, principal of the Framingham Normal School, desires to put on record its deep sense of the far-reaching, wide and beneficent service she has rendered the State during the thirty-five years of her connection with the school. She has imparted to it as a unit, and to the pupils individually, a high sense of the dignity of the profession of teaching, of the thorough training requisite for instructors, and of refined and Christian graces of womanhood.

> The State of Massachusetts, the Board of Education, the town of Framingham and the innumerable pupils who have been under her charge, owe her a vast debt of gratitude for her able administration of the school and her sincere devotion to the highest interests of education.[58]

Despite the unstinting praise and tributes for her long years of dedicated service, there are hints beneath the polite phrases suggesting that her resignation came with some bitterness, or that she resigned on a matter of principle. Some of the issues are suggested by subsequent announcements. First, the advanced class, or four-year program, was to be closed.[59] Miss Hyde had considered the advanced students important role models for the younger students, and felt that their advanced studies raised the intellectual level at the school. But by this time the women's colleges had gained a firm footing, and the board of education did not wish to have state facilities in competition with private institutions.

A second development was the establishment at Framingham of the Household Arts Program, the first such program in the United States.[60] It is possible that Miss Hyde was troubled by the narrow focus of that program in the face of her own commitment to a broad, liberal education. The curriculum under her direction had emphasized art, music, and literature in addition to the common branches, and was probably not consistent with the demands of the new program for practical instruction in all phases of household management.

Finally, it was mentioned discreetly that Miss Hyde did not feel supported by the board of education. That was probably a reference to Mrs. Kate Gannett Wells, the official visitor. From the beginning, these visitors had played an important role in the life of the school. When Miss May died unexpectedly in 1886, Mrs. Wells was appointed in her stead. Mrs. Wells took a rather different view of the appropriate role for women in society. She was a member of the Massachusetts Association Opposed to the Further Extension of Suffrage to Women.[61] Both women were too well-bred to show any ripple of disagreement publicly, but Miss Hyde must have been dismayed by Mrs. Wells's little talks to the "girls" (always young ladies to Miss Hyde) about the young men waiting for such accomplished young women as their education would make them. Miss Hyde never spoke pejoratively of marriage and the family, but she did expect a commitment to their profession from the young women for as long as they wished to teach.

After her resignation, Miss Hyde continued to reside in Framingham, and for several years she conducted a school for girls. She served on the board of the Framingham Hospital and was an active member of the Plymouth Church.[62] She continued to be interested in the affairs of the Normal School and continued to serve as president of the alumnae association.

In 1914, the Normal School began preparations for the seventy-fifth anniversary of the founding of the state normal schools. As president of the alumnae association, Ellen Hyde presided over the festive banquet held on 1 July 1914. In her welcoming address, she reviewed the history of the Normal School, mentioning in particular that one member of the first class remained, although she was too feeble to be present. Miss Hyde asked that they all stand to honor Adeline Ireson, "the last human link between that past, that long past, and the present."[63]

Later in the evening, Sarah E. Pratt, a graduate of the advanced class of 1874 and a twenty-year teacher at the Normal School, delivered an "appreciation" of Miss Hyde and her work, even though Ellen, as a member of the program committee, had vetoed its inclusion on the program. The appreciation is a touching account of Ellen Hyde's work, and it supports the suggestion that Ellen resigned because of her differences with Mrs. Wells.

Antoinette Roof, class of 1886 and principal of the Practice School, prepared the historical address for the evening. She also offered her tribute to Ellen Hyde:

[A]s one of her girls I would lay a tribute at her feet. By word and deed she placed constantly before us high ideals and inspired us with a sense of personal responsibility for making our own lives beautiful. Her intolerance of all that was false or mean, her patience with every struggle to overcome weakness, her love for all that was good and beautiful and true were forces that molded and shaped our lives. . . . The years have brought a growing realization that all life has been richer and stronger because of her teachings and her influence.[64]

Ellen Hyde was president of the alumnae association until 1916, and she remained an active supporter of the Framingham Normal School until she was confined to her home by ill health. The alumnae association established a scholarship fund in her name to assist students in financial need, and the Ellen Hyde Scholarship is still available today for students at Framingham State College.

Miss Hyde died at her home on 25 February 1926. The Framingham *Evening News* headlined her passing and praised her years of service: "No adequate history of education in this state could be written without according her a high place. . . . The influence both upon education and character, which emanated from her remarkable mind and vivid personality is incalculable."[65] Antoinette Roof, by then a professor at Simmons College in Boston, wrote: "This is not a time of mourning or sadness, but rather a rejoicing together because we have had the power and the influence of Ellen Hyde's life while she lived in our midst and shall have forever, as a precious heritage, her spirit in this school."[66]

Ellen Hyde was not a pioneer of those earliest days in Lexington and West Newton, but she knew the women who were. As principal, she sought to preserve the traditions as she led the institution toward higher standards and a wider mission. Her steadfast pursuit of both access to public schools and excellence in education, goals of the normal-school founders, was significant for the Massachusetts public schools of the nineteenth century. By the end of her twenty-three-year administration, high school education was required for admission to all of the normal schools, model, or practice, schools had become an integral part of teacher preparation, and teacher certification and employment were linked to preparation. The battle for free public high schools had been won, and 90 percent of the youth of the commonwealth lived close enough to attend one. Ellen Hyde carried with her always the ideals and goals of Cyrus Peirce and Horace Mann, and she kept abreast of the developments in education that translated them into effective modern practice.

Framingham Normal School campus, circa 1898.

NOTES

1. Obituary, *Framingham Evening News*, 26 February 1926.

2. J. Messerli, *Horace Mann: A Biography* (New York: Alfred A. Knopf, 1972), 298.

3. Alpheus Crosby, "Proper Sphere and Work of American Normal Schools," in *America's Normal Schools: Their Theory, Their Workings, and Their Results As Embodied in the Proceedings of the First Annual Convention of the American Normal School Association, Trenton, N.J., August 19, 20, 1859* (New York: A.S. Barnes & Burr, 1860), 57.

4. "Catalogue of the State Normal School at Framingham (1861)." Framingham State College Archives, Framingham, Massachusetts.

5. Ibid.

6. Beverly J. Weiss, "Growth and Outreach: 1864–1889," in *Pioneers in Education: A History of Framingham State College* (Framingham: Framingham State College, 1989), 27.

7. Ibid., 21–22.

8. Unsigned letter. The Framingham State College Alumni Association files. In preparation for the seventy-fifth anniversary celebration in 1914, the Alumnae (now Alumni) Association solicited information from graduates about their days at the Normal School. Many letters were received, and some were used by Grace Shepard to prepare her chapter "Historical Sketch, 1889–1914," in *Historical Sketches of the Framingham State Normal School* (Framingham: Alumnae Association, 1914). Many of the letters were not used, and some were used only in part, but all were retained and stored in boxes. Because they were not filed systematically, identifying information has often been lost.

9. Grace Shepard, "Historical Sketch, 1889–1914," in *Historical Sketches of the Framingham Normal School* (Framingham: Alumnae Association, 1914), 58.

10. Electa L. Walton, "Historical Sketch, 1864–1889," in *Historical Sketches*, 42.

11. Shepard, *Historical Sketch*, 59.

12. Weiss, *Pioneers in Education*, 18.

13. Dickinson, in *America's Normal Schools*, 98.

14. Ibid.

15. Jurgen Herbst points out that the Westfield principals had "no experience as common school teachers." J. Herbst, *And Sadly Teach: Teacher Education and Professionalization in American Culture* (Madison: University of Wisconsin, 1989), 87. It seems to me that it was precisely that lack of experience with elementary school children that prevented them and many of the other principals from appreciating the value of the model school.

16. "Catalogue of the State Normal School at Framingham (1868)."

17. *Report of the School Committee of the Town of Framingham (School year 1873–74).*

18. School Diary, 27 January 1876.

19. Weiss, *Pioneers in Education,* 24.

20. School Diary, 17 March 1876.

21. Electa Walton, "Historical Sketch, 1864–1889," in *Historical Sketches,* 44.

22. Ibid.

23. *Annual Report of the Massachusetts Board of Education (1877),* 136.

24. *Annual Report of the Massachusetts Board of Education (1878),* 14.

25. Letter file, FSC Alumni Association.

26. Catalog of the State Normal School at Framingham (1877), 11.

27. Nellie Dale, letter file; see also *First State Normal School in America: The State Teachers College at Framingham, Massachusetts* (Framingham: Alumnae Association, 1959), 56.

28. *Annual Report of the Massachusetts Board of Education (1883),* 10.

29. Ibid., 23.

30. Alex, letter file, FSC Alumni Association.

31. Letter file, FSC Alumni Association.

32. Ibid.

33. George Walton, *Annual Report of the Massachusetts Board of Education (1897),* 268.

34. Samuel E. Armstrong, *Memories of Old Hampton* (Hampton, Virginia: Institute Press, 1909), 1–11. Hampton University Archives, Hampton, Virginia. Thanks are due to archivist Fritz J. Malval, who assisted me and facilitated my search at the Hampton University archives.

35. Wilma K. Hunter, "Three Women at Tuskegee 1882–1925: The Wives of Booker T. Washington." Manuscript, undated and unpaged, Hampton University Archives, Hampton, Virginia.

36. School diary, 29 June 1881, Examination Day.

37. Weiss, *Pioneers in Education,* 26.

38. Jessie P. Guzman, "Olivia Davidson Washington: Educator and Co-Founder of Tuskegee Institute." Manuscript. Department of Records and Research, Tuskegee Institute, Alabama (18 September 1956), 5. Hampton University Archives.

39. Ibid., 9–10. Guzman gives the date of their marriage as 11 August 1885, but a news clipping from the *Messenger* in Athens, Ohio, where they were married, is dated 11 August 1886. Clipping from Ohio University archives.

40. Wilbur W. Howard, "Anna Dawson Wilde: 1868–1968." Manuscript. Hampton University archives. An accompanying letter (30 July 1970) indicates that the writer is Mrs. Wilde's foster son, and that the article was written in 1967 for a church publication.

41. Letter, Ellen Hyde to Cora M. Folsom (19 June 1889). Hampton University Archives.

42. Howard, "Anna Dawson Wilde."

43. School Diary, vol. 5 (1876–81).

44. Ibid., 5 May 1877.

45. Ibid., 20 December 1877.

46. Ibid., 20 February 1877.

47. Mary J. Studley, *What Our Girls Ought to Know* (New York: M. L.

Holbrook & Co., 1881), title page. Personal library, Beverly J. Weiss.

48. *Annual Report of the Massachusetts Board of Education (1877)*, 15; School Diary, 20 February 1877.

49. Catalog of the State Normal School at Framingham.

50. Antoinette Roof, "Tribute to Miss Hyde," 19 June 1926. Probably delivered at the Annual Alumnae Association meeting. Hyde folder, files of the FSC Alumni Association.

51. Quoted by Roof, "Tribute to Miss Hyde."

52. Ibid.

53. Ibid.

54. Lillian Ordway, letter file, FSC Alumni Association.

55. *Historical Sketches*, 78.

56. Weiss, *Pioneers in Education*, 22.

57. Mary Swift Lamson, ed., *Records of the First Class of the First State Normal School in America* (Boston, privately printed, 1903), 169.

58. *Annual Report of the Massachusetts Board of Education (1899)*, 33.

59. School Diary, 11 March 1898 and 26 April 1898.

60. *Annual Report of the Massachusetts Board of Education (1899)*, 35.

61. Manuscript files of the Massachusetts Historical Association, Boston, Massachusetts.

62. John Temple, "Plymouth Church Historical Notes," membership list. Framingham Public Library, Framingham, Massachusetts.

63. *Proceedings of the Seventy-Fifth Anniversary State Normal School Framingham (July 1 & 2, 1914)*, 10. Pamphlet file, FSC Alumni Association.

64. Ibid., 36.

65. Obituary, *Framingham Evening News*, 26 February 1926.

66. Roof, "Tribute to Miss Hyde."

MASSACHUSETTS NORMALITES MIGRATE WEST

This volume began with teaching in the public schools of New England, because it was there that many educational problems and conflicts were first confronted. Many of the traditions in schooling had their origins in Europe, and New Englanders often looked in that direction for guidance, as the advocates for the normal schools in Massachusetts had done. In contrast, the settlers in the Northwest Territory, from which the older states west of the Alleghenies were formed, tended to bring with them institutions and ideals that had evolved in the East, influenced though they were by the demands of frontier life and the rise of new cities.

Educators had watched the experiment with normal schools in Massachusetts, and because it was deemed successful in producing better prepared teachers, the normal school movement spread rapidly. Graduates of the normal schools in Massachusetts were in demand not only as teachers for the public schools but also as instructors for teacher institutes and for normal schools in more distant places. One outstanding example was Anna C. Brackett from the Framingham Normal School class of 1856, who was called to the St. Louis, Missouri, Normal School, where in 1862 she became the first woman to be appointed principal of a normal school in the United States.

The two women whose stories are told in this section were also graduated from the Framingham Normal School and migrated westward: Lelia Patridge taught in normal schools and teacher institutes in Pennsylvania, Illinois, Florida, and Kentucky; Catherine Tilden Avery lived and taught in Cleveland, Ohio, for the remainder of her life.

In Ohio, the first settlement, in 1787 at Marietta, was planned as a "second New England," and schools were an integral part of the plan.[1] Life on the frontier, a growing number of settlements, and the rise of cities soon challenged the newly established state to devise solutions of its own to provide its citizens with access to schools of higher quality. In 1825 a law was enacted that provided for the organization of school districts, for county school taxes, and for the certification of teachers by county examiners, who were also required to visit the schools at intervals. That was, in effect, the beginning of a public school system in Ohio.[2] By the law of 1829, cities were permitted to organize separate districts, and Cincinnati was the first to take advantage of the new law, followed later by Akron and Cleveland. Ohio did not support state normal schools, probably because of the number of colleges that sprang up, some with departments offering instruction in pedagogy, and because cities established and maintained normal schools.

It was against this background that Catherine Tilden Avery was educated and began her career in public-school teaching. She was educated first in the public schools of Michigan, another of the states carved from the Northwest Territory that was strongly influenced by Massachusetts school legislation. She was graduated from Detroit High School and then went to Massachusetts to study at the Framingham Normal School, where she received the benefit of both the advanced class and the elementary program. The young Ellen Hyde was then teaching at the Normal School, and Annie Johnson became principal during Tilden's years of study. Tilden certainly had the opportunity to know former graduates and teachers, including Electa Lincoln Walton and Lucretia Crocker, all women of superior intellect, education, and dedication to public education.

In a few years Catherine, or Kate as she was called, returned to the Midwest, but first she taught in Wayland, Massachusetts, where she demonstrated the value of the classical education she had received at the Detroit High School and the pedagogical training she got at the Normal School. She made contact during her youthful years in Massachusetts with Wendell Phillips and Lydia Maria Child, both of whom were active in the movement for universal suffrage. From them and from the women associated with the Normal School she acquired a life-long respect for the rights of all people, the efficacy of education in ameliorating inequities, and the necessity for political activism.

Kate Tilden married her childhood friend, Elroy Avery, and with him she migrated to Cleveland, Ohio, in 1871. The Cleveland assignment proved congenial to both of them, in good measure because of Andrew Jackson Rickoff, the superintendent of the Cleveland schools. Although he had come to Cleveland recently, Rickoff had already acquired a reputation for innovative pedagogy and school management in Cincinnati, and he had embarked on a similar program in Cleveland. Kate and Elroy Avery were teachers and administrators in the high school and later in the city normal school for a decade, and Kate continued to teach in various classrooms and forums throughout her career.

Lelia Patridge, a high school graduate from northeastern Vermont, came to the Framingham Normal School to study in the elementary program. During the fall term in 1864, she and Kate Tilden were both students at the Normal School, and they certainly would have met. Lelia, of course, shared all of the same teachers and would have been present at the celebration of the twenty-fifth anniversary of the founding of the normal schools, where in 1864 Electa Lincoln Walton spoke and the first graduates were honored. It was at the Normal School also that Lelia Patridge met Dr. Dio Lewis, who, for a brief time, provided physical education instruction at the Normal School. For Lelia, the new field of physical education shaped her aspirations and career for a number of years.

Lelia Patridge's far-flung career allows us to trace educational developments in several localities. She distinguished herself particularly by writing two widely distributed textbooks for teachers. The first was written in 1883 in collaboration with Francis Wayland Parker, who gained a reputation as an early proponent of the progressive education movement. The second book, copyright 1885, was Lelia's own description of the daily classroom practices developed by teachers influenced by Parker in Quincy, Massachusetts, during his superintendency there from 1874 to 1879. Interestingly, Parker credited the work of A.J. Rickoff in Cleveland, Ohio, where he had been a visitor in the early 1870s, as the inspiration for his success. One can argue that Lelia Patridge was drawn to Parker's work because she recognized in it much that Cyrus Peirce, the first normal-school principal, had espoused and taught.

Both Catherine Tilden Avery and Lelia Patridge contributed to the education of the growing number of competent women teachers imbued with the ideals and philosophy pioneered by the first public normal school in Massachusetts.

NOTES

1. Edwin G. Dexter, *A History of Education in the United States* (New York: Macmillan, 1919), 104.
2. Ibid., 105.

5 TEACHING IN THE MIDWEST: CATHERINE TILDEN AVERY (1844–1911)

Beverly J. Weiss

Catherine Tilden Avery.

Catherine Hitchcock Tilden first demonstrated her skills as a teacher in the schools of Massachusetts, where she had attended the Framingham Normal School. Early in her career, however, she returned to the Midwest, where she was born, to serve as high-school teacher and principal. She married her childhood friend, Elroy M. Avery, also an educator, and together they served in the schools of Cleveland, Ohio. Catherine Tilden Avery became a political activist at an early age, espousing universal suffrage, enabling education for immigrants, and better working conditions for women. For her outstanding leadership, she was accorded the honorary title First Woman of Cleveland. Throughout her life she saw her political activities as an extension of her role as an educator, and education as the key to a better and more harmonious life for all.

Early Years

Catherine Hitchcock Tilden was born in Monroe County, Michigan, on 13 December 1844. Her parents were Zeruah Rich Tilden and the Honorable Junius Tilden, a lawyer who was well known in southern Michigan. Her mother died when she was ten years old, and some time later Junius Tilden married Ellen Haskell. Young Catherine, or Kate as she was called, attended primary and grammar schools in Monroe, Michigan, but when Junius died in 1861, Ellen Tilden moved to Detroit with Catherine and her sister. A cousin, Dr. Joseph Hildreth, became their guardian, and Kate attended the high school in Detroit.[1]

The Detroit school report for 1863 lists Kate Tilden as one of seventy-four girls and forty-eight boys attending Detroit High School. The high school conducted two courses of study: the English department, where literature, reading, spelling, composition, rhetoric, history, geography, philosophy, geometry, trigonometry, various applications of mathematics, botany, and anatomy and physiology were emphasized; and the classical department, where Greek and Latin were studied extensively, and the more practical aspects of mathematics, science, and English received much less attention.[2]

At that time, the Civil War was having an impact on the young people of the community. Young men were leaving school to enlist in the army at the rate of more than one hundred a year. Young women were needed increasingly as teachers, although the women who were being graduated from the high school did not have access to a college or university to continue their studies and prepare appropriately for the responsibilities of teaching.

After Kate had graduated from high school in 1864, the family moved to Natick, Massachusetts, and that September she entered the Normal School at Framingham. In that year the Normal School was under the direction of

Mr. George N. Bigelow, who had been the principal of the Clinton, Massachusetts, High School; just previous to his appointment to the Normal School in 1855 he had spent two years in Europe in "pedagogical study." It was said of him that his ideas concerning teaching were "advanced and progressive," and he took great interest in helping young teachers. A publication of the Alumnae Association states that "no event of great moment occurred during his administration," but that the school continued to send out "many well-fitted for their work."[3]

Perhaps that "even course of useful service" made possible the appointment of a woman, Miss Annie Johnson, as principal when Bigelow resigned in 1866. Miss Johnson had been his assistant since 1861 and had acted as principal for a number of months during his extended illness the previous year. She had shown herself to be thoroughly competent to succeed to the position. Though there were those who feared this new "experiment," Governor Bullock himself came to preside at the inaugural ceremonies for the first woman normal-school principal in the commonwealth. Miss Johnson had had a reputation for being helpful to young teachers, and now she had set a precedent and established a goal for the young women to aspire to.[4]

In 1865, the prescribed program for elementary-school teachers was extended from eighteen months to two years. There was also an advanced course, usually of a year, for those who wished to prepare for high-school teaching or who felt the need for a broader education. Annie Johnson was a highly visible and articulate advocate for state approval for advanced courses in the normal schools, so that young women could have an educational experience comparable to that available to young men in colleges. Competent young women like Kate Tilden, studying at the Framingham Normal School, found opportunity to be educated and the encouragement to go as far as they could.

FIRST TEACHING POSITION

Catherine H. Tilden completed the elementary program in 1866 and the advanced course in 1867.[5] Her first teaching assignment was to the grammar school, district 4, in Wayland, Massachusetts. The school committee report of 1867–68 for the town of Wayland noted that the grammar school had had four different teachers in the previous four terms and that the school was in a "low state." Miss Tilden, however, met with better success:

> We were very fortunate in securing the services of Miss Kate H. Tilden, of Natick, for the past two terms. From a state of almost open

rebellion, she has by peculiar tact and perseverance, brought the school to a very high degree of perfection. We do not like to see so many tardy marks on her register, however. Earnestness, faithfulness, and an intense love for her pupils, cause them to love her in return, and to be faithful to their duties. She is succeeding admirably though this is her first school.[6]

The school committee went on to say that because of a lack of fuel, the school had been kept in one of the "lower rooms, used formerly as a playroom, where the scholars were so crowded as to make the room both uncomfortable and unhealthy." There were twenty-eight students during the fall term, six of whom were over the age of fifteen, and thirty-one during the winter term, with twelve over the age of fifteen.[7] One of the arguments against employing women to teach in the grammar and high schools had been that they would be unable to command the respect of the older boys and maintain order. Successes, such as Miss Tilden's under adverse conditions, began to challenge the accepted wisdom of the day.

Miss Tilden earned $10 per week, as compared with the $6 or $7 paid primary-school teachers. The committee noted that Miss Tilden's school "really is a Classical Grammar School, extra pay being given the teacher by private subscriptions that the higher English branches and Latin and French may be taught."

Kate Tilden's success at the Wayland Grammar School brought her an offer to teach at the Prentice Allen Classical School in West Newton, Massachusetts, at double the salary she had earned in Wayland. She accepted the position much to the disappointment of the Wayland school committee, who noted that she had departed with many tokens of esteem from the community. In West Newton, she taught mathematics during the 1868–69 school year to prepare boys for entry into Harvard.[8]

During the summer of 1869, Kate Tilden visited her early home in Monroe, Michigan. While there she renewed her friendship with a classmate, Elroy M. Avery, whom she had known in primary and grammar school, and they were engaged to be married. In September 1869 Kate went to teach in the Chicago public schools and Elroy became the principal of the high school in Battle Creek, Michigan. A few months later, Elroy Avery decided to return to the University of Michigan to complete the college course he had begun in 1867, and Kate Tilden applied for the position he vacated at the Battle Creek High School.[9]

One of the letters submitted to the Battle Creek School Committee in behalf of Catherine Tilden was written by Wendell Phillips, a well-known

Boston abolitionist, orator, and reformer. He was a temperance advocate and a champion of women's rights, and they shared an interest in universal suffrage advocacy. In one of the letters to Battle Creek he wrote: "To all who know me or value my opinion, let this introduce Miss Kate H. Tilden, a graduate of the best schools we have, and one who has, with rare success and exemplary fidelity, improved all her opportunities."[10]

Kate Tilden became the principal of the Battle Creek High School in December 1869. She and Elroy Avery were married on 2 July 1870, and she continued to serve as the principal in Battle Creek for another year. In 1871, Elroy Avery graduated from the University of Michigan, and the couple moved to the village of East Cleveland, Ohio, where Elroy became the superintendent of schools and Kate the principal of the high school.[11] There they made their home, and Catherine Tilden Avery devoted her life to teaching, social reform movements, and educational activities in the city of Cleveland.

GETTING SETTLED

Kate and Elroy Avery arrived in East Cleveland during a period when the city of Cleveland was expanding and incorporating adjacent small towns. Barely one year later, in October 1872, East Cleveland was annexed to Cleveland, and its six schools became part of the Cleveland school system. The high school now became East High School, with Elroy as its principal at a salary of $2,500, and Kate as the assistant principal with a salary of $1,100.[12]

The first high school for boys had been opened in 1846 by order of the city council. Rooms were rented in the basement of a church for the classes, and the following year the city council directed that a department for girls be added. There had been considerable opposition to the high school by taxpayers who, while favoring public schools, did not support free high schools or colleges. Nevertheless, legislation passed authorizing and requiring the maintenance of a high school. All of the instruction was given by two teachers until 1852, when an assistant was employed. Although all the customary high-school subjects except languages were taught, the schedule was unusual. Since the teaching staff could not meet with all of the classes during school hours, recitations were often heard after school hours and in the evening.[13]

In 1856 a new high school was built, later to be called Central High School, for about 116 students. When Ohio City was united with Cleveland in 1864, another high school was annexed, bringing with it fifty-four students, which became West High School. The third high school was the East High School, which added another sixty students to the high-school system.

All three schools used the same criteria for admission and provided the same courses of study.[14]

The Cleveland superintendent of schools was Andrew Jackson Rickoff, who in 1867–68 had succeeded to the position and presided over a number of significant changes in the Cleveland school system. Among these changes were the organization of the schools into four years of primary study and four years of grammar school with specified levels of achievement; combining classes of girls and boys for instruction; and the consolidation of higher classes from adjacent districts into a single school. Rickoff had named a number of senior women teachers as principals at grammar and primary schools because the male principals were being promoted to positions as "local superintendents."[15] Although he considered placing women as principals an experiment, he was gratified by the results of his appointments. In the *Thirty-fifth Board of Education Report on the Cleveland Public Schools (1871)*, he wrote at some length on the positive aspects of having women at the head of grammar and primary schools:

> "It cannot be denied that our schools are more efficiently taught than when there was a man at the head of every house. The improvement in the respect and attention paid by the older pupils to their teachers is remarkable. Classes of boys corresponding to some that in times past drove one principal after another from his post, are today so quiet, orderly and studious, that it is wondered that their predecessors should ever have given trouble. . . . What physical force failed to control, subtler influences have completely mastered."[16]

Given his inclination to appoint women, Rickoff may have been willing to have had the experienced Kate Avery as principal of East High School. But Elroy Avery, with his college degree, was better qualified for the position. In any case, they seem to have worked well as a team for the next decade, and Kate did carve a niche for herself.

The Cleveland school system, like others at that time, had difficulty reaching all of the youth eligible for public education. During that period, there were 37,877 youths between the ages of five and twenty-one, but only 13,647 were enrolled in school, and fewer still attended school regularly. With the annexation of East High School in 1872, the city of Cleveland now had three high schools for about four hundred high school students. Although it would have been more economical to have had a centralized high school, historical agreements and geographical constraints made the three necessary.[17]

During the first two years of the Averys' tenure at East High School, the superintendent's report gave few details about the school, but it is clear that the school was generally considered inferior to the other two high schools. By 1875, he noted that the growth of the high-school population barely kept pace with the population growth, indicating that the number of students staying in school longer was not increasing markedly. He remarked, however, that at East High School, the smallest of the three schools, the number of students completing the year's study had been increasing steadily. He attributed that increase to not only the "greater average prosperity" of that section of the city but also the satisfaction of the parents with the school. Under the Averys' administration, the withdrawal rate had declined from 41.7 percent to 13.1 percent in the three-year period. The withdrawal rate at Central was 20.9 percent and at West, 34.8 percent.[18]

East High School had also brought with it a plan for "single daily sessions," that is, the school hours were continuous until 2 P.M., with no break for an extended lunch period at home. The Cleveland Board of Education seems to have adopted the plan in the other high schools as well. Elroy Avery explained the rationale in his report for 1876: "Boys and girls must have recreation [after school], they ought to have it, and at all events, they will have it."

Mrs. Avery taught geometry, algebra, English literature, English history, and botany, while Mr. Avery taught chemistry, physics, and trigonometry. The prescribed texts were: Schuyler (algebra); Davies' Legendre (geometry); Goodrich (English history) ; Wood (botany); with English literature ad lib. Since the examinations were held in common with the other schools, pace as well as subject matter must have been dictated by the system. One of the problems discussed by the superintendent was class size. Since there were four courses of study for relatively few students, some classes were, indeed, very small, especially those in advanced Latin, Greek, and German. Kate Avery's classes were larger, however, probably because her courses were the basic ones. The average size of her classes was nineteen, compared with seven for the other three teachers.[19]

But if the framework for Kate Avery's teaching seems circumscribed to us, she seems to have surmounted the constraints. Alvan Ingersoll, who entered East High School in 1876 at the age of seventeen, remembered her many years later:

> Her method of teaching was such that she made every point clear to every student. . . . By a few well-directed questions she soon discovered whether the pupil understood the principles involved, and if not,

instead of scolding him for his stupidity or lack of memory, she, by questions and suggestions led the pupil so that he could think out the demonstration for himself. In other ways, such as giving propositions that were not demonstrated in the book, for the pupil to work out for himself, she constantly encouraged originality.[20]

He went on to say that she was also sympathetic and showed an interest in each student, so that "each regarded her as his personal friend and helper." She was capable, however, of disciplining students who seemed to be intentionally misbehaving. At such times "her eyes snapped, and her words stung like whip lashes," but still she appealed to the best in the student and expected the best. She was not easily provoked, and was known for her patience with "trifling faults and shortcomings."[21]

The superintendent's report for 1875 had given the statistics for the three high schools as the background and justification for considering their reorganization. Newburgh had been annexed by Cleveland in 1874, adding another small high school branch with sixteen pupils that was quickly disbanded and the pupils transported to Central High School. The superintendent was concerned not only about the increased per-capita cost associated with the small schools, but also with the problem that fewer courses and programs of study could be offered. Noting that there was "a special and well-defined programme for the preparation of boys for college . . . which today overlaps very considerably the work of the Freshman year in some institutions of real merit and enviable reputation," he went on to say that there was, however, insufficient scientific education. Courses preparing "our boys" to enter apprenticeships in "machine shops, manufactories, chemical works, offices of architects" were not offered, and graduates often needed special preparation to enter polytechnic schools.[22]

Moreover, the superintendent asserted that the design of the required curriculum was too general to serve any group well: not enough mathematics, physics, and chemistry for the scientifically inclined, but too much physiology, botany, and zoology for the classical students. Seeking a solution to the problem he referred to the Boston schools, where students might choose between the Latin High School and the English High School. In addition he proposed a high school for girls where "they might prepare thoroughly for the Normal School, the duties of home, or those callings which are open to women." He hastened to add:

In speaking of a separate school for girls, I do not wish to be understood to entertain a notion that girls should be excluded from the classical or the scientific school. I only contemplate a system of high schools which would afford the people of Cleveland opportunity of choosing just that education for their sons and daughters which to each one might seem most desirable or appropriate."[23]

Despite the superintendent's preference for building at least two new high schools, he recognized the constraints and proposed as an alternative one conveniently located building that would be, in effect, two schools or divisions—until such time as other buildings could be added. The plans for consolidation went forward and, in 1878, the new Central High School, more centrally located on Willson Avenue, was dedicated, incorporating Central, East, and Newburg high schools. The old West High School remained to serve that section of the city.[24]

For the second time, the consolidation of the Cleveland schools prompted a change in the Averys' teaching assignment. In 1878 they were appointed to the Normal School, Elroy Avery as principal and Kate Avery as assistant principal, and it seems to have been a challenging assignment.

TEACHING AT THE CLEVELAND NORMAL SCHOOL

The city's Normal School had begun its operation on 1 September 1874, with Alexander Forbes as its principal, and two women as training teachers, Kate E. Stephan and Julia E. Berger. In the report for 1874, Superintendent Rickoff wrote that it was not because of opposition or indifference that he had delayed the establishment of a normal school, but rather the desire to make such a school a "homogeneous part of the system already in operation." The superintendent went on to say that although he and the board wished to maintain certain principles and methods of instruction, they also wished to avoid:

> the establishment of a fixed routine, a mere mannerism in teaching, under the pretentious name of a method. . . . As the best education is the development of the faculties of a child, each according to its native power and susceptibility, so the best normal training is that which sets free the native talent of the individual, and makes each one a teacher perfect as may be, but perfect only after her kind."[25]

In an historical sketch, Superintendent Rickoff states that there was no opposition to establishing the school, "and there has been none since its opening." The first year there were three possible ways to qualify for admission: graduation from the Cleveland City high schools, certification from the city board of examiners, or certification from county boards of examiners and one year of teaching experience. The superintendent noted that much less was required scholastically by the city board of examiners than by graduation from high school, and still less was required for the county certificate. Keeping the standards high was a goal, but the board was concerned with the problem of recruiting enough students to supply the teachers needed in the public schools. The length of the program was also a concern, and they noted that the programs in Cincinnati, Chicago, and St. Louis were two years in length while Cleveland's was to be but one. They concluded that the admission standards must be higher, or the education of Cleveland teachers would "on comparison, soon show itself to our great disparagement."[26]

At the end of the first year, there was praise for the Normal School staff and its first graduates. The Cleveland Board of Education president, M.G. Watterson, wrote that "the excellence of the work they are doing fully justifies the Board in incurring the trifling expense of maintaining the school."[27] The superintendent noted ruefully that it was necessary to do "a great deal of academic work" in the Normal School, and perhaps it would always be necessary because of the immaturity of the students. Facts, he thought, were easily learned but not the underlying philosophy, and they were determined not to graduate mere imitators of the master teachers. The remedy was to lengthen the Normal School course, so that the subjects to be taught in school could be reviewed in connection with the methods of presentation and a more extended practice in the training school.

Accordingly, by 1876, high-school graduation was required of all applicants. Students who graduated from the four-year high-school course entered a one-year course at the Normal School, while graduates of the three-year program entered a two-year Normal School course. (Despite Ellen Hyde's efforts in Framingham, Massachusetts did not require high-school graduation for admission to the normal schools until 1894.) Principal Forbes found it necessary to emphasize that the purpose of the Normal School was to supply well-trained teachers for the schools and not to "directly benefit those who attend."[28] That, of course, was a policy articulated wherever and whenever normal schools were proposed, to counter the argument that states and cities should not be providing education at public expense beyond the basic level or to mature students.

Having established more stringent requirements for admission to the Normal School, the following year, 1877, the board of education formally adopted the policy. It stated that "inasmuch as the existence of the Normal School is justifiable only on the ground that it educates and trains teachers for our schools, it cannot be made a place for the general education of those who have no natural aptitude for teaching."[29]

It seemed that some opposition to the Normal School was developing, as the composition of the board of education changed. In Cleveland, the budget was tight and the expected savings from the newly consolidated high school not yet realized. Rickoff found himself defending the cost of the Normal School, despite the fact that the public schools were anticipating an increased student enrollment and would need more teachers. The Ohio legislature had passed a compulsory school attendance act for children between the ages of eight and fourteen years. There were 22,840 eligible children, of whom 13,705 attended public schools and 6,433 private schools, leaving 2,702 children not attending school. The law provided a fine for parents who did not send their children to school, and many of the children were expected to be enrolled.[30]

It was at that time, 1878, that the Averys began their administration of the Normal School. The board of education had instituted two measures in an effort to decrease the school budget. The first was a reduction in salary for all teachers. The second provided that $2 per absence would be taken from a teacher's salary. The Normal School student who substituted for the teacher would receive fifty cents and the remainder would be credited to the Normal School's account. "In this way the Normal School has become more than self-sustaining," President Smith noted.[31] Beginning in 1880, students in the first, or most advanced, class were required to hold a teacher's certificate from the city's board of examiners because they were frequently called upon to act as substitutes for the regular teachers. On average, the Normal School had graduated twenty-six students each year since its establishment in 1874, and the number graduating increased to an average of thirty-six during the Averys' tenure.[32] Looking at the list of graduates, they all appear to have been women, although nothing in the text suggests that men were excluded.

The teaching staff consisted of Elroy and Kate Avery and two "practice teachers," who were assigned as supervisors in the schools receiving the students. Elroy Avery received a salary of $2,100, Kate received $1,000, and each of the practice teachers received $800. Superintendent Rickoff continued to regret the time that had to be spent going over "the studies of the grammar and high school," but he found the graduates "thoughtful, earnest students of education." And he seemed pleased with the instruction in the Normal School: "It is high praise, to say of the teachers of the Normal and Training schools, that their pupils come out, modest, tractable and well prepared to acquire the art of governing and teaching and not as having mastered all that is known of the science and art of teaching."[33]

The Cleveland board of education seems to have entered a period of instability. Dr. D.B. Smith served as president for only three years and he was followed in the next four years by four different presidents, apparently with various differing views. At the end of the 1882 school year, Superintendent Rickoff also resigned in favor of B.A. Hinsdale, who continued to defend the work of the Normal School. In his report, the superintendent reviewed the history of the Normal School and concluded by saying that "many of our strongest and best known teachers" were graduates of the Normal School. He commended the school to the "confidence of the Board and the public."

MOVING ON

During that year, 1882–83, the Averys resigned from the Normal School, perhaps because of the controversies and the departure of their long-time colleague A.J. Rickoff. It seems just as likely, however, that Elroy Avery was simply ready to move on to other interests. Since 1879 he had been lecturing on the new electric light, and in the period from 1879 to 1885 he "directed the formation of more than 40 Brush Electric Company subsidiaries throughout the country."[34] He wrote a series of high-school physics texts, wrote extensively on U.S. and Cleveland history, and served as a member of the City Council and then the Ohio State Senate. Both Averys became prominent, influential figures in the affairs of the city and the state.

The Cleveland schools and teaching seem to have remained the central focus of Kate Avery's life. She continued to teach in the high schools of Cleveland, apparently much of the time as a substitute. Edward L. Harris, principal of Central High School, said that she had taught with him for twenty-five years. He spoke of her qualities as a teacher, saying that she "believed the best and saw the very best in her pupils." She had few restrictive rules in the classroom, preferring "do" to "don't"; her most important qualities were love and enthusiasm, and the children knew that she loved and trusted them.[35] Kate seems to have had a particular affinity and gift for teaching boys. Harris attributed this to the experiences early in her career at the Allen School in West Newton.

In addition to her teaching, Kate filled her life with cultural and civic activities. According to a newspaper article written about her, apparently in 1896, when she was a candidate for the Cleveland Board of Education, she was a member of "Conversational, the oldest literary club in Cleveland," and its president for three years. She belonged to the Woman's Press Club, was twice its president, and was its representative to the International League of Press Clubs. She was also a member of the Federation of Women's Clubs and the Women's Christian Temperance Union.[36] As early as 1893 she was listed in a volume called *Women of Cleveland and Their Work,* in a chapter entitled "Sixty Well-known Women of Culture." The citation read, "Kate H.T. Avery, well-informed and brilliant, wields a sprightly pen; [she] is looking up those revolutionary dames, our foremothers, indeed, she is constantly engaged in historical and genealogical research."[37]

DAUGHTERS OF THE AMERICAN REVOLUTION

On 19 December 1891, Mrs. Avery and sixteen other women met at the Case Library to establish the Western Reserve Chapter of the Daughters of the American Revolution (DAR). Kate was elected regent and became the first charter member of the chapter, and number 135 in the national DAR Register. They met monthly, and their early activities centered on researching and presenting papers on historical events and people. Over a period of several years, Kate read papers on "Bunker Hill," the "Evacuation of Boston," "Arnold's March to Quebec," and many other subjects. In 1893 the group changed their meeting place to the Western Reserve Historical Library. They began to collect material for the Western Reserve Historical Society in exchange for the use of their facilities.

Kate Avery was elected the DAR Ohio state regent in 1895, a position that entailed organizing chapters throughout Ohio. At the end of her term, she was elected vice-president general in the national organization and honorary state regent for life. At the turn of the century she became editor of *American Monthly Magazine,* the official organ of the DAR, a service she performed for twelve years until her death in 1911.

During the last two years of her life, 1909 to 1911, Mrs. Avery worked with the DAR's Committee on Patriotic Education to design a patriotic lecture course, a series of twenty lectures. The lectures were given by Mr. Charles W. Burrows and by Mrs. Avery. According to the DAR minutes, they proved so successful that they were invited by the Cleveland Board of Education to repeat them in other schools. One account spoke of a meeting at the Central High School building. A "citizen" presided at the program, assisted by "the principal, teachers and students, who furnished patriotic singing."[38] Kate commented that more than 8,000 students, of many national backgrounds, had attended the lectures. "All audiences have so many who speak simple English, that this work must be presented in simple language. The program must be short in duration and have the element of entertainment and recreation." The lecture was, she said, "profusely illustrated with beautiful colored slides."[39]

In 1892 Ohio sanctioned the right of women to serve on school boards, and in 1896 the name of Mrs. Elroy M. Avery was placed in nomination. Alice Webster, a newspaper columnist, wrote that "there is every reason to think that a woman can be elected to the School Council in Cleveland this spring." She went on to say that, as they hoped to broaden the franchise to women, it was important to choose a woman with whom "the members of the board can not only work in harmony, but from whom they can draw inspiration for conscientious work, and to whom they can look with pride as a specimen of magnificent womanhood." Webster felt that this was an opportunity for a woman to demonstrate that qualified women should be given more "places of public trust," and she saw the participation of women as essential to a "true republic."[40] She wrote:

> [H]er life has been passed in study, and in imparting to others the knowledge gained. In this one city alone there are more than three hundred of her former pupils employed in the public schools, while hundreds of other young women and men will find an added pleasure in casting their first ballot for her who taught them not only mathematics, but that a teacher may be loved second only to one's parents.

> There is no branch of the public school system with which Mrs. Avery is not thoroughly familiar, and she has the rare faculty of presenting her convictions in a manner so convincing that any board with which she sits in council must give weighty consideration. Mrs. Avery is a strong advocate of having the kindergarten become a part of the public schools, a step with which every mother must be deeply in sympathy."[41]

A biographical sketch by Sophia E. Roberts accompanied the endorsement outlining her education and her experience in the Cleveland schools as well as her many civic activities. She mentioned also that she has a happy home life working side by side with her husband. Perhaps because she had mentioned Kate's "Puritan and Pilgrim" ancestry in New England prior to 1650, Sophia Roberts asserted that Mrs. Avery was "free from all blue-stocking proclivities" and very "helpful in work for the public welfare."

Kate Avery was, indeed, the first woman elected to the Cleveland Board of Education in 1896. According to Mrs. Sarah E. Hyre, a member of the board of education at the time of Kate's death, Kate "blazed the way, and gave to the city intelligent service with much thought for the teacher and the inner life of the school."[42] Following her term on the board of education, Mrs. Avery was appointed to the city's board of school examiners, and at the time of her death she was its president. She was also the first woman to hold a seat on the Cleveland Library's board of trustees.

When the city of Cleveland celebrated its centennial year in 1896, the woman's department of the Cleveland Centennial Commission, with Kate Avery as chairman of the executive committee, decided to reach out to the women of the future. The *Cleveland Leader* for 19 December 1896 gave full coverage to the ceremony, at which an aluminum box was filled with memorabilia and sealed for the women of 1996. Women representatives from a variety of organizations came to place in the box documents and artifacts reflecting the history and work of the women of the city. Finally, a letter to the women of 1996 written and read by Kate Avery "on behalf of the Woman's Department of Cleveland's first Centennial Commission" was added to the box. Kate tied the red ribbons together at the top of the box, sealing them with white wax, and "Mrs. Avery placed upon the wax the seal of the Centennial Commission, pressing it on with the badge which she was wearing." The cover was riveted in place and Mrs. Avery presented the box to Mrs. W.A. Ingram, the president, who made the formal presentation of the sealed box to Mr. H.C. Raney, president of the Western Reserve Historical Society, for safekeeping until 1996.[43] This is the letter prepared by Kate Avery:

To Women Unborn. 1896 sends greeting to 1996

We of today reach forth our hands across the gulf of a hundred years to clasp your hands. We make you heirs of all we have and enjoin you to improve your heritage. We bequeath to you a city of a century; prosperous and beautiful, and yet far from ideal. Some of our streets are not well-lighted, some are unpaved; many are unclean. Many of the people are poor, and some are vainly seeking work at living wages. Often, they who have employment are forced to filch hours for work from the hours that should be given to rest, recreation and study.

Some of our children are robbed of their childhood. Vice parades our streets and disease lurks in many places that men and women call their homes.

It sometimes happens that wealth usurps the throne that worth alone should occupy. Sometimes some of the reins of government slip from the hands of the people and public honors ill-fit some who wear them. We are obliged to confess that even now 'Man's inhumanity to man Makes countless thousands mourn.'

How are these things with you?

Yet the world-family is better and happier than it was a hundred years ago; this is especially true in this American republic and has come by wisdom working through law. We love our country and seek its prosperity and perpetuity; we love our country's flag and pray for its greater glory; in this country, our men have marched to victory under its folds, in three great wars; we are ready to defend it against all the world.

Are you?

This hundred years has given the world the locomotive and the steamboat, the telegraph, telephone, photograph, electric light, electric motor and many other wise and beneficent discoveries. Have you invented a flying machine or found the north pole? What have you done? In this first centennial year of our city we have planned many important works for the 'Greater Cleveland' of tomorrow, and have appropriated millions of money for the execution of the plans. Among these are the improvement of the harbor; the widening, straightening and cleaning of our narrow, crooked and befouled river; the sanitary disposal of garbage; a fitting home for the public library; the extension and completion of an adequate park and boulevard system; the addition of kindergarten to our public schools.

What are you doing for Cleveland?

Standing by this casket soon to be sealed, we of today try to fix our vision on you who, a century hence, shall stand by it as we now do. The vision can last but a moment, but before it ends and we fade into the past, we would send up our earnest prayer for our country, our state, our city, and for you.

On behalf of the Woman's Department of Cleveland's First Centennial Commission.

Mrs. Elroy M. Avery
Chairman of the Executive Committee[44]

In her work with the DAR, Kate Avery put into action her conviction that citizens need to know as much as possible about their country and how to participate in making life better for all. She believed in the efficacy of using the legal system to improve the quality of life for those less favored than herself. She worked with children of immigrant parents, teaching them not only academic skills, but also the information they needed to participate in the affairs of the city and the nation. She sought to give them a sense of belonging and of pride in their new country. She was patriotic because she believed that in this country, as in no other, informed citizens could and would use established, lawful means to correct injustices. Kate was fully aware that life in Cleveland and elsewhere fell short of the ideal. She was particularly aware that women and children were often the last to benefit from the republican ideal, and she became an active worker for legislation to improve their lot.

Kate was president of the Cleveland Council of Women, an organization that urged the legislature to establish a committee of women to inspect living conditions in all state institutions. They urged, also, that a separate reformatory for women be provided. When the Consumers League of Ohio was formed in Cleveland in 1900, Kate Avery was an early member and chairman of its committee on legislation. The purpose of the Consumers League was "to further the welfare of those who make or distribute things bought." Early on, the league issued "white lists" of stores that sold goods produced by "adults, employed at a fair wage and working under favorable conditions."[45] Beginning about 1909, the league moved from a position of seeking voluntary action by informed consumers to a "policy of endorsing and campaigning to secure labor legislation mandating better working conditions and wages."[46] In 1911, the league was concerned with a bill to limit the hours women could be required to work. Kate wrote and sent letters to 118 legislators in support of the legislation and made several trips to Columbus to testify at legislative hearings. By October the bill had passed as the "54 hour a week bill," but it was being contested as unconstitutional by a group of manufacturers.

In December, while the fate of the "54 hour bill" awaited the decision of the Ohio Supreme Court, Kate Avery introduced a letter to the board requesting that the members of the Consumers League write to their delegates to the Ohio Constitutional Convention urging them to empower the legislature to "regulate all conditions of employment and all contracts and relations between employer and employed." The league endorsed the position, and Kate wrote to each delegate to the Ohio Constitutional Convention.[47]

Catherine Tilden Avery died on 22 December 1911 at the age of sixty-seven. The *Cleveland Plain Dealer* noted her passing in an editorial entitled "Cleveland's First Woman," and the *Cleveland Leader* wrote, in part:

Mrs. Avery

> The death of this teacher, promoter of beneficent public enterprises and activities, patriot and writer, organizer of useful and honorable societies, and guide and friend of a multitude of women and not a few men, directs attention to the vital importance of the part which women of talent and energy and broad public spirit play in the development and welfare of American cities. . . . Her place in Cleveland was won by the useful and worthy activities of a clear head and a good heart. She had great abilities and used them for the welfare of the city as well as those nearer and dearer to her. She was always awake to public needs and civic obligations. In many ways her life might well serve as a pattern of unselfish usefulness and high-minded endeavor, for men as well as for women so situated that they could give their time and strength to large interests as she gave hers. In school affairs, in patriotic societies, in literary pursuits, in movements for the rights of women and men, also, in city planning and city building, in philanthropy and charity, Catherine Tilden Avery was a notable factor in Cleveland's progress and development.[48]

A public memorial meeting was arranged by a committee of women representing the organizations with which she had worked. The memorial was held on 4 January 1912 in the auditorium of the Cleveland Chamber of Commerce. The program comprised a series of tributes by those who had known and worked with her for many years, including the mayor of Cleveland, Newton D. Baker. Elroy Avery paid his own tribute by publishing a "small book," a short biography and a collection of the remembrances of her friends and colleagues. In the foreword Elroy wrote: "I have written much, have received some literary recognition and many academic degrees, and have had my fill of political honors—all of which are as dust beside the fact that she loved me."[49]

Kate Avery's life was one long tribute to her belief in the power of learning and education. One of her friends suggested that the secret of her teaching success was her "great sympathy for young people" and her philosophy that "a teacher should never see more than half that is going on and speak of only half that she sees."[50]

And clearly Kate did not believe that learning and teaching stopped at the doors of the school, or at any particular age. She demonstrated a belief in the need for constant learning, and she believed that well-informed citizens would change the city and the nation for the better. Today, facing new versions of the same old problems, perhaps some will find her faith in the nation and the power of law to bring about equality and justice naive. Hers however, was not a blind faith, and she used the skills she had honed in the classroom to gather information and present it effectively in a variety of forums. Kate Avery continued to teach within the confines of the classroom, but she seems to have been teacher to a city and state as well.

NOTES

1. "Mrs. Elroy M. Avery (Catherine Tilden Avery): A Memorial." Also titled "The First Woman of Cleveland" (Cleveland: privately printed, 1912), 4. Courtesy Framingham State College Alumni Association, Framingham, Massachusetts.

2. *Twenty-first Annual Report of the Board of Education for the Public Schools of the City of Detroit (Year Ending December 31, 1863)*, 82–85. School Reports Collection, Gutman Library, Harvard University.

3. *Historical Sketches of the Framingham State Normal School* (Framingham: Alumnae Association, 1914), 40–41.

4. Beverly J. Weiss, "Growth and Outreach: 1864–1889," in *Pioneers in Education* (Framingham: Sesquicentennial Publications Committee, 1989), 17.

5. *State Normal School Framingham, Massachusetts, Catalogue of Teachers and Alumnae 1839–1900* (Boston: Wright & Potter, 1900), 58, 114.

6. *Report of the School Committee of the Town of Wayland, Massachusetts (1867–68)*, 8.

7. Ibid., 8–9.

8. Sophia E. Roberts, "Mrs. Elroy M. Avery." Unidentified newspaper clipping, Framingham State College Alumni Association files.

9. "Mrs. Elroy M. Avery: A Memorial," 4.

10. Quoted in "Mrs. Elroy M. Avery: A Memorial," 4.

11. William J. Akers, *Cleveland Schools in the Nineteenth Century* (Cleveland: William Bayne Printing House, 1901), 153.

12. Ibid.; see also Andrew J. Rickoff, *"Superintendent's Report" Thirty-seventh Annual Report of the Cleveland Board of Education (1873)*, 228.

13. Andrew J. Rickoff, *Fortieth Annual Report of the Cleveland Board of Education (1876)*, 39.

14. Ibid., 40.

15. Ibid., 39.

16. Rickoff, *Board of Education Report (1871)*, 78.

17. Akers, *Cleveland Schools*, 152; also Rickoff, *Board of Education Report (1873)*, 38.

18. Rickoff, *Superintendent's Report (1875)*, 76.

19. Rickoff, *Board of Education Report (1875)*, 79–80.

20. Alvan F. Ingersoll, in "Mrs. Elroy M. Avery: A Memorial," 17.

21. Ibid., 18.

22. Rickoff, *Board of Education Report (1875)*, 81–82.

23. Ibid., 84.

24. Watterson, *Board of Education Report (1878)*.

25. Rickoff, *Board of Education Report (1874)*, 58.

26. Rickoff, *Board of Education Report (1874)*, 60.

27. Watterson, *Board of Education Report (1875)*, 35.

28. Forbes, *Board of Education Report (1876)*, 165.

29. Akers, *Cleveland Schools*, 183.

30. Watterson, *Board of Education Report (1878)*.

31. D.B. Smith, *"President's Report," Board of Education Report (1879)*, 19.

32. *"Table of Graduates," Board of Education Report (1883)*, 84.

33. *Board of Education Report (1881)*, 70.

34. David D. Van Tassel, ed., *The Encyclopedia of Cleveland History* (Bloomington: Indiana University Press, 1987), 60.

35. Edward L. Harris, quoted in "Mrs. Elroy M. Avery: A Memorial," 15–16.

36. Sophia Roberts, "Mrs. Elroy M. Avery." Unidentified newspaper clipping, Framingham State College Alumni Association files.

37. Mrs. W.A. Ingham, "Sixty Well-known Women of Culture," in *Women of Cleveland and Their Work* (Cleveland: W.A. Ingham, 1893), 285–86.

38. "Report of the Committee on Patriotic Education." Records of the DAR (May 1910).

39. Ibid.

40. Alice Webster, "The School Council." Unidentified newspaper clipping. Framingham State College Alumni files.

41. Ibid.

42. Mrs. Sarah E. Hyre, in "Mrs. Elroy M. Avery: A Memorial," 22.

43. The *Cleveland Leader*, 19 December 1896. Western Reserve Historical Society manuscript collection.

44. Ibid.; also quoted in "Mrs. Elroy M. Avery: A Memorial," 23–24.

45. "The Records of the Consumers League of Ohio." Introduction to the microfilm collection, Western Reserve Historical Society manuscript collection.

46. Ibid.

47. "Minutes of the Consumers League of Ohio (April to December 1911)." Myrta Jones, quoted in "Mrs. Elroy M. Avery: A Memorial," 24–25.

48. Quoted in "Mrs. Elroy M. Avery: A Memorial," 6–7.

49. Elroy M. Avery, quoted in "Mrs. Elroy M. Avery: A Memorial."

50. Sarah E. Hyre, "Mrs. Elroy M. Avery: A Memorial," 22.

6 TEACHING IN NORMAL SCHOOLS: LELIA E. PATRIDGE (1844–1920)

Beverly J. Weiss

Lelia Patridge.

Lelia Patridge had a propensity for showing up in places where something new was happening that would influence the practice of teaching and the education of teachers. She was among the first teachers trained in physical education and gymnastics, and she was an early proponent of activity-based learning and child study. Lelia Patridge taught in four normal schools: the Philadelphia Girls High and Normal School; the Cook County (later renamed Chicago) Normal School; Stetson University in De Land, Florida; and the Eastern Kentucky State Normal School in Richmond, Kentucky. She was a member of the faculty at the Florida and Kentucky schools just as they were being established. She received more recognition, however, for her descriptions of other people's teaching methods than for her own. It is puzzling that she is so seldom acknowledged in the accounts of the progressive educational movement, since the books she wrote and edited set sales records in their time.

EARLY YEARS

Lelia E. Patridge came to the Framingham Normal School at the age of eighteen from her home in Passumpsic, in northeastern Vermont near St. Johnsbury. Her father was Ora B. Patridge, whose occupation was listed in the registration book for the Normal School as "merchant." Lelia had graduated from the public high school in her Vermont town in December of 1861. The course of study in the Normal School at that time was a year and a half in length. The principal was George Bigelow; Ellen Hyde and Annie Johnson were her teachers. She was graduated in December 1864 at the age of twenty.[1]

At some time during the next three years, Lelia completed a course of study at the Boston Institute for Physical Culture. For Lelia Patridge, that course became an important qualification for the teaching positions she held over the next two decades and, if one can judge from her vigorous longevity, an important influence in her own life.

THE PHYSICAL EDUCATION MOVEMENT

From the 1820s and 1830s, seminaries and schools for girls had been criticized for a lack of attention to the health of girls, since they focused on lessons and "lady-like" behavior without regard for physical exercise. Calisthenics were introduced in some schools as early as 1825, and Catharine Beecher had introduced exercise into the Hartford Seminary early in the century. Exercise programs, however, were not general until "after the epoch-making work of Dio Lewis."[2] Dr. Dio Lewis deplored the socialization imposed on girls. On hearing that a group of girls had "finished" their education, he remarked, "If you had said the girls themselves were finished, I should have understood you. . . . pale, thin, bent—they had been outrageously humbugged."[3] Lewis regarded women's styles as a "chief cause of illness and weakness," and he maintained that ill health, in turn, interfered with their independence. He advocated putting aside corsets in favor of garments that would give "perfect liberty about the waist and shoulders."[4]

In 1860, Dio Lewis began offering classes in gymnastics in Boston and was invited to present his new system of gymnastics before the prestigious American Institute of Instruction. He gained considerable support for his system from that presentation, and in 1861 he established the Boston Normal Institute for Physical Education. Over the next seven years, more than four hundred men and women, including Lelia Patridge, studied at the institute, and went out to introduce his methods into the schools. The program announcement for the institute declared that all those who entered the school would be examined "with reference to strength, form and health" and "any deficiency thus disclosed will be at once placed under the most thorough treatment."[5]

The course at the institute lasted ten weeks, during which time Dio Lewis himself drilled the students "with such care that he or she cannot fail to become a competent teacher of gymnastics."[6] He promised to teach them more than two hundred exercises, which were detailed in *New Gymnastics*, the book he wrote, the following year. Lewis also popularized dance, particularly square dances, as a form of exercise rather than as a diversion or social accomplishment. Lelia Patridge began her career in the vanguard of the new physical education movement.

THE PHILADELPHIA GIRLS NORMAL SCHOOL

The first documented position held by Lelia Patridge was that of teacher of Physical Exercises at the Philadelphia Girls Normal School. Miss Patridge was listed on the roster of teachers for the term ending 9 July 1868 at an annual salary of $660. She joined a staff which comprised ten women, a man who taught music, and the principal. The addition of teachers in music and in physical exercise reflected some of the changes in the school curriculum based on the recommendations of the Philadelphia Board of Contollers Committee on Revision of Studies. The curriculum revisions were accompanied by a change in the school name from the Girls' High and Normal School to the Girls' Normal School. Principal George W. Fetter approved the change in title on the grounds that "the title now indicates its mission, which is, to prepare teachers for both public schools and private seminaries," and that preparation continued to "embrace all the subjects necessary to a good English Education."[7] The Girls' Normal School continued to be the only public high school available to the young women of Philadelphia at that time.

Early on in Pennsylvania, public schools were established for the benefit of poor families. It was not until 1834 that a state law "erased the reproach that the schools were founded only for the poor."[8] Primary schools were established in 1836 and the Central High School for boys opened in 1838. Although discussions began as early as 1840 about the need for a comparable high school for girls, it was evident that the "importance of female education in the general opinion" did not rate very high.[9]

The training of teachers in Philadelphia, however, had a longer history, which historian John Trevor Custis proudly points out antedated the first state Normal School at Lexington by twenty-one years. It began under the Act of 1818, which called for the establishment of schools at public expense and authorized the Philadelphia Board of Controllers to provide "a Model School, in order to qualify teachers for the sectional schools and for schools in other parts of the State."[10] The Model School attracted a great deal of attention, especially since it advertised its ability "to furnish well qualified teachers at reasonable salaries,"[11] and at one time had "nearly six hundred Pupils."[12] Of course, the "reasonable salaries" reflected the fact that the teachers were, for the most part, very young women who had few choices. The Model School continued to operate until 1836.

As the trend toward the establishment of schools to train teachers spread, the Philadelphia Normal School, forerunner of the Girls' High and Normal School, opened in the old Model School building on 1 February 1848 with an enrollment of 106 girls. Of this development Custis said, "Philadelphia must be credited with being the first city in the United States to establish a city school exclusively for the training of teachers."[13] He comments that although the curriculum was meager (mathematics, history, grammar, reading, music, drawing, and writing) and required but two years of study, "it was greatly in advance of other schools for girls of that period."[14] In 1859, the board of controllers, to lower costs, extended the course of study to three years, abolished the practice school, and changed the name to Girls' High School. The school continued to prepare teachers, but without a practice school the students' experience was limited. It was soon recognized that this arrangement was unsatisfactory, and a compromise was sought. The senior high school year was dedicated to the teacher preparatory program and experience in the practice school was reinstituted. The title of the school now became the Girls' High and Normal School.[15]

The president of the Board of Public Education, M. Hall Stanton, wrote glowingly of the Normal School as offering "girls the same opportunities for a collegiate education which the boys were enjoying" as a matter of "equity and justice,"[16] but a comparison of the courses of study suggests that the opportunities for advanced education were far from equal inasmuch as the girls' curriculum did not prepare them to enter college. Boys were studying "belles-lettres, higher mathematics, natural history, natural sciences, mental and moral philosophy, physiology, Latin and German languages, commercial calculations and business forms, etc."[17] The girls at the Normal School were offered grammar, composition, English and literature, American and ancient history, geometry and practical mathematics, algebra, geography, rhetoric and elocution, drawing and penmanship, music, and physical exercise.

Lelia Patridge came to the Girls' Normal School as a result of revisions in the courses of study, made in response to a law of 1867 that stiffened the requirements for obtaining a teacher's certificate and required that pupils complete at least two years at the Normal School before sitting for the teacher's examination.[18] Principal Fetter noted, however, that the plan of study remained essentially the same. That is, the first year was dedicated to "the extension and systematizing of the subjects taught in the grammar school." The remainder of the course was "occupied in a higher range of study," and students were instructed in the theory and practice of school management.

Apparently, Miss Patridge's contributions were well received, and Fetter's report for 1869 included an appraisal:

> The Department of Physical Exercises is now an essential feature of the school. The effects of this study are obvious to all who witness its operations. Through the indefatigable efforts of Miss Patridge, all obstacles have been removed and prejudices overcome, and the pupils appreciate its worth both physically and mentally: vigor of body, gracefulness of action, and vivacity of spirits are the evident results; languor, headaches, depression, and excessive mental fatigue, are to a great extent, things of the past, and the future graduates will go forth as well qualified to teach this subject as any other pursued in the school.[19]

Lelia Patridge remained at the Girls' Normal School, apparently in the same position, until 1874. The Normal School had a student body of about four hundred women during this period.[20]

As important as the Normal School's contribution was, in 1870 only 43.8 percent of Philadelphia's teachers had received normal training, and more than 70 percent of them were under twenty-five years of age.[21] Here, as elsewhere, salaries were inadequate, the majority of women teachers earning $400 to $500 per year. Women principals earned $540, and the majority of the principalships for the lower grades were held by women. Thus, the graduates of the Normal School could look forward to employment in the schools of the city and state, but their salaries would be meager.

About 1875 Lelia Patridge began teaching in Pennsylvania Teacher Institutes. Pennsylvania had mandated teacher institutes throughout the state in 1867 to improve the qualifications of those already teaching. As a result, the attendance at the institutes tripled in the following year and continued to grow throughout the 1870s.[22] The institutes excited popular interest, and thousands of citizens, as well as school officers and teachers, attended them. "The Institutes have thus become a great educational power, not only providing instruction for teachers but conveying valuable information concerning educational affairs to whole communities."[23]

THE SEARCH FOR BETTER TEACHING

Miss Patridge was teaching in the Pennsylvania Teacher Institutes in 1879 when a series of articles appeared in the Philadelphia *Ledger* describing the reforms taking place in the Quincy, Massachusetts, schools under Superintendent of Schools Francis Wayland Parker. By her own account, because of her dissatisfaction with the results of teaching methods then in vogue, Lelia had been studying the work of the German educator Froebel on the education of young children and had received instruction at the Philadelphia Kindergarten Training School. When she heard an address given by Colonel Parker before the National Educational Association at Chautauqua in 1880, she felt that she had been in the presence of not merely the "coming educator" but one who was "already doing his work among us."[24]

Lelia determined to visit Quincy to see for herself how teachers were implementing Parker's ideas in their classrooms. What she found during her visit in September of 1880 was "teaching of a remarkable character. . . . It was development, not acquisition; growth instead of accretion," and all accomplished through "self-activity."[25] For her it was the embodiment of the Froebelian principles advocated by those in the kindergarten movement.[26] By this time, Parker had completed five years in the Quincy Schools, and had accepted an appointment as a supervisor in the Boston schools.

The following summer, 1881, on the Island of Martha's Vineyard, Parker offered a course on "Didactics," in which he again expounded his philosophy and recommendations on teaching. Fifty people including Lelia Patridge attended. That same fall again found Lelia in the Quincy schools, observing the teaching. With the approval of the new superintendent of schools, she was allowed to observe the training classes for teachers and to attend their weekly discussion meetings. Lelia departed with "copious notes" from which she prepared presentations on "the distinguishing features of the Quincy work" for the Pennsylvania Teachers Institutes. She found teachers eager to learn ways to improve their teaching and their schools, and to gain a better understanding of "child gardening."[27]

At the close of her institute commitments in 1882, Lelia decided to return to Quincy. Amos M. Kellogg, the editor of the New York *School Journal*, asked her to prepare a book of "sketches of actual lessons taken directly from the schoolrooms of Quincy." Lelia commented that "had the requirement been for a book on the philosophy of teaching I should never have entertained the proposal; but I thought I could be the eyes and ears for such as could not go to Quincy to see and hear for themselves. . . ."[28] She spent the remainder of the 1882 school year observing in Quincy, and then went to Martha's Vineyard for Parker's second course of lectures.

The second session in 1882 attracted a larger audience, about 150 people, and Lelia Patridge was listed among the instructors and lecturers, as was Dr. William T. Harris, later to be the U.S. Commissioner of Education. Miss Patridge spoke on "Gymnastic Drill."[29] It was at this time that Lelia conceived the idea of publishing her notes on Parker's lectures. She wrote: "Listening day after day, note-book in hand, to those wonderful 'Talks on Teaching,' the highest expression of pedagogical truth ever uttered in this country, it occurred to me that the publication of my notes of these lectures (the principles of Quincy teaching) would fitly precede the coming book of practice."[30]

When Lelia approached Parker with her idea, he "generously replied" that the notes were her own and she might do as she liked with them. He went on to say, however, that if he were to endorse them, he must first revise them. Patridge gave him her manuscript and he rewrote the notes extensively: [T]he proposed revision became really a re-writing. . . ."[31] The first edition of the book carried an endorsement that read: "I have carefully examined the MS. of the 'Notes of Talks on Teaching' prepared by Miss Patridge, and find it substantially correct. FRANCIS W. PARKER Chicago, Ill. April 19, 1883."

Although Colonel Parker had attracted considerable attention for his work in the Quincy school system, he had not written anything more than a few tracts for teachers on topics such as spelling and numbers. He evidently recognized in Patridge's proposal the opportunity to have a book about his theories promoted by a major publisher of educational texts.

During the 1882–83 school year, Miss Patridge continued her observations in the Quincy schools, and in the summer of 1883 attended the third and last of Parker's lecture series in the East. *Notes of Talks on Teaching* was published in 1883 under a copyright held by Lelia Patridge, and it was immediately successful. Kellogg's promotional literature proclaimed: "The book became famous; more copies were sold of it in the same time than any other educational book whatever. The daily papers, which usually pass by such books with a mere mention, devoted columns to review of it."[32]

Dr. William T. Harris wrote later that it was a "small but remarkable book." "It is," he said, "like gold."[33]

PARKER'S *Talks on Teaching*

Notes of Talks on Teaching began with a brief biographical sketch of Colonel Francis W. Parker, which Miss Patridge said she wrote so that readers might understand the man and his experience: He had begun teaching at age seventeen in his native New Hampshire, although his own education had been spotty. He enlisted in the Union Army with the New Hampshire Regiment in 1861, rose through the ranks to become a colonel, and was wounded in action in 1864. After the war, he went to Dayton, Ohio, where he began his work in primary schools and served as principal of the Dayton Normal School and then as assistant superintendent of the city schools. His theories led him into conflicts with other professionals, and he resolved to go to Europe "to consult the highest authorities in the art of teaching." There he found confirmation of his theories, and he returned to the United States eager to put his ideas into practice. In Quincy, Massachusetts, he found a receptive school committee and a superintendency from which he could direct a program of educational reform.

The rest of the book purported to present the words of Colonel Parker as he spoke to those who gathered to hear him on Martha's Vineyard. It reads like a transcript of the twenty-five lectures in which he presented his concepts of how children learn and how they should be taught reading, writing, spelling, composition, arithmetic, geography, and history. He spoke also of examinations, school government (that is, discipline), and moral training. In the introductory lecture he set forth his philosophy, acknowledging his debt to Comenius, Pestalozzi, and Froebel, of whom he said he had summed up "the wisdom of those who preceded him, and embodying it in one grand principle . . . announced the true end and aim of all our work—the harmonious growth of the whole being." Parker went on: "Every act, thought, plan, method, and question should lead to this. Knowledge and skill are simply the means and not the end, and these are to work toward the upbuilding of the whole being. Another name for this symmetrical upbringing is character, which should be the end and aim of all education."[34]

Parker believed also that there were "mental laws" which would enable teachers to adapt the subjects taught to children so that their minds would be developed. He believed that learning about the mind and the means by which it could be developed required a lifetime of unceasing study, and that instruction in methods of teaching by itself was insufficient. He was clear, however, on the knowledge and skills needed by the teacher. First of all, teachers cannot teach without having themselves the knowledge and skills they wish to impart. Beyond that, teachers should have a "clear, musical voice," perfect pronunciation and articulation, the ability to sing well, skill in writing and drawing, the ability to model in sand or clay, and a knowledge of gymnastics.

Parker emphasized the need to build on those things which are already familiar to the child. So, for example, in learning to read, the child is already prepared by spoken words and thoughts. Familiar objects can stimulate associations and simple sentences, which the teacher can write on the blackboard for the class to read. Words should be learned in the context of a thought or sentence, not individually in a spelling list, nor should the beginner be troubled with using phonics to analyze a word. Keeping the child's interest and the sense of enjoyment were key ingredients of the learning process for Parker. Children were expected to be active physically and mentally, learning through varied sensory experiences rather than through memorization from textbooks.[35]

From these examples, one can see why Lelia Patridge felt it was important for teachers to understand his philosophy before reading about what the teachers were doing in the Quincy schools. Some critics at the time said that Parker had nothing new to say, and Parker agreed—but pointed out that few schools had translated the principles into practice. Later, Parker also acknowledged that his ideas for the methods he introduced to the Quincy schools originated from his observations in the Cleveland schools during the period when he was a teacher in Dayton, Ohio.

That this is more than a courtesy to Superintendent Andrew J. Rickoff is evidenced by reading the detailed "object lesson" presented by Mrs. Rebecca Rickoff at a Cleveland Teachers Institute during those years. The lesson she presented began with the distribution to each child of a single, perfect maple leaf that was used to elicit observations and encourage verbalization, and as a model for drawing. Using the blackboard, the teacher assisted the children in arranging their observations into a category system that they would use to observe and discuss leaves from other trees, as well as their appearance in different seasons. In bringing in specimens from other trees, the children were asked to observe and describe their locations and growing conditions. Literary and imaginative activities were encouraged by visualizing trees in winter and reading poetry. As Mrs. Rickoff presented the model lesson, a simple leaf introduced an integrated lesson on natural science, observation, organization, oral expression, reading, and writing, in which every step created opportunities for the child's active participation, discovery, and invention as well as the acquisition of information.[36]

Original or not, Parker's work received a great deal of attention in Quincy because he succeeded in introducing methods that revitalized teaching in those schools. Lelia Patridge's conception of the companion books and her difficult labors to bring them to completion documented Parker's philosophy and provided teachers with examples of lessons created by teachers to implement his ideas. The large audience attracted by the books helped to create support among educators for his subsequent work in Chicago.

Parker had been offered the position of principal at the Cook County Normal School in what was then a suburb of Chicago. Some years later it became the Chicago Normal School. Colonel Parker summoned a number of the teachers from Quincy for his faculty, and Lelia Patridge was also invited to join his staff. She went to Normal Park, Illinois, in September 1883 as a member of the faculty, although she was not paid by the Normal School until September of 1884. At that time she received a salary of $400 for teaching gymnastics. Parker's salary had jumped to $5,000, although none of the other men on the faculty received more than $2,200, and the women faculty generally earned $1,200.[37] It is unclear why Lelia's salary was so low. It is possible that she did not teach full-time, inasmuch as she was working on the manuscript for *Quincy Methods* until 1885.

Lelia began "the great labor of selecting, arranging, and writing out my voluminous reports of lessons," but completing the book was delayed by "over-work and ill-health."[38] Although she had originally planned to write about teaching in all of the eight years of basic schooling, she settled for the four primary years, leaving the grammar school years for another volume that seems never to have been finished. *Quincy Methods Illustrated: Pen Photographs from the Quincy Schools* was copyrighted in 1885.

PATRIDGE'S *Quincy Methods*

The interest in the Quincy Schools had stemmed from reports of great improvement under Parker's direction. The book Lelia Patridge wrote, *Quincy Methods,* is unmistakably her own product, reflecting not only what she had studied with Parker but also her understanding of the craft of teaching drawn from her education at the Framingham Normal School and her own experiences. Her own values and expertise are evident throughout. *Quincy Methods* runs to 660 pages, a monumental work of selection, organization, and narration based on many months of observation.

The annual report of the Quincy School Committee for 1873 had reflected the dissatisfaction of its members with the ability of the town's children to read, write, spell, and use arithmetic. The committee concluded that "the children, as a whole, could neither write with facility nor read fluently. . . . The ever-present object in the teacher's mind was to pass a creditable examination; and to insure this, he unconsciously turned his scholars into parrots, and made a meaningless farce of education."[39]

The town's money was being wasted, but the cost of securing better prepared teachers would impose a tax burden the citizens would not bear. Their solution to the problem, in 1875, was to place the Quincy schools for the first time in the hands of a superintendent; having concluded that the existing system was wrong, they were quite willing to engage a superintendent with radical theories of his own. The man they chose was Francis Wayland Parker.

According to the account by one of the school committee members, Charles F. Adams, Jr., by 1878 the changes in school practices and children's attitudes were so marked and so favorable that visitors were flocking to Quincy to visit the schools. Adams was gratified by the improvement in the quality of the education the children were receiving, and he noted that the annual cost to educate each pupil had been reduced from $19.24 in 1875 to $15.68 in 1878.[40] While some of the visitors came to learn how to reduce the cost of education in their towns, others came to judge its educational success. Lelia Patridge came to study and evaluate the teaching methods. In strong agreement with the philosophy and practices she observed, she recorded the classroom activities so that other teachers would have examples from which to learn how to create a better learning climate in their own classrooms.

In the preface to *Quincy Methods,* Lelia explained that she had taken notes in regular classrooms, and that her sketches were not intended as models to be copied but as examples to be studied. Indeed, today's teachers could still read these examples and come away with sound principles and ideas for their own classrooms. Both Lelia and Parker intended that teachers create their own lessons, in keeping with sound pedagogical principles. Lelia organized the material she had gathered to stress the use of a variety of readily available materials and to demonstrate a variety of teaching techniques. The examples were arranged as a progression from the first year to the fourth.

Each chapter and lesson had an introduction consisting of four parts: "Purpose of the Lessons" was intended to give the reader, especially the inexperienced teacher, a clear picture of the main theme and how the lesson builds toward it; "Preparation Made by the Teacher" called the reader's attention to the teacher's planning process and what must be obtained or prepared in advance; "Preparation Made by the Pupils" was designed to remind readers how important it is to "begin where the children are" so as to move from the known toward the unknown; and "Plan of the Lesson," which Lelia said is the most difficult because the teacher should state what she proposes to do in a step-by-step order while observing her pupils and being responsive to them. Although she should not lose sight of the main goal, the details of the lesson might vary from the plan.[41]

Some of the chapters began with the presentation of a principle. For example, in the chapter illustrating a beginning lesson in reading, Lelia wrote: "The thought being the unit of mental action, it follows that the sentence is the unit of expression, and should be reached, in the teaching of reading, as soon as possible. After a few object-words have been learned (and the greater the skill of the teacher the less the number of words required) the first sentence may be properly taught."[42]

Readers who had followed the publisher's recommendation to buy both books would have been able to look up the chapter on reading in *Talks on Teaching* for a more detailed exposition of Parker's theory on the subject.

In preparing the framework for the book, Lelia had drawn on her own experience. She wished to emphasize the necessity for a well-defined goal for the lesson as well as for reflection on the experiences the children would bring. She emphasized detailed planning and practice on the part of the teacher. She may have interviewed teachers about their goals in some cases, but she has said that for the most part she was just another visitor taking notes. Nevertheless, Lelia commented that the teacher's goal and plan should be obvious to the observer, even though the teacher is responsive to the children and the teaching seems spontaneous. Here again she demonstrated her grasp of a pedagogical principle as important today as it was then. The teacher must have a clear goal for the work she introduces, as well as sufficient knowledge to guide the children in their exploration.

Following the introduction, Lelia presents her account of the lesson that followed. The narrative includes the quoted dialogue between the teacher and her pupils as well as a description of the materials and the action. It is not, however, an objectively worded report. Lelia wrote in a more colorful, reportorial style. The opening section of the lesson introduced above conveys the flavor:

> The teacher stands by the blackboard with her little class—which she has just called up—gathered around her. Looking at them keenly a moment, and detecting a certain lack of animation in their manner, she steps to the door, sets it open, and says to the group, "I am going to play that you are all kittens. How do kittens run?" "Fast." "Quick." "Softly." "Yes; fast and softly. Now let me see which of my kittens will run fast and softly out of the east door, half around the house, in at the west door, and get here again first. Go."
>
> Like a flock of startled birds they fly, and in two minutes are back, panting and breathless, from their rapid run, but alive from top to toe.[43]

Lelia then recorded the steps by which the teacher led the children to imagine a hen outside the window, a frequent event, so that they volunteered the sentence "I see a hen."

> "I will put what you said on the blackboard," says the teacher, and writes, "I see a hen." "Somebody tell me what I wrote." All the hands are flying. "Mary." "I see a hen." "Johnnie." "I see a hen"; and so on, till every member of the group has read the sentence, and no two with the same tone or inflection.[44]

The lesson continued with graphics drawn by the teacher so that the children were reading pictures as well as words. For example, the teacher drew a fence underneath the hen, so that the children read, "I see a hen on the fence." While Lelia took the teacher's skill in drawing for granted, the modern reader now understands why Colonel Parker felt that the ability to draw was an important qualification for a teacher. Each teacher was expected to be able to sketch on the blackboard the simple illustrations often found in children's books today.

At the end of each lesson Lelia included a section called "Notes and Comments," in which she pointed out observations she felt were particularly important, sometimes with an explanation of the principle involved. In this example, she notes the contrast between the former repetitive methods of teaching reading and a more joyous approach:

Something of a contrast—this lesson—both in manner and matter, to the old fashion of presenting a Webster's spelling book to the innocent little miserables, and expecting them to learn to read (in spite of being taught the alphabet) such exciting things as these—"An ox." "Is it an ox?" "It is an ox." To say nothing of those later days, when the primer came to alleviate their sufferings, filled with inspiring information like this—"The bug is on the mug." "The mug is on the rug." "The rug is on the tug."[45]

Most of her comments made important pedagogical points, and taken together with the narratives they convey a clear picture of what Lelia (and Parker) considered the goals of teaching and the best methods of achieving those goals. Throughout the narratives, lessons were based on familiar objects used to engage the children's attention. The children handled the objects, observed them, described them, wrote about and drew them. The role of "concrete" experiences was stressed for young children whenever a new subject was introduced, for language and reading as well as for number work. Teachers relied on eliciting information, words and sentences from the children rather than telling them. Lelia applauded a teacher who waited patiently when the answer to her question was slow in coming. "Here is a teacher who possesses this rare gift of silence. She knows not only when to speak, and what to say, but where to stop. If teachers would talk less, they would make a far stronger impression when they do speak, and give poor children a chance to talk, besides."[46]

Giving the children a chance to talk was more significant than allowing them to discharge energy, although that was also a consideration. More important, the teacher's questions in the group setting were designed to facilitate the children's sharing of information or making discoveries together. Good comments and answers received praise and attention, and children were encouraged to help each other. Lelia emphasized this point:

The device of the young teacher-pupil was excellent, for children love children, and children are impressed by children. The little child will learn far more rapidly from one of his own age than he will from the most skilful or gifted of grown-up teachers. "We send our children," says Emerson, "to school to the teacher, but it is the pupils who educate them."[47]

In short, many of the educational practices put forward today as a part of educational reform were the focus of attention in the Quincy schools and in Lelia Patridge's book. An integration of subjects was recommended, so that time and effort would not be fragmented by the study of many different subjects. One topic or project might be used as the vehicle for instruction in reading, writing, spelling, and botany. Critical thinking and problem solving were emphasized over memorization of facts and rules. And above all, teachers were urged to observe the children, to learn what they already knew, to evaluate how well they were able to grasp a new presentation, and to study the process of intellectual growth. To Lelia it was this "keen, unremitting observation of the pupils" that made the Quincy schools notable. "In brief, their [the teachers] never-ending study of the children . . . gives these teachers the foundation of the skill which enables them to control the children. It is the great secret of their success."[48]

One big difference between the classrooms Lelia described and those of today is in the general decorum expected. Although Lelia found the teachers more relaxed and accepting of the children than most teachers, readers today would find the routines done in unison, marching in and out, standing together, and the words used in disciplining, restrictive and, perhaps, incompatible with the child-centered attitudes professed. The teachers also must have experienced some confusion. Parker was fond of saying that teachers were given guidelines and that they were free to work out the best strategies for themselves. In giving freedom to the teacher, more freedom would be given to the children. But he was well-known for bellowing down a corridor at a teacher who was not teaching as he thought she should.[49] Still, his success in Quincy captured the interest of educators desirous of improving their teaching, and Lelia Patridge's *Quincy Methods* provided examples of how that might be accomplished. Only a person with a deep understanding of educational philosophy and practice, and a gift for observation and writing, could have produced such a book.

JOHN B. STETSON UNIVERSITY

Lelia Patridge was engaged to teach in the normal department at Stetson University in DeLand, Florida, for the 1891–92 school year. According to the minutes of the annual meeting of the board of trustees, her teaching assignment included methods of teaching, elocution, rhetorical work for the upper classes, and light, or class, gymnastics. Her qualifications seemed to fit with the needs of the university at that time very well.

Stetson University had its origin as the DeLand Academy, founded in 1883 by Henry A. DeLand. John B. Stetson, the hat manufacturer from Philadelphia, donated funds to reorganize the school, which was granted a charter in 1887 under the name Stetson University. In 1891 the university was still young, and both the normal department and the physical culture department were new. The normal department was organized in response to the need for special professional training for teachers for the public schools; it was, in effect, the fourth year of high school.[50]

A new gymnasium had been built to accommodate men and women at different times of day. The trustees' report stated that the new gymnasium had "apparatus for making measurements and tests for determining accurately the condition of a pupil, and the proper exercises can then be prescribed and any defect remedied." The reader will recognize the similarity between this description and that of Dr. Dio Lewis. Lelia was hired as an "expert in class and light gymnastics" and may have influenced the outfitting of the new gymnasium.[51]

From the records at Stetson University, it appears that Lelia stayed there only one year.[52] Precisely where Lelia went and what she did for the next fifteen years is unclear. At least part of that time she was living in Massachusetts. It seems likely that she met Ruric Nevel Roark at Clark University, where he was an "honorary fellow," and where she attended child-study classes with the noted psychologist G. Stanley Hall. Roark subsequently invited her to join him at Eastern Kentucky Normal School when he became its first president.

THE EASTERN KENTUCKY NORMAL SCHOOL

In 1908, Lelia Patridge began her work at the Eastern Kentucky Normal School as a teacher in the model high school. In Kentucky she found a place where her skills and experience were valued, and she became an active member of a faculty who were attempting to establish a new normal school in a state badly in need of educational reform. After the first year of teaching in the model school, she found her niche teaching courses in principles and methods of teaching and as director of the rural school program. Lelia seems to have committed herself completely to the challenges of the developing school. In some ways it does seem remarkable that the woman from New England, with a lifetime of experience in Northern cities, chose to spend the most extended and the final period of her career in the South, in rural schools, and that she should find so much dignity and respect there.

Writing in 1909, the superintendent of public instruction of Kentucky, John Grant Crabbe, described the status of schooling and literacy in the state. Only 46 percent of the white children in the state were enrolled in school. Kentucky was surpassed in the number of native, white illiterates only by North Carolina, Louisiana, and New Mexico; in one county he found that one-third of the white population could neither read nor write. Nor, he said, was illiteracy confined to the mountains. "There are more native white illiterates in the blue grass counties than in the entire states of Massachusetts or Maine. The foreign-born citizen in Kentucky is better educated than the native born."[53]

Superintendent Crabbe did not give the statistics for African Americans. He did address the issue to some extent by saying that most of the "colored race" lived in cities where a system of segregated, graded schools had been maintained for many years under the control of elected trustees, and that the system had given "great satisfaction." The implication was that schooling was better for both blacks and whites in the cities. The state's problem was the "deplorable condition of the common schools" in the rural areas, for which there were no local taxes to provide schoolhouses and supplies or to hire adequately prepared teachers. Overall, there were no instructional plans, no supervision, no school libraries, and few high schools in the rural areas.[54] The rural schools served both black and white children poorly. The new School Law in 1908 was directed toward rectifying some of these conditions by organizing county systems of graded schools similar to those in the cities. Apparently, there was some opposition in the countryside because of apprehension about the "race question," that is, the threat of integrated schools. Superintendent Crabbe addressed the issue: "There is no reason for this. The constitution of Kentucky provides that separate schools for the two races shall be forever maintained."[55] The intent of the law was to extend the city-tested graded system to the country schools with the county as the unit of organization.

In short, schools in the rural areas of Kentucky in 1909 suffered from many of the same deficiencies Horace Mann found in Massachusetts seventy years before, and Kentucky proposed to try the same remedy—normal schools to prepare professional teachers who could carry out the necessary reforms. As early as 1872 there had been a proposal originating from the teachers institutes that one or more normal schools be established, but it was not until March 1906 that the schools were authorized. The cities of Richmond and Bowling were selected as the sites for the normal schools. The Eastern Kentucky Model School opened in September 1906, and the Normal School began admitting students in January 1907.

President Roark described Richmond as a "little city" with a population of about 6,000, "on the border line between the bluegrass and the mountains." The campus and buildings, once the site of Old Central University, were given to the state by the city. Roark found the campus "one of the most beautiful in the South" with its "splendid sweep of bluegrass turf, thickly set with fine maples and other trees." He began to press at once for more buildings, and urged the "further beautifying of the campus and its careful reservation as an aesthetic feature. This would preclude the pasturing of any kind of livestock upon it."[56]

In July of 1908, Roark prepared his report for the first year and a half of the new school. The number of matriculated students had already reached 550 in the Normal School and 157 in the Model School, and he commented that the majority of the students were teachers rather than young people expecting to enter the career. He saw that as a wholesome tendency, boding well for improving the quality of teaching. Roark was not satisfied with the quality in some of the Model School departments and predicted that the new faculty would improve the high school and increase attendance. Lelia was one of the new teachers to be assigned to the Model High School.

Before the school year 1908–09 was completed, Dr. Roark died quite suddenly. His loss was lamented greatly, especially by Miss Patridge, who wrote the memorial tribute to his memory. Roark's wife, Mary C. Roark, became acting president, and writing the second part of the biennial report fell to her. She reported that the enrollment had increased steadily and now stood at 882 students, some of whom were high-school or college graduates. Mrs. Roark noted that having students with good preparation enabled the school "to better accomplish the work for which the Normal School was created—the professional training of teachers."[57] In January 1909 the Normal School had secured one of the rural schools to be used as a country practice school, and Mrs. Roark reported that "Miss Lelia Patridge was made Supervisor and the work done by her for our more advanced pupils has been a source of pride and gratification to the school. Theory and careful observation in the Model School always precede the practice work."[58]

Superintendent Crabbe had also taken note that the Kentucky Federation of Women's Clubs under the leadership of Mrs. Charles Weaver had organized more than forty school improvement leagues in cooperation with the County Teachers' Institute, and Lelia had plunged into this work as well:

> Miss Lelia Patridge says: "A general report of school improvement work this year suggests that not only has a good beginning been made, but that the second stage of progress seems to have been reached. While a few immature or easily discouraged teachers have fallen out of ranks, the older and stronger majority has become more interested and more in earnest. Not only has the work been organized in every section of the State, but in some cases, large results have been accomplished, as in that rural district in Campbell County, where teacher, with the aid of pupils and patrons, cleared up the yard, set out trees,

improved and decorated the school house, bought a fair sized library and organized a course of popular lectures, free to the people of the neighborhood."[59]

Meanwhile, the legislature had appropriated the funds for three new buildings. Ruric Nevel Roark Hall, named for the late president, was the largest of these, and it accommodated the administration and business offices, the Model School, a large classroom, and a science laboratory for the normal classes. The heating and power plant occupied the second building, along with manual training shops on the second floor. The yearbook for 1914 crowed that the "power plant is considered the best power plant in the State of Kentucky."[60] The third building provided living quarters for 124 young women. Two dormitories and three brick cottages accommodated the young women, who were under the "special oversight" of the dean of women, a post held by Mrs. Roark for many years after she passed the presidency to J.G. Crabbe. The young men were boarded in town, although Mrs. Roark felt that a similar dormitory for them was urgently needed.

In the biennial report for the two years ending June 1911, President Crabbe presented a long and formal report giving full details of the faculty assignments, the physical plant, the curriculum, and the campus resources. Besides president Crabbe and dean of women Roark, there were twenty-three faculty members including the teachers in the Model School. All of the professors of academic subjects—English, mathematics, Latin, French, German, pedagogy, history, natural science, and civics—had one or more college degrees, as did the principal and assistant principal of the high school and the director of the gymnasium.

The seriousness of purpose reflected by the state's investment in the Normal School was evident also in the school's statement of the worth of the normal certificates, of which there were three: the state elementary certificate, the state intermediate certificate, and the state advanced or life certificate. "These certificates will stand for (1) character; (2) a high standard of scholarship; (3) a thorough study of the science of teaching; (4) observation and practice in teaching under competent supervision."[61]

The curriculum for the certificates was continuous; that is, the elementary certificate could be obtained after one year of study, the intermediate after two years, and the advanced after three years. Noncredit review and preparatory classes were offered in the common-school branches for those who wished to prepare for county teacher examinations and for those who wished to enter the state certificate programs but were deficient in the basic qualifications. Throughout his report, President Crabbe stressed the professional nature of the education, and the unique character of a normal-school education in which child psychology and the art and science of teaching are stressed. The importance of observation and of practice is stressed, and we find Lelia Patridge listed as "Professor of Methods and Supervisor of Practice Teaching" in the 1911 report.

The *Bluemont,* a publication issued by the life certificate class of 1910, features a photograph of Lelia, a pleasant, dignified woman, still looking youthful and vigorous. Beneath the photograph there is the following paragraph:

> She is truly a friend to the mothers, a Godsend to the children, and a benefactor to her race. "Have we our manners? Good afternoon." "You must not come to the Normal School without getting the three M's, matter, method, and a goodly share of my mind if you whisper in my class." "Children, dear, minimum of punishment means maximum of excellence." The students adore her though she frowns. But woe unto you poor Seniors when it comes to Method exam.[62]

The same publication contains Lelia's tribute to Dr. Roark, and it is of interest for its language, as well as for its sentiment:

> I wish to pay this tribute to one of those rare men whom we women, who are in public life, know best how to appreciate. He was a twentieth century knight, whose chivalry was no mere matter of sentiment, but a feeling of loyalty to women that was pure, true and high. To women not of his own household or kindred he was like a kind-hearted and gentle brother, a fair-minded and cordial comrade—a charming combination.
>
> You think that Dr. Roark belongs to you, but I tell you he was known and loved in other states besides Kentucky. Everywhere he went he left a trail of friends behind him. Men loved him for his high sense of honor, his sterling worth, his inspirational power, but women admired him for rarer qualities yet. They appreciated his exquisite courtesy that came from the heart, his purity of life and his nobility and largeness of soul.[63]

The next biennial report, ending 30 June 1913, found Miss Patridge with a new assignment. She had been given responsibility for the new Department of Rural Schools. President Crabbe explained that hundreds of young women and men came to the Normal School to take the review course so that they would be able to pass the county teachers examination. They had no professional training and they returned to their counties "as untrained as they left them."

> This state of affairs is greatly to be deplored. . . . A new department has been created with Miss Lelia E. Patridge as its head, the Department of Rural Schools, and from this time, every student who attends (even for a single term) the school will be required to take at least one period each day in professional work, that shall enable him to go back to his school with some knowledge of approved up-to-date methods of teaching and some ideas of better ways of conducting a school than the traditional ones previously followed.[64]

They also initiated a rural school supervisors' course for the seventy supervisors already in the field. The course was directed at a consideration of such issues as the function of the rural school, qualities of a first class rural school, school management, evaluation and school-book selection, and issues of consolidation. Considering the enormity of Kentucky's problem in the rural areas, this was also a challenging position for Miss Patridge.

Normal School faculty committees were listed in the 1913 report, along with faculty assignments. Lelia Patridge was a member of the committee on recommendations and the teachers' bureau. Early on, the Normal School had initiated the teachers' bureau to assist students in finding "a position best suited to his qualifications," and at the same time to assist school officials in locating well-qualified teachers for their schools. In reviewing the record, President Crabbe reported that Eastern Normal School had trained 3,500 teachers and that nearly every one of them was teaching in Kentucky, 75 percent in rural schools.[65]

Lelia's assignments did not change substantially over the next few years. She continued to serve on the committee on recommendations and the teachers' bureau, the new committee on faculty club, and as "officer" for the class of 1918, apparently a class-advisor role. The teachers' bureau published an elaborated version of its work, mentioning specifically the availability of special teachers in subjects such as art, music, domestic science, and agriculture. The Normal School had followed the trends along "more utilitarian lines," adding manual training, domestic science, agriculture, horticulture, and similar subjects to the curriculum.

By the time of the biennial report of 1917, the effects of the Great War were being felt. The school's gardens and the purchase of a "modern pressure canner" made it possible for the home economics department to can berries, beans, potatoes, apples, and tomatoes for use in the school's kitchens, and for the public. To promote conservation, the Normal School held a four-day conference with speakers from farm organizations, churches, women's clubs, and others—amounting to "thousands of people"—all addressed by Governor Stanley.

Miss Patridge had never been busier. Her area of responsibility was "methodology and professional reading," and she was a member of the committees responsible for certification and graduation, the literary magazine the *Talisman*, classification and student schedules, and chair of the committee on courses of study. She also continued to be the officer for the class of 1918. According to the president, as much of the work of the Normal School as possible was conducted through these committees, and faculty met regularly to confer and report on their actions.[66]

By 1919, the Normal School curriculum and organization had begun to resemble that of the colleges. The faculty now held more advanced degrees, especially those in the traditional disciplines of mathematics, history, and English. A semester hour was defined as one recitation per week for a semester or for two terms, and courses were assigned credits accordingly, except that laboratory classes earned half as much credit. Requirements for the certificates were noted in terms of academic credits and professional credits. Mrs. Roark had retired, and the faculty had been organized into "departments of instruction." Lelia Patridge was still teaching methodology, and she had been granted a leave of absence for the following semester "to visit other schools."[67]

Career's End

Shortly after 8 P.M. on Saturday, 4 December 1920, Lelia Patridge was struck by an automobile on Main Street in Richmond, Kentucky. It was a rainy night and she had been shopping. As she crossed the street with her arms full of packages and her umbrella raised, she was struck by a car driven by the druggist's son, Hume Griggs. Dr. O.F. Hume was nearby and took her to the hospital. It was clear that she had sustained fatal injuries, and she died a few hours later. She was seventy-six years old. Mr. Griggs stated that he had been driving slowly, but had not seen her until it was impossible to avoid striking her.

A member of the Eastern Kentucky Normal School contacted with the news of Miss Patridge's death said that her position would be difficult to fill:

She possessed a broad knowledge of method and practice of which she had made a special study for years. After her employment here, she made trips to western states where she inculcated the original and successful ideas in colleges and institutions of learning. She was the author of text books treating upon these matters which have been taken up extensively in this and other countries.[68]

The Eastern State Normal School Board of Regents met on 8 January 1921 and adopted "Resolutions of Respect" written by President T. J. Coates:

Whereas Miss Lelia Patridge entered the Eastern Kentucky Normal School as instructor in 1909 [actually 1908], and served the Institution faithfully, efficiently and well from the time she entered the Institution until the time of her death . . .

Whereas, the School has suffered a very great loss in her death, therefore, be it resolved by the Board of Regents of the Eastern Kentucky State Normal School, first, that the faithful and efficient services of Miss Patridge are highly appreciated by said Board; second, that the Board deeply regrets her death; third, that the Board sympathizes with her friends and relatives in their loss; fourth, that a copy of these resolutions be spread upon a page of the minutes of the Board of Regents, and a copy of the same be furnished her surviving brother.[69]

Lelia Patridge's will, written in 1915, directed the bulk of her estate, about $20,000, to a trust fund "to assist aged unmarried women preferably teachers so that their last days may not be made miserable by extreme poverty."[70]

In 1960, the Board of Regents announced that seven units of a married-student housing project were to be named "in honor of seven prominent members of the Eastern faculty who served the college [now Eastern Kentucky State University] well in its formative years."[71] One of those honored was Lelia E. Patridge. Thus her name has been preserved on the Eastern Kentucky State University campus as one who made an important contribution during the formative years of the college.

For more than fifty-five years Lelia Patridge was a teacher, a teacher who was among the first to study and teach physical culture and gymnastics; a teacher who sought more effective methods of teaching and in the process wrote two widely disseminated books about a significant educational movement of the nineteenth century; a teacher who in her mature years brought her experience and her energies to yet another new enterprise, where she won recognition for her abilities and respect for the quality of her work.

NOTES

1. Register of the State Normal School, "Entrance and Graduation Register," Framingham State College Archives.

2. Thomas Woody, *A History of Women's Education in the United States*, vol. 1 (New York: Octagon Books, 1966), 415.

3. Ibid., vol. 2, 101.

4. Ibid., 103.

5. Ibid., 134.

6. Ibid., 134.

7. George W. Fetter, "Report of the Principal of Girls' Normal School," in *Fiftieth Annual Report of the Board of Controllers of Public Schools of the First School District of Pennsylvania Comprising the City of Philadelphia (For the Year Ending December 31, 1868)*, 47.

8. M. Hall Stanton, "Report of the President of the Board of Public Education," in *Fifty-seventh Annual Report of the Board of Public Education of the First School District of Pennsylvania Comprising the City of Philadelphia (For the year ending December 31, 1875)*, 14.

9. J.T. Scharf and T. Westcott, *History of Philadelphia 1609–1884*, vol. 3 (Philadelphia: L. H. Everts & Co., 1884), 1932.

10. John Trevor Custis, *The Public Schools of Pennsylvania* (Philadelphia: Burk & McFetridge, 1897), 153.

11. J.P. Wickersham, *A History of Education in Pennsylvania* (New York: Arno Press and the New York Times, 1969), 610.

12. Custis, *Public Schools*, 153.

13. Ibid., 154.

14. Ibid., 157.

15. Ibid., 158.

16. Stanton, *Fifty-seventh Annual Report*, 20.

17. Ibid.

18. Wickersham, *History of Education*, 560; also Fetter, *Fifty-first Annual Report (1869)*, 31.

19. Fetter, *Fifty-first Annual Report (1869)*, 34.

20. Custis, *Public Schools*, 170.

21. R.B. Fishbane, "The Shallow Boast of Cheapness: Public School Teaching As a Profession in Philadelphia 1865–1890," *Pennsylvania Magazine of History and Biography*, vol. 103 (Historical Society of Philadelphia, 1979): 70.

22. Wickersham, *History of Education*, 559.

23. J.P. Wickersham, "Report of the Superintendent of Common Schools" in *Forty-first Annual Report of the Commonwealth of Pennsylvania (For the Year Ending June 1, 1874)*, xi.

24. Lelia Patridge, *The "Quincy Methods" Illustrated: Pen Photographs from the Quincy Schools* (New York and Chicago: E.L. Kellogg, 1891), xii.

25. Ibid.

26. For a discussion of the kindergarten movement see Michael Steven Shapiro, *Child's Garden: The Kindergarten Movement from Froebel to Dewey* (University Park: Pennsylvania State University Press, 1983).

27. Patridge, *Quincy Methods*, xiii.

28. Ibid., xiv.

29. Lelia Patridge, comp., *Notes of Talks on Teaching* (New York and Chi-

cago: E. L. Kellogg, 1883), xxi. When the memorial edition was printed after Parker's death in 1902, Lelia's introduction was truncated and it no longer included the list of lecturers and teachers at Martha's Vineyard. The title was simply *Talks on Teaching*, and an endorsement by Parker was not included.

30. Patridge, *Quincy Methods*, xiv.

31. Ibid.

32. Several pages of book advertisements were appended to *Quincy Methods* when it was published in 1891. *Talks* was being marketed under the title *Parker's Talks on Teaching*, with Lelia Patridge as editor, and this quotation was a part of the advertisement.

33. Quoted by Amos Kellogg in his tribute to Parker in the memorial edition of *Talks on Teaching*, 33.

34. Patridge, *Notes of Talks on Teaching*, 22.

35. Ibid., passim.

36. Andrew J. Rickoff, "Superintendent's Report" in *Cleveland Public Schools Board of Education Report (1874–75)*, 89–95.

37. Henry F. Donovan, "Report of the President of the Cook County Board of Education," in *Biennial Report of the County Superintendent of Schools (Cook County, Illinois, July 1, 1882 to June 30, 1884)*, 50.

38. Patridge, *Quincy Methods*, xv.

39. Charles F. Adams, Jr., *The New Departure* (Boston: Estes and Lauriat, 1879), 33.

40. Ibid., 46.

41. Patridge, *Quincy Methods*, 2.

42. Ibid., 128.

43. Ibid., 129.

44. Ibid., 131.

45. Ibid., 134.

46. Ibid., 370.

47. Ibid., 127.

48. Ibid., 213

49. Edmund W. Kearney, *Chicago State College: A Centennial Retrospective* (Chicago: Chicago State College, 1969), 9.

50. Gilbert Lycan, "The Stetson Story." Pamphlet. Stetson University, 1977; see also "Seventh Annual Catalogue of John B. Stetson University," 34.

51. "Minutes of the Annual Meeting of the Trustees of John B. Stetson University (1892)," duPont-Ball Library Archives, Stetson University.

52. I wish to thank archivist Gail Grieb at the duPont-Ball Library for locating and sending me the materials from Stetson University. We shared the pleasure of searching for clues.

53. John G. Crabbe, *Biennial Report of the Superintendent of Public Instruction of Kentucky (For the two years ending June 30, 1909)*, 14.

54. Ibid., 19.

55. Ibid. Blacks were served by the Kentucky Normal School and Industrial Institute for Colored Persons, authorized in 1886 "to prepare colored teachers for the colored common schools of the Commonwealth of Kentucky." *Biennial Report of the Superintendent of Public Instruction of Kentucky (1913)*, 669.

56. Ruric N. Roark, in ibid., 55.

57. Mary C. Roark, in ibid., 353.

58. Ibid.

59. John G. Crabbe, in ibid., 46.

60. "Year Book Eastern Kentucky State Normal School," *Eastern Kentucky Review* 8 (October 1914): 17.

61. John G. Crabbe, "Report of Eastern Kentucky State Normal School," in *Biennial Report Superintendent of Public Instruction of Kentucky (For the two years*

ending June 30, 1911), 167.

62. Life Certificate Class of 1910, in *Bluemont* (Richmond: Eastern Kentucky Normal School).

63. Ibid.

64. Crabbe, in *Biennial Report (June 30, 1913),* 479.

65. Ibid.

66. T.J. Coates, in *Biennial Report (December 31, 1917),* passim.

67. T.J. Coates, in *Biennial Report (December 31, 1919),* 314. This may have been one of the lecture tours mentioned in the *Richmond Daily Register* article of 1920 reporting on her death.

68. *Richmond Daily Register,* 6 December 1920.University Archives, Eastern Kentucky University.

69. Eastern State Normal School Board of Regents Minutes, 8 January 1921, 32. University Archives, Eastern Kentucky University.

70. Archivist Charles C. Hay III at Eastern Kentucky University located and sent me a copy of Lelia Patridge's will as well as copies of the *Bluemont,* the Regents Resolutions and Minutes, and other documents. I deeply appreciate his assistance and encouragement.

71. Eastern State Normal School Board of Regents Minutes, vol. 11, 16 November 1960, 312–13.

SECTION THREE

TEACHING ON THE EAST
AND WEST COASTS

In the nineteenth century most women teachers taught in rural communities, often in one-room country schools, and on the West Coast rural
schoolteaching has continued well into the twentieth century. With the
growth of metropolitan school systems in large cities and suburban systems
in smaller towns, however, the urban schoolteacher has emerged as the dominant type in the twentieth century. This section profiles rural and urban
women teachers of Massachusetts and California, comparing the evolution
of public schools on the East and West Coasts.

Public schools were established in California even before the state
joined the union in 1850, and the first teacher was a woman, Mrs. Olive
Mann Isbell. She taught in 1846 at the Mission Santa Clara and in 1847 at
the customhouse in Monterey. But the official founding of a public-school
system dates from 3 April 1848, when San Francisco opened the first public school in a redwood schoolhouse erected on Portsmouth Square.[1] In April
1850 the city council of San Francisco passed an ordinance establishing a
system of public schools, and the first state constitution included a provision that a school "be kept up in every school district at least three months
in every year."[2] In 1860 and again in 1866 additional state laws were enacted ensuring the financing and managing of public schools, guaranteeing
to children in both rural and urban areas access to free public schools.

In rural and urban communities on both the East and West coasts
during the nineteenth and twentieth centuries, women teachers have been
at the center of public-school education. They have been the main workforce.
In the city of Los Angeles, the first public school opened on 19 March 1855
with William A. Wallace in charge of the boys' department and Louisa Hayes
in charge of the girls' division.[3] The first teacher to teach at San Diego's public
schoolhouse in 1865 was Mary Chase Walker, a young woman from Massachusetts who had attended Framingham Normal School.[4] Every change,

whether in the philosophy of teaching or in the politics of school administration, has been carried out by teachers, the majority of whom have been
women.

At the same time, the growth of public education increased women's
influence on American society. Women were able to gain elementary, secondary, and university educations, and with increased demand for teachers
the number of jobs for women outside of the home expanded. In both rural
and city schools, women established professional careers as teachers, principals, and administrators.

In rural areas in the nineteenth century, the job of schoolteacher offered women one of the few possibilities to be self-supporting. Although the
stereotype of the maiden schoolmarm remains a vivid image from fiction,
this chapter portrays both married and unmarried women. In describing the
teachers' lives we document real-life classroom practices, which included
regimented reciting and writing exercises on the one hand and individualized assignments and group learning on the other hand. The rural teacher,
as the central component of the public-school system in her community,
taught the curriculum that her society and generation required. The teachers profiled in this chapter, Josephine Newhall of Stow, Massachusetts, and
Gene Bond of Santa Paula, California, instructed children how to become
moral Americans.

In the twentieth century American women could exercise a degree of
choice in career, and teaching became only one possibility. Women who in
previous generations might have dedicated their lives to the classroom, could
now become white-collar workers, nurses, and social workers, or could enter other professions, albeit in small numbers. Nevertheless, schoolteaching
continued to offer employment opportunities for American women, and to
some segments of the population it provided entry into U.S. society. Women
whose families had immigrated to the United States in the nineteenth century often found in schoolteaching a channel for social mobility. In this section, we profile the life of Mary O'Neill Mulcahy, a schoolteacher of Irish
descent. Her story in large measure could be that of women whose families
emigrated from an array of European countries. Public schools not only
taught English to the children of immigrants, but also offered instruction in
the American way of life. If a girl excelled in school, she could usually be
assured of employment as a schoolteacher.

The chapter on urban schoolteachers also examines the role of the
teacher as the instrument for carrying out policy changes. In the twentieth
century, American public schools underwent a fundamental shift in their
methods of teaching. John Dewey's philosophy of progressive education

transformed the public schools. In the profiles of Mary Mulcahy of Cambridge and Lucy Jenson of Los Angeles, we are able to compare how progressive concepts were applied in Massachusetts and in California. We also demonstrate how the teacher, as part of a school system, fit into the changing classroom scene, blending individual and societal interpretations of progressive education.

NOTES

1. Federal Writers' Project, *WPA Guide to California* (New York: Pantheon Books, 1935; reissued 1984), 132.

2. Ibid., 133.

3. John and LaRee Caughey, *Los Angeles: Biography of a City* (Berkeley: University of California Press, 1976), 137.

4. Ben F. Dixon, *Don Diego's Old School Days* (San Diego: San Diego Historical Days Association, 1955), 23.

RURAL SCHOOLTEACHERS, 1870S–1940S: JOSEPHINE NEWHALL AND GENE BOND

Madelyn Holmes

[Josephine Newhall] has been faithful and earnest, and her gentle and yet most effective government was in every way successful. Her scholars made excellent progress. . . . Miss Newhall retired from the school . . . bearing with her the love and esteem of her pupils.[1]

The job of rural schoolteacher in the nineteenth century was in some sense an exercise in pleasing the local community. Teachers were selected and paid by a local district committee. They lived in the community, either as boarder or as local resident. They taught rural children what the community wanted them to teach. Classes were held usually in one-room school buildings maintained by the local community.

For Miss Josephine Newhall, who taught school in Stow, Massachusetts, for more than twenty years, it was an ideal position. "Country schoolteachers had to reflect faithfully the values of the rural communities in which they taught," according to Andrew Gulliford, author of *America's Country Schools*.[2] For Miss Newhall this was no problem. She herself was a product of the community, and her personal life was fully enclosed within Stow society.

But for other rural schoolteachers, the role of pleasing the community was not as automatic. Middlebury College Professor Margaret Nelson, who interviewed rural teachers in Vermont, identified a tension between the schoolteacher's central role as community builder and her more peripheral role as community servant.[3] What she found was that teachers were expected to serve the community, but often were not able to become full participants in community life. They were outsiders.

Educational historian David Tyack suggested a possible explanation: the "rural teacher was sometimes regarded by the community as an intellectual."[4] This reputation, often based upon a teacher's longer attendance at school, could understandably have resulted in a degree of social isolation in a small rural community. But Professor Nelson detected another cause for teachers' outsider status. Because of their daily contact with young children, teachers learned about conditions at home that families may have wanted to keep secret.[5] Even if a teacher were no more intellectual than anyone else in a rural community, she may still have been socially isolated because she knew too much.

By the early twentieth century the job of rural schoolteacher had become more than one of pleasing a local community. National and regional educators criticized rural schools, the teachers, and their teaching methods as unmodern. On the West Coast however, country schools did not disappear with the dawning of the twentieth century. Even as late as the 1970s in the state of California alone, fifty-five one-room schoolhouses were still in operation.[6] Former teacher Mrs. Gene Bond, whose one-room school is described below, carried on rural traditions for nearly twenty years from the mid-1920s through June 1942 at Santa Clara Elementary School District in Santa Paula, California:

> The school day began with a daily pledge to the flag and the singing of "America." One of the students played the tune on the piano. We then had sharing time, when everyone from the youngest to the oldest discussed current affairs. That was really good for the young children. They could learn about events which would have passed them by completely unnoticed. After that we went on to regular lessons in spelling, arithmetic, geography, history, and composition. She gave everyone individual assignments and had all students progressing at the best of their abilities.[7]

Even though a number of country schools remain in the Western states, many more have consolidated into large, standardized, graded elementary schools. As the twenty-first century approaches, a few educators are looking back longingly at the one-room school and what it contributed to public schooling in the United States. "The closing of one-room country schools forever changed the rural American landscape and diminished close community ties and a sense of social cohesion among rural Americans."[8] Perhaps Gulliford has overly romanticized the loss, but as Tyack points out, more "reminiscences of rural schools are highly favorable" than are the personal accounts of city schools.[9] To Fred Schroeder, the "icon of the little red schoolhouse" embodied "yet more transcendant ideals . . . the ideal of organic harmony of building, people and environment . . . an institution serving people as individuals, within a non-compartmentalized community, and as sympathetic parts of an accessible natural environment."[10] But to other historians, it was not the icon or the landscape or even the sense of community that made the country school something special in the history of American education. "Where the teacher in the one-room school had the sole responsibility for what took place there, it was obvious to the most casual observer that the teacher made the school."[11]

TEACHING IN STOW, MASSACHUSETTS

It may seem paradoxical to describe historical rural teachers in Massachusetts, a state far better known as the birthplace of the American industrial revolution. Yet in the nineteenth century, at the same time as workers flocked to cotton mills, banks, and shipyards in the cities, the rural population continued to raise cows, plant corn, and pick apples.

In fact, in 1800 more Massachusetts residents lived in rural areas than in urban ones. Out of a total Massachusetts population of 423,000, 358,000 were rural residents and only 65,000 urban.[12] In 1850, for the first time, the numbers of urban dwellers surpassed the numbers of rural residents. Only by the latter decades of the century did the Commonwealth of Massachusetts assume its urban character.

It was not difficult, therefore, to locate a rural school system for study. I chose Stow, a small town in eastern Massachusetts, which today with its population of 5,650 may still retain a rural appearance but whose employment profile is decidedly suburban and high tech. Twenty percent of the population work for a neighboring computer giant, the Digital Equipment Corporation.[13]

Stow in the nineteenth century was genuinely agricultural. In 1855, the 1,485 inhabitants earned their livings mainly as farmers, and in 1900 there were still more cows than people in Stow.[14] The school system consisted of five one-room district schools. The town did not operate a public high school until the 1870s, and only in the early twentieth century did the school committee consolidate and construct modern, graded schools. Even though the town was only twenty-five miles from Boston, superintendent of schools J.S. Moulton in 1899 could lament that the teachers were far away from "the stimulus which comes from contact with those who are experts in education."[15]

The townspeople of Stow have shown a lively interest in their own school history. In the 1970s, a group of Stow residents applied for and received a bicentennial matching grant to help restore a red-brick schoolhouse, built in 1825. Called the West School because it served children in the western part of the town, the building had been converted into a four-room private residence after school consolidation in the early 1900s. The town of Stow repossessed the house in 1970 when the owner defaulted on payment of property taxes. The citizens' group restored the building, furnished it with early-nineteenth-century school desks, and assembled photographs, schoolbooks, and other artifacts out of its past from townspeople whose ancestors had attended district school number three, the West School.

The history of schools in Stow, as in most other Colonial settlements in Massachusetts, goes back to the period of the town's establishment. The 10,000 acres of "country's land," which became an official township in 1683, were originally divided into twelve "Lotts" of fifty acres each. The town's first permanent minister, appointed in 1699, was John Eveleth; he was also the schoolmaster. Although church and school were inextricably united during Colonial times, nevertheless the town of Stow chose a separate schoolmaster in 1714. Thomas Brown was the first of a constantly changing list of young men hired to keep school before the town constructed three schoolhouses in 1733–34. In 1752 there were 118 families living in Stow, comprising a population of 260.[16]

With the establishment of a new government in 1789, the state of Massachusetts formalized its requirements for education. Each town was to institute a district school system. Stow divided into five districts with five schoolhouses, each supported by the families who lived in that district. In the early years of the nineteenth century Stow's schoolhouses were wooden structures, usually consisting of one room with an open fireplace. One local historian recounted a resident's memory of attending school in 1810: "I have heard her speak of the intensity of the cold of that school-house in the winter."[17]

By the 1820s Stow was constructing brick schoolhouses like the West School. That school, which was built in six months by local firms, cost the district taxpayers only $246.50. Not until 1831, however, was it furnished with a stove and not until 1836 did it acquire the luxury of an outhouse. In the mid-1830s mice were still found at the West School; one five-year-old was pleased to catch a mouse with the teacher's tongs.[18]

Each of Stow's district schools of the 1820s and 1830s served anywhere from sixty to one hundred students, with the youngest aged two or three and the oldest in the late teens. Girls sat on benches at one side of the room and boys at the opposite side, with the teacher's desk in between. An open space, usually in the center of the room, was reserved for lesson recitations.

Teachers were employed by the term, approximately nine weeks in either summer or winter. The winter term was taught by male teachers, a large proportion of whom stayed for one year only and went on to become lawyers. The earliest documentation of a female summer-term teacher that I have uncovered was in 1822, when local young women were hired to teach the summer term at the Old South School. Dorcas H. Scott worked as a summer term teacher in the early 1820s and remembered her pay as having been $1 per week in addition to the $1 per week the committee paid to the family with whom she boarded. She was lured away from Stow, however, when a nearby school offered her $2 a week with board included.[19] Male winter-term teachers earned between $46 and $60 in the 1830s, and female summer term teachers continued to earn $1 per week for a ten-week term.[20]

A popular summer-school teacher in the early 1830s was Miss S.L. Gerry. She taught sixty-two students during a school term that was now of twelve weeks duration. Her oldest scholar was thirteen years old and the youngest three years old. She taught reading, grammar, spelling, written and mental arithmetic, and geography. Although teachers still whipped rowdy students, Miss Gerry chose to reprimand in a gentle manner. When she heard a boy swearing, she is said to have reproved him saying, "To swear is neither brave, polite nor wise."[21]

In 1824 the town of Stow, in line with many other New England towns, established a private academy that emphasized the teaching of languages and English.[22] Stow Academy flourished for thirty years, educating boys and girls from nearby towns but also boarding students from as far away as Louisiana and Canada. Several of the district schoolteachers in the 1820s and 1830s attended Stow Academy. In 1855 the academy closed its doors, but the building was later reconstituted in 1871 as Hale High School, Stow's first public high school.

By the 1840s townspeople who were interested in school matters began to complain about the way the school system was managed.[23] The school committee report of 1845, which appears to have been the town of Stow's first published report, is scathing in its criticisms of school buildings, schoolteachers, and "that destroying bane of useful education—the Dancing school."[24] Although two members of the school committee who signed their names to the document commended a teacher for doing "the best she possibly could," they recommended general strategies for improving the quality of the teaching force. They sought teachers who would discipline children on "the principle of love, confidence, affection and respect."[25] The committee wanted to reject teachers who were prone to inflicting harsh punishments, perhaps remembering Harriet Conant, who taught during the summer of 1840 and eventually died of insanity.

She was of a nervous temperament, and probably at times was sorely tried with the conduct of her scholars. Being somewhat impulsive in her feelings, and not always taking sufficient time to inquire into each individual case of a supposed offender, she would, it is said, aim a blow at the supposed guilty one, and which would sometimes fall upon the head of an innocent 5-year-old, whose wounded feelings would not readily heal.[26]

By the end of the 1840s, the school committee had determined what they required of a schoolteacher. "We shall be exact in requiring testimonials of good moral character. . . . We could even wish that every teacher . . . should be decidedly religious."[27] They were concerned about profane talking, scholars' missing school to pick berries, and lack of parental interest in the schools. They praised teachers who could interest children in their studies and keep them happy.[28]

It was during the 1840s that female teachers were finally permitted to teach the winter term. Up to that time, only male teachers had been employed, because older boys who assisted with farmwork during the summertime attended school only in the winter. Rural school systems throughout New England had considered female teachers incapable of teaching older boys. The Stow School Committee in 1849 experimented, engaging Sarah Eveleth as the first female teacher of the winter term. She not only had had previous experience teaching in Stow, but she had also attended the Normal School at West Newton, presumably equipping her for dealing with older boy scholars.[29] Following upon the precedent established by Miss Eveleth, the committee decided to appoint another female to teach the winter term at the Grove School.

The committee was effusive in its praise of Mary T. Stevens, who had also taught the summer terms in 1848 and 1849. As a local historian reported, "The committee, elated with the improvement of the school, consented to allow the same teacher to take the winter term, notwith-standing there were eight "big boys" between sixteen and twenty years of age."[30] They were well pleased with the decision, for the boys respected their teacher and she added history, physiology, and algebra to the curriculum. She also managed to exhibit forty faultlessly neat student writing books.[31]

While publicly acknowledging that female teachers were capable of handling winter-term conditions, the town expressed interest in another type of sexual division of labor, called the Littleton Plan—a scheme from a nearby town. According to the Littleton School Committee:

The younger portion of scholars might be taught by females, more successfully and with less expense than by males. God seems to have made woman peculiarly suited to guide and develop the infant mind, and it seems to your Committee very poor policy to pay a man 20 or 22 dollars a month, for teaching children their A,B,C's, when a female could do the work more successfully at one-third of the price.[32]

In fact, the town of Stow did not systematically divide scholars into age-segregated schools. There is evidence, however, that during the 1850s and 1860s some of the districts hired male teachers to instruct children aged twelve and above. In 1860, for instance, Mr. Beane from the Divinity School in Cambridge taught forty-seven scholars in school district number one. He was paid $45 per month, whereas the female teacher in the same district was paid $25 per month. The committee was enthusiastic about Mr. Beane, for he not only taught "higher branches of study" but was able to inspire students to write "new and original" compositions and declamations.[33] At the end of the term Mr. Beane staged a "highly satisfactory and interesting" public exhibition in the town hall.[34]

By the 1850s the school committee had stopped writing as critically about Stow teachers as they had done in earlier years. Nonetheless, in the school report of 1860, the three-man committee published a portrait of an ideal schoolteacher: "full of life and energy, with clear eyes and a feeling heart; agreeable in person, and faultless in manners as possible; capable of using fitting words promptly and with ease, at every emergency. Children are by nature designedly creatures of imitation, and the teacher ought to be an attractive example set before them of the best social and cardinal virtues."[35] They listed a number of specific virtues that an ideal teacher should possess, including good humor, sincerity, and punctuality.[36]

Not only did the school committee discuss the type of teacher desired for employment, they also recommended curriculum changes. During the 1860s teachers in Stow were encouraged to pay more attention to reading aloud from a new series of readers. They were to "drill their scholars in the elementary exercises and rules of elocution."[37] Angeline E. Cogswell, a teacher at the Grove School from 1862 to 1865, taught her twenty-eight students to pronounce syllables more clearly and distinctly, varying their emphasis and voice inflection, and to express the meaning of the reading more naturally, intelligibly, and forcibly.[38]

Major changes, however, began to overtake the school system by the end of the decade. Stow discarded the district system of administration in 1869 and replaced it with a general school committee and a superintendent of schools. The first school superintendent was Theodore Cook, who was succeeded by a number of the town's leading citizens, including at least two Unitarian ministers. The school year was divided into three terms, and in 1871 Stow opened a public high school for twenty-nine students. The school was named in honor of Elijah Hale, a Stow resident who donated $5,000 toward its construction.

The school committee hired Miss Annie M. Howe of Marlboro to organize the high school.[39] She was a graduate of Wilbraham Academy and a scholarly and experienced teacher. The school committee was enthusiastic about the success of the first two terms,[40] but it was not until seven years later that they established a course of study for the high school. Miss Howe stayed only two years, and afterward the school had deteriorated.[41] The prescribed curriculum set forth a two-year English course of study as well as a three-year Classical course. Mathematics covered both algebra and geometry, and sciences included botany, geology, physiology, chemistry, and astronomy. Latin and French were offered in the Classical course, and bookkeeping in the English course. Both curricula included composition, rhetoric, English literature, philosophy, and history.

Even though changes were afloat in the school system in the 1870s, the schoolteachers of Stow remained local residents and intimately connected with community life. The lives of Stow schoolteachers, Susan Proctor Lawrence and Josephine Newhall, were representative of rural teachers in many towns throughout Massachusetts.

Susan Proctor Lawrence

Susan Proctor came to Stow to teach in the West School in 1862 when she was not yet sixteen years old. She had grown up in the nearby town of Carlisle and attended Howe Academy in Billerica. After two years as a schoolteacher, she married U.S. Army Sergeant Samuel Lawrence of Stow. According to Stow folklore she had kept her romance a secret. On a Friday afternoon in July 1864 she matter-of-factly announced to her class that when school commenced on Monday morning the name of their teacher would be changed from Miss Proctor to Mrs. Lawrence. She was married on the weekend, and her husband returned to army duty during the Civil War.[42]

Mrs. Lawrence continued to teach school in Stow through the 1880s. Altogether she taught for nearly thirty years at three Stow schools: the West School, the Centre School and the Lower Village School. During her years in the 1870s as a teacher at the Centre School she taught approximately forty children, ranging in ages from four to sixteen. For thirty-six weeks of teaching she was paid $312.50.

The town's school committee continually found new words to praise her teaching. Superintendent of schools Edwin Whitney wrote: "Scholars in all branches of study, by their long and accurate recitations, well indicated the faithfulness with which she attended to all her duties to the uttermost."[43] Unitarian minister Thomas Weston, who served as superintendent of schools in the 1880s, succinctly commented: "She seems peculiarly fitted to develop the capacities of her pupils." And yet at the same time, "Mrs. Lawrence has possessed the love and confidence of her pupils, and this continuing from term to term, has produced the best results."[44]

During all those years she managed successfully to combine marriage, motherhood, and teaching. She gave birth to four children, two of whom died in infancy. Both of her surviving children, a daughter and son, followed her into the teaching profession. Her husband worked at the textile mill in neighboring Maynard but died in 1900, twenty-seven years before Mrs. Lawrence.

In 1892 Susan Lawrence embarked upon a second career, as founding librarian of the Stow town library, a job she held for twenty-six years. For this contribution to community life, as well as for several service roles and positions held in the local Unitarian church, Mrs. Lawrence was remembered in Stow as "a prominent factor in the educational, social and religious life."[45]

As town librarian, Mrs. Lawrence continued to exert her influence on the children of Stow. She wrote in the town report of 1904 how important the library was to the education of children: "An increasing number of parents have taken out cards for the use of their children who wish to draw out books for the help they may get in their work at school. By the myth, the fable and the fairy tale the child is led by these stories to use better judgment, which in time will stimulate a desire to read the best kind of literature."[46]

Susan Lawrence died at the age of eighty in Stow on 18 July 1927. She participated actively in Stow affairs until two years before her death, and the pastor of the Unitarian church paid her "a high and deserving tribute" at her funeral.

From the personal yet unsigned obituary that extended for a full two columns in the local newspaper, we can learn something about her personality:

> Mrs. Lawrence was industrious; she was public-spirited, and she was a good woman. Her word was as good as her bond. She never forgot her friends, and she was willing to help anybody who needed help.

She had high ideals, and maintained them. She was usually right. Such opposition as she encountered resulted naturally from her dominating enthusiasm. Generous with others, with herself she was severe. She would lean over backwards to keep from humoring herself.[47]

Josephine Newhall

Josephine Newhall of Stow, Massachusetts.

The teaching career of Miss Josephine Newhall, spanning the years from 1873 to 1915, may appear as somewhat anachronistic. In 1912 she was teaching first-, second-, and third-graders together in one classroom at the Centre Primary School in Stow. Yet Mr. Francis S. Brick, superintendent of schools, said of her:

During my professional experience I have never had a better school. Miss Newhall has had an enrollment of fifty-two pupils since September. In a primary school fifty-two pupils is nearly double what it should be. Yet this school with its teeming roomful, its many classes, its multitude of problems is making progress such as never has been surpassed in my work during the eighteen years' experience.[48]

Miss Newhall's tenure as an elementary schoolteacher may have represented the end of an era, the end of the differences between rural and urban schoolteaching in Massachusetts. In the early 1900s she was the only Stow teacher who had not been educated beyond high school. She was a hangover from the nineteenth century, when rural Massachusetts schoolteachers grew out of the local community. Although she did not teach her entire life in Stow, nonetheless she remained within a ten-mile radius and returned to her hometown to become a Stow legend.

By the time Josephine Newhall was born in the mid-nineteenth century, apple orchards, saw mills, and pastures were only one aspect of the economic life of Stow. A woolens factory and a shoe factory, each employing approximately one hundred workers, and a number of shops and taverns servicing stagecoach passengers en route to Boston had added diversity to the formerly agricultural community. The population reached 1,485 inhabitants in 1855.

Josephine Newhall was born on 24 May 1854 in Stow to Lucy A. Fletcher and Nehemiah Abbott Newhall, a farmer. Her older sister, Sarah Maria, also taught school in Stow but died at the age of twenty-six in 1875. "Josie," as Josephine Newhall was known locally, was born into the Stow establishment. The Fletcher and Newhall families had been part of Stow community life for several generations. Josie was a lifelong active member of the First Parish Church, whose history dated back to the town's founding in 1683, changing from congregationalism to unitarianism in 1833.

Josie attended elementary school in Stow, receiving special recognition for good attendance at the Centre School in 1870. In 1871 Josie Newhall attended newly founded Hale High School. The seventeen-year-old scholar joined twenty-eight other members of the first class.

Miss Newhall started teaching school in the Gleasondale section of Stow at the age of nineteen in 1873. Her first job was at the Grove School, where her older sister, Sarah, had previously taught. Since it was several miles' distance from her family house on Boxmill Road, she boarded there with Mrs. Folsom. An outbreak of scarlet fever cut short Josephine's tenure at the Grove School, however, for several children died and the school closed.[49]

From 1877 to 1881, she was a teacher at the Lower Village School. This was one of the five one-teacher elementary schools in the town of Stow that educated children between the ages of five and fifteen. There were approximately twenty-seven students, still called "scholars" at that time, in Miss Newhall's school. During the winter term, which ran from the beginning of December until March, four scholars over the age of fifteen attended as well. The school year of thirty-six weeks was divided into three terms, starting in April. She received $8.50 per week for the first two terms and $9.00 per week for the winter term. During the 1880–81 academic year, teachers' wages in Stow were reduced.[50] Accordingly, Miss Newhall earned $7.50 per week but also taught fewer children, on average only sixteen children per term.

Josephine Newhall was well received as a teacher, but the descriptions in the annual reports of the school committee were not as enthusiastic as they were about other elementary schoolteachers during those years. She overcame disciplinary problems, held closing examinations, prepared her scholars for an exhibition of singing and public speaking, and received silver presents from her students "as tokens of their love and esteem."[51] The school committee praised Miss Newhall in 1879 for her exemplary record of pupil recitations, "which was remarkable for the number of perfect lessons. The written exercises in spelling were equally perfect."[52] In 1881 the Reverend Thomas Weston, superintendent of schools, described Miss Newhall at the time of her retirement from the Lower Village School: "She has been faithful and earnest, and her gentle and yet most effective government, was in every way successful. Her scholars made excellent progress. . . . Miss Newhall retired from the school at the close of the Winter term, to the great regret of all, bearing with her the love and esteem of her pupils, and lasting tokens of their regard."[53]

From the year of her retirement in 1881 until 1897, there exists no record of Josephine Newhall as a teacher in the town of Stow. She was reported to have taught for seventeen years in the nearby town of Littleton, although her parents continued to live in her childhood house on Boxmill Road until 1890. In that year the Newhall family, including Josie, moved to the house on Great Road across the street from the First Parish Church. Josie lived there even after her mother died in 1907. It is a large, gray, shingled house with a porch in front.[54]

It was during the late 1890s and continuing until her death in 1915 that Josephine Newhall's reputation as a "much loved and successful teacher" became part of Stow's recorded history.[55] She returned to Stow to care for her ill mother and arranged with the school committee to teach singing on a voluntary basis during the school year 1898–99.[56] It was at this time that the elementary school curriculum in Stow was also being enriched by a visiting teacher of drawing, presaging modern changes to come.

Josie was elected teacher at the Centre School during the following academic year, replacing Miss Harriet Faxon who resigned because of illness. Miss Newhall taught grades one, two, and three for a total of thirty-six weeks and received a salary of $323.10. Her salary increased to $409.00 by the 1911–12 academic year.

During the early 1900s the school committee consolidated the entire public-school system and constructed a new school building known as the Union School. All primary, grammar, and high-school-age students attended this school until it burned down at the end of 1908. Children rode to school from outlying rural areas of the town on a covered, horse-drawn "school barge." Wendell Stephenson, a former student of Miss Newhall's, remembers riding on the barge from his family's farm. During the winter term in 1911 the town added a second school barge to transport the growing number of students from the western part of the town.

Not only were the school buildings consolidated, but the content of the curriculum was also changed during these early years of the twentieth century. In line with progressive thinking in education, Stow schools added more manual training to the standard program of the three Rs. Superintendent of schools Francis Brick explained: "There is a cry for skill—for such training as will not only develop a boy mentally but will train his hand and eye to be skillful."[57] Accordingly, the art course became more practical, and paper cutting, knitting, weaving, molding, sewing, and modelworking were introduced.

Furthermore, Stow schools made a decisive effort to teach patriotism.[58] Pupils saluted the flag, pledged allegiance to the flag, and sang "America" every morning. There were twenty-nine flag days when the flag was to be on display.

Textbooks reflected the new attitudes in education. When Josie started out in the late 1870s, Stow schools were introducing a new reading textbook called the *Franklin Readers*. The books were written by Hillard and Campbell and published in Boston. The authors wrote in their preface to the *Second Reader* that they "have endeavored to inculcate correct moral sentiments and kindly affections, including the good treatment of domestic animals."[59] They included poems and short stories primarily about dogs, cats, birds, horses, plants, and children, as well as a few didactic pieces such as "Be Kind," "The Selfish Boy," and "How to Read Well."

When Josie returned to the Stow schools at the end of the nineteenth century, superintendent of schools Sidney Moulton recommended the use of a new set of readers by Ellen Cyr. Published by the Boston firm of Ginn and Company in the 1890s, *Cyr's Second Reader* introduced children to the poetry of Longfellow and Whittier. Other stories in the reader were "closely allied to Nature-work and child-life." The author, aligning herself with the modern, progressive, child-centered attitudes of the period, stated her purpose: "While it is of the greatest importance that the practical side of life should open before them, and that they should look duty and responsibility squarely in the face, the imagination should be carefully cherished, for it is a God-given faculty and plays an important part in every life."[60]

Superintendent of schools Brick, writing in his 1911–12 report, tried to summarize many of the changes that had been made in Stow's schools. He ascribed "this word planning" as the key factor accounting for efficiency in the work of the elementary schools.[61] The school committee prepared a course of study for each subject in every grade of school. Teachers were required to cover the subject matter indicated for each half year.

For many years, the school committee reported a problem with attendance and tardiness. By 1912, the committee had come up with a solution. They bestowed at graduation ceremonies in June special certificates for perfect attendance. In 1911, however, only four students out of a total school population of more than one hundred were so honored.

By the early twentieth century the Stow school system employed special supervisors for singing and drawing. In the primary grades, "appropriate rote songs for each month are taught."[62] In drawing, young children used crayons to draw objects from nature as well as to construct "with and without the use of patterns." They were taught paper-cutting "both free and directed."[63]

After the Union School fire in 1908, Miss Newhall returned to teach in a one-room schoolhouse, the Centre School. Her fifty-two students in first, second and third grades sat in a classroom that, although old-fashioned, was used as a primary school until the late 1920s. During her tenure at the Centre school, the school committee complained about the poor condition of the building. It lacked proper ventilation, suffered from unsatisfactory seating and broken blackboards, and had no indoor toilet. In 1915 the superintendent of schools described the out-building at the Centre school as "an eyesore to the public."[64]

When Josephine Newhall died at age sixty-one in 1915, "she was known and loved by all, parents and children as well. The influence of her life will tell forever in the lives of the many children who have spent such happy years with her."[65] One of her students, Francis Warren, who for many years was town clerk of Stow and most respected citizen, wrote about her generosity in his unpublished memoirs. He remembered that she had often given presents to children and had bought two pairs of eyeglasses for students who couldn't afford them.[66]

Her obituary informs us that "her whole life was filled with service and thoughtfulness for others." During the last fifteen years of her life, "she has been in the primary grades in Stow, where her care and forethought for the children was uppermost in her mind."[67]

Neither Mrs. Lawrence nor Miss Newhall is a familiar historical figure in New England, but in the town of Stow their names are still known more than fifty years after their deaths. Local historians are well aware of the central role many schoolteachers have played in their communities. Both of these teachers participated in a range of activities outside the classroom. Both women were active members of the Unitarian Church, and Miss Newhall maintained links with her former high school as an active alumna. Mrs. Lawrence played an extensive role in Stow community life as an organizer of celebrations, reporter of local events, librarian, and historian.

Not only were they active community citizens, they also reflected the values and educational ideas of the Stow School Committee. They met the ideal qualifications for schoolteacher: each woman had "a feeling heart"; was "agreeable in person"; and was "full of life and energy." Each schoolteacher taught the curriculum that the Stow community required, and when teaching methods changed Mrs. Lawrence and Miss Newhall actively implemented the changes. Mrs. Lawrence drilled her scholars in the rules of elocution in the 1860s and inculcated correct moral sentiments as expressed in the *Franklin Readers*. Miss Newhall used *Cyr's Readers* with her students in the early 1900s, introducing progressive, child-centered attitudes. When new courses were added to the elementary school curriculum, Miss Newhall was the teacher who introduced singing.

The teaching careers and community lives of Susan Lawrence and Josephine Newhall could be duplicated in communities throughout New England. They were rural schoolteachers. They not only taught children reading, writing, and arithmetic, but they were also an intrinsic part of the community.

TEACHING IN SANTA PAULA, CALIFORNIA

Country schoolteachers are not relics from the past in the western region of the U.S. Even in the 1990s a number of one-room schools still remain in California. One such, the Santa Clara Elementary School District, is located three miles east of Santa Paula in Ventura County. In this little red school-house, Ruth Metcalf and Mary Marsh in 1992 were teaching twenty-eight children in grades kindergarten through sixth.

Santa Clara Elementary School in Santa Paula, California, built in 1896.

The school is situated in a valley surrounded by citrus and avocado trees, with South Mountain clearly visible from the playground. The Santa Clara River is close by, and in the early 1900s students would run down for illicit swims during recess. According to local lore one student commuted to school, swimming across the river every day. The now seldom-used spur lines of the Southern Pacific Railroad border the school in the back, and a four-lane highway runs by the front of the building. Although the school-house consists of only one large room, the belfry and veranda give it an appearance of spaciousness. The schoolyard is enclosed behind a fence and equipped with a basketball court, baseball field, volleyball court and backboard, playground, and picnic area.

When I visited the school a local policeman was discussing drugs with the fifth and sixth graders, while Mrs. Metcalf stood on the white porch teaching the younger children a reading lesson. Later in the day, Mary Marsh took several students into the cloakroom for a computer lesson, while Mrs. Metcalf, in the classroom, assigned the fourth graders a writing exercise in social studies.

The Santa Clara School is located in the vicinity of the city of Santa Paula in an area to the east, where homesteaders in the late nineteenth century had moved onto land lying between two former Mexican land grants. In the 1870s the community, numbering fewer than one hundred inhabitants, was predominantly agricultural, with oil exploration beginning in the late 1870s. The first schoolhouse for Santa Paula opened its doors to forty-nine children in 1874, five years before the Santa Clara School was organized in the outlying region. The one-room redwood school building also served as a local church, with five Protestant denominations sharing it on a rotating schedule.

The community of Santa Paula and the surrounding area changed dramatically in the 1880s. Not only did the Southern Pacific Railroad make its way into town in 1887, but in addition oil deposits were discovered in nearby canyons. In 1886 the Hardison & Stewart Oil Company moved its main office to Santa Paula and built an oil refinery the following year. In 1890 three local oil companies, the Mission Transfer Company, the Torrey Canyon Oil Company, and Hardison and Stewart merged to establish the Union Oil Company. Citrus orchards bore fruit by the end of the decade, and Limoneira Ranch, a large lemon orchard, was started soon after in 1893.

With enterprises expanding rapidly in Santa Paula, the demands on the school system also increased. In 1884, with the town's population reaching three hundred, "the new Ventura Street School, the pride of Santa Paula," was opened.[68] The school, serving 180 students, used three classrooms in two buildings. Thomas O. Toland taught the older children; Miss Anna Parsons had charge of the fourth, fifth, and sixth grades, and Miss Victoria Shore had responsibility for the primary grades.

By the end of the 1880s many inhabitants began to sense a need for post–grammar-school education in Santa Paula. Several of the town's leading citizens, including its cofounder, Nathan Blanchard, convinced the Congregational Church in 1889 to establish Santa Paula Academy. The Reverend T.D. Murphy from Ventura served as principal/teacher, and the private school taught a demanding four-year college-preparatory course. Many Santa Paulans, however, objected to the tuition costs, which effectively excluded some potential secondary-school students. Residents in 1891 voted to convert the private school into a public town high school, part of a statewide movement toward the creation of public high schools.

Santa Paula High School graduated its first four students in 1894, all young women. By 1900, with the town population climbing to 1,500, more than sixty young men and women were attending the school. In 1901 the curriculum was broadened and the faculty expanded to three. The high school began to offer a two-year commercial course in addition to the original college-preparatory curriculum.

Santa Clara School

In the late 1870s when settlers began to homestead on lands beyond the boundaries of the town, the school in the town did not meet the needs of those outlying families. Therefore in 1879 another school, the Santa Clara Elementary School District, was founded. Settlers to the north of town created Mupu Elementary School District, and to the west settlers created the Briggs District. The original Santa Clara school building was a small, wooden lean-to structure with only two windows.

First school building for Santa Clara Elementary School District in the 1880s.

The first teacher was Miss Martha Seward, who taught thirty-five children during a school term lasting eight and a half months. Local Santa Paulan historian Mary Alice Orcutt Henderson found a district record-book in which Miss Seward entered her monthly wage of $60 and annual earnings of $510. Her students wrote out their lessons on slates and played in a schoolyard cleared of cactus and sagebrush. From the very beginnings of the Santa Clara School, parents played an active role. They made benches for the children and contributed a small table and kitchen chair for Miss Seward. In 1885 a parent donated land on which to move the schoolhouse. In adherence with California state law, parents bought their children's textbooks. By the 1880s, the Santa Clara School owned library books, an anatomical chart, and a manikin.

Teachers did not remain long at the Santa Clara School. By mid-1885 five women teachers had served in the one-room schoolhouse. In 1886 E.E. Gerry, the first male teacher, was hired, but he did not stay long either. During the more than one-hundred-year history of the school only one other male teacher ever taught there. Mr. Asa Whittaker, who served for one term in 1899, was not a popular teacher. He was replaced by "Miss Edith Boor—a welcome relief from the too-strict Mr. Whittaker. . . . She rode her saddlehorse daily from town to the school. She was a good sport and the kids liked her a lot."[69]

As was customary in rural communities, teachers boarded at the farms of the childrens' families. The fate of one 1892 schoolteacher, Miss Catherine Steepleton, has been long remembered. "It seems a brush fire was triggered by sparks from a passing train. Dismissing the class because of the possible danger, Miss Steepleton returned to her home where she boarded with the Henry Cook family. The fire spread, endangering the ranch buildings. While helping to fight the blaze, her long skirts caught on fire. She died twelve days later from the severe burns."[70]

In the mid-1890s residents in the Santa Clara School District discussed ways to modernize their elementary school. The economy in nearby Santa Paula was expanding, and farmers were enjoying good harvests. The one-room school building appeared no longer large enough. In 1895 the district voted to build a new schoolhouse, the school building still standing today. The land, comprising nearly two acres, was purchased from a local farmer and total construction costs amounted to $2,634.35. In comparison, the district spent $75,000 in the 1970s to rehabilitate the school to meet earthquake safety requirements.[71]

On 17 August 1896 at 9:00 A.M., the school bell rang for the first time, summoning approximately thirty children into the "pretty and convenient" schoolhouse, which was painted a cream color until the 1960s. Former teacher Miss Carrie Arnold continued in her post, serving as the first teacher in the new building. Remembered by a graduate as "very kind and very much loved," she left the school after only a few months to get married.[72]

Schoolteachers at the Santa Clara School earned $65 a month in the

1890s. No teacher could be hired under the age of eighteen or without a legal teaching certificate. Most of the young women had only a grammar-school education, for secondary schools such as recently established Santa Paula High School were not yet commonplace in California.

The schoolteacher's job was not an easy one. She had only a janitor to assist with maintenance, and taught primary-age children until 2:40 P.M. and older children until 4:00 P.M. The California Board of Education spelled out curriculum requirements. Each teacher was to teach reading, orthography, arithmetic, grammar, geography, history, penmanship, and elements of bookkeeping. In addition, "instruction must be given . . . in manners and morals, and upon the nature of alcoholic drinks and narcotics, and their effects upon the human system." Furthermore, they were expected to teach the "principles of morality, truth, justice, and patriotism; to teach them to avoid idleness, profanity, and falsehood, and to instruct them in the principles of a free government, and to train them up to a true comprehension of the rights, duties, and dignity of American citizenship." Teachers of primary-school-age children were also instructed to conduct "free calisthenics and vocal and breathing exercises at least twice a day and for a time not less than from three to five minutes for each exercise."[73]

Teachers, however, operated country schools, such as the Santa Clara School, with minimal supervision. The county superintendent usually visited once a semester, and school trustees visited occasionally. Educational resources were limited, but by the mid-1890s teachers reported the existence of a school library consisting of 173 volumes. Although the curriculum may have been challenging for the teacher and the teaching methods routine for the children, at least one former Santa Clara student found schooling in a one-room school a fast way to learn. "Ruby Boosey, Mrs. Philip Corrin today . . . recalls that when in the classroom, she could hear the older children reciting . . . while sitting on the recitation bench in front of the teacher's desk. And because she often just sat and listened to them, learning through listening, she was falsely accused of day dreaming. However, through this absorption, she became a whiz at arithmetic."[74]

Gene Bond

Mrs. Gene Bond, who taught at the Santa Clara Elementary School District for seventeen years from the mid-1920s until June 1942, was the school's longest-serving teacher. The three-member board of trustees hired her to replace Maud Adamson, who retired at the end of the school year in 1923. Before Mrs. Bond could legally sign her contract of employment she was required to acquire a Ventura County teacher's certificate. It is interesting to note that during the 1920s the superintendent of schools in Ventura County, the deputy superintendent, as well as the three assistant superintendents were all women. Women assumed these administrative positions during World War I and after the war did not relinquish the jobs.

Gene Bond and class of 1942 at Santa Clara Elementary School District in Santa Paula, California.

By the time Gene Bond came to the Santa Clara School, the town of Santa Paula had grown into the third-largest city in Ventura County, with a population in 1920 of 3,967. During the booming 1920s the Santa Paula area, although retaining its agricultural character, attracted a rapidly increasing number of inhabitants, totaling 7,395 by 1930.

Yet outside the town, where large farms and ranches continued to dominate the landscape, the population was stable, and the number of children in attendance at the one-room schoolhouse remained small. Between twelve and fifteen students attended Mrs. Bond's classes during the 1920s. The school accommodated children up through the eighth grade, after which they could continue onto Santa Paula High School. It was only in the 1950s that the school dropped seventh and eighth grade, adopting a K–6 curriculum.

Gene Bond came to the area with her husband, George Bond, also a teacher; he became principal of a school in Santa Paula. Previously they had taught in the Philippines. They brought their two daughters with them to Santa Paula. In 1926 Mrs. Bond earned a salary of $170 per month, or

$1,600 for the school year.[75]

Although the roads in the Santa Paula area were rapidly filling up with automobiles and school-bus service was operating in the town, children attending the Santa Clara School still had to get to school on their own. Either they walked—sometimes several miles—or their parents drove them.

Two of Mrs. Bond's students, citrus farmers still living in the area, shared with me their memories of their former schoolteacher. Bob Culbertson, born in 1919, attended the Santa Clara School from 1925 to 1933, and his six sons followed in his footsteps. Robert Dudley attended from 1935 to 1943; his three daughters graduated from the school, and even a granddaughter attended.

When Robert Dudley turned six years old, his parents drove him to the Santa Clara School from the family's citrus and walnut farm one and a half miles away. Although he was the son of a second-generation farmer, many of his classmates were the children of farmworkers. "Some of them had come from the Midwest, but we all got along fine," he asserted, as he resurrected childhood memories of nearly sixty years ago.[76] In the late 1930s a few Hispanic children had attended the one-room school as well, and their number increased during World War II as Mexicans replaced Midwestern farmworkers, drafted into the armed forces. Today one-quarter of the school-children at the Santa Clara School are Mexican-Americans.[77]

Robert Dudley's memories of his schooldays focused primarily on what took place in the classroom. He remembered that the school was quiet, for the most part. "Mrs. Bond kept perfect control in the classroom. But there was one time when one of the older boys—he must have been six foot tall—disrupted the class. She didn't allow that in her school and boxed his ears. He didn't disrupt anything after that."

What he recalled in more detail was what he had learned at school. "We didn't have report cards," he explained, "but she managed to convey to my parents that I was having trouble learning to read." She gave him individual reading assignments, as she did for all the other students. When I asked him what he remembered about social studies lessons he replied, "Mrs. Bond was patriotic and taught love and respect for the country." He added that she also taught "morality, honesty and respect for parents and other adults."

Schooldays began at 9:00 A.M. with a daily pledge to the flag and the singing of "America." He remembered regular lessons in spelling, arithmetic, geography, history, and composition. Mrs. Bond gave everyone individual assignments; he emphasized that "she had all students progressing at the best of their abilities." The school day ended at 1:45 P.M. for children in grades one, two, and three, and at 3 P.M. for grades four through eight.

The one negative note he mentioned was the physical-education program. "She wasn't involved with sports, and we weren't taught athletic skills preparing us for high school." Nonetheless, they did participate in track meets with other nearby country schools, such as Mupu and Briggs. On the other hand, he did remember instruction in music. "We all learned to play flutettes," he noted. "We also had annual Thanksgiving, Christmas and Easter celebrations at school."

Mrs. Bond was on her own at the school. There were no aides and no specialists sent in from the county. She did, however, administer standardized tests and hearing tests. They did not take field trips, although Mr. Dudley remembered a one-day excursion to the planetarium in Los Angeles on a Santa Paula High School bus.

When children had completed the eighth grade, they received a promotion certificate. Robert Dudley went on to high school in Santa Paula. "That was a culture shock for me," he repeated several times. "There were six hundred students there compared with the thirty or so at the country school. We changed classrooms and teachers every hour. Up to then I had known only one teacher, Mrs. Bond, and one classroom for eight years. It was a difficult adjustment for me," he confessed. Yet he went on to college, graduating with a B.S. in agricultural economics from the University of California at Davis. His youngest daughter, also a graduate of the one-room school, was graduated *magna cum laude* in 1992 from Biola University in Los Angeles.

During the 1920s and 1930s, educational leaders throughout the United States were continually pointing out problems with rural education. The California State Department of Education considered the problems of rural schools "one of the most difficult in education."[78] In 1921, the department had instituted a program of rural-school supervision. Because county superintendents of schools were preoccupied with administrative responsibilities, the department of education determined that "a coordinated program of county supervision is imperative if county children are to have opportunities equal to those which urban children have had for many years."[79] Yet in the face of unrelenting pressure to consolidate country schools, the state of California did not consider that course of action a panacea. "During the school year 1934–35, California operated 1,360 one-room schools, and in 32 California counties one-room schools represented more than 50 percent of the school buildings."[80]

In fact, several features of one-room schooling that educators in the 1920s and 1930s regarded as problems are today considered advantageous.

For example, many graded elementary schools are reverting to heterogeneous age and grade grouping. And old-fashioned teaching methodologies, such as individualizing reading and writing assignments and older children assisting younger ones, are coming back into fashion.

Valerie Sare, who taught at the Santa Clara School in the 1970s, summarized the advantages she saw in a one-room school. "In the multi-grade classroom younger children are exposed to advanced skills early and older students are allowed continuous review, giving them second and third chances."[81] With cross-age tutoring, older students learn how to teach and to be patient with younger students. Because classes are small and only one student may be at a particular grade level, teachers normally offer individualized instruction.

For the teacher, the one-room school can be unusually rewarding. Says Carolyn Colburn, who served as a teacher's aide at the Santa Clara School in the 1970s: "Our one-room school has given me so much personal satisfaction in the four years I have been here. I've been able to watch the academic growth of students over a period of years."[82] Other teachers have relished the autonomy, the opportunity to administer their own school.

On the other hand, many teachers in one-room schools reported that "this solitary responsibility . . . also brings a great workload. A lot of work is necessary to prepare for, present to, and grade a multigraded class. A year's program in art, music, drama, social studies, creative writing, etc. cannot be repeated next year. A teacher needs three to four years' worth of materials and ideas to keep the one-room school a stimulating environment."[83]

In the eyes of educators there will always be advantages and disadvantages to one-room schooling. In the local communities in which they are located, however, they remain as historical symbols and vibrant, living institutions. The Santa Clara School belongs to the rural community it serves and always has since its establishment in 1879. Present teacher Mrs. Ruth Metcalf, sitting on the banister of the school's porch so that she could keep an eye on the children at recess, called me back after our interview had ended to emphasize one final point. "I couldn't manage as well without the involvement of the families of the children. Someone comes in every day to assist in the classroom. They also drive on the field trips, patch up the fence, and fix the plumbing."[84]

NOTES

1. Stow School Committee, *Annual Report of 1881*, 6.
2. Andrew Gulliford, *America's Country Schools* (Washington, DC: Preservation Press, 1984), 63.
3. Margaret Nelson, "Female Schoolteachers as Community Builders," in *The*

Teacher's Voice, ed. Richard J. Altenbaugh (London: Falmer Press, 1992), 78–89.

4. David B. Tyack, *The One Best System: A History of American Urban Education* (Cambridge, Mass.: Harvard University Press, 1974), 20.

5. Nelson, "Schoolteachers," 87.

6. Introduction, *California School Boards* (November 1977): 3.

7. Personal interview with Robert H. Dudley, former student of Gene Bond's, Santa Clara Elementary School District, Santa Paula, California, 16 March 1992.

8. Gulliford, *Country Schools,* 44.

9. Tyack, *History Urban Education,* 15.

10. Fred E.H. Schroeder, "The Little Red Schoolhouse," in *Icons of America,* ed. Ray B. Browne and Marshall Fishwick (Bowling Green, Ohio: Popular Press, 1978), 158.

11. Wayne E. Fuller, *The Old Country School* (Chicago: University of Chicago Press, 1982), 192.

12. Bureau of the Census, *Historical Statistics of the United States, Colonial Times to 1970* (White Plains, N.Y.: Kraus International Publications, 1989), 29.

13. Ethel B. Childs, *History of Stow* (Stow, Mass.: Stow Historical Society, 1983), 149.

14. Ibid., 145. There were 1,002 people and 1,026 cows.

15. Stow School Committee, *Annual Report of 1899,* 71.

16. Childs, *History,* 32.

17. A.G.R. Hale, *History of the Old South School* (Stow, Mass.), 5.

18. Ibid., 15.

19. Ibid., 10.

20. Northwest School notebook in Stow town vault, copied by Connie Schwarzkopf in 1976.

21. Hale, *Old South School,* 13.

22. R. Crowell, *History of Stow, Massachusetts, 1683–1933* (Stow, Mass.: Rev. and Mrs. Preston, 1933), 42.

23. Stow School Committee, *Annual Report of 1845,* 1.

24. Ibid.

25. Stow School Committee, *Annual Report of 1845,* 3.

26. Hale, *Old South School,* 20.

27. Stow School Committee, *Annual Report of 1849,* 3–4.

28. Ibid., 6.

29. Ibid., 7. Miss Eveleth attended Framingham Normal School when it was located in West Newton. (See chapter 3.)

30. Susan M. Lawrence and S. Smith, *A History of the Grove School, Stow, Mass.* (Hudson, Mass.: E.F. Worcester Press, 1898), 37.

31. Ibid., 38.

32. Stow School Committee, *Annual Report of 1849,* 9.

33. Stow School Committee, *Annual Report of 1860,* 14–15.

34. Ibid.

35. Ibid., 18.

36. Ibid.

37. Stow School Committee, *Annual Report of 1863,* 3.

38. Ibid.

39. Stow School Committee, *Annual Report of 1872,* 9.

40. Ibid.

41. Stow School Committee, *Annual Report of 1879,* 5.

42. Crowell, *History of Stow,* 92.

43. Stow School Committee, *Annual Report of 1878,* 4.

44. Stow School Committee, *Annual Report of 1881,* 6.

45. Obituary, *Hudson News Enterprise,* 22 July 1927.

46. Librarian of Stow's Randall Memorial Library, *Annual Report of 1904,* 50.

47. Obituary, 22 July 1927.

48. Stow School Committee, *Annual Report of 1913*, 16–17.

49. Lawrence and Smith, *Grove School*, 49.

50. Stow School Committee, *Annual Report of 1881*, 9.

51. Stow School Committee, *Annual Report of 1878*, 6.

52. Stow School Committee, *Annual Report of 1879*, 7.

53. Stow School Committee, *Annual Report of 1881*, 6.

54. Personal interview with Thelma Fletcher, niece of Josephine Newhall, 7 October 1988.

55. Crowell, *History of Stow*, 44.

56. Stow School Committee, *Annual Report of 1899*, 72.

57. Stow School Committee, *Annual Report of 1910*, 20.

58. Stow School Committee, *Annual Report of 1909*, 16.

59. G.S. Hillard and L.J. Campbell, *Franklin Second Reader* (Boston: Brewer and Tileston, 1875), preface.

60. Ellen M. Cyr, *The Children's Second Reader* (Boston: Ginn and Company, 1894), preface.

61. Stow School Committee, *Annual Report of 1912*, 15.

62. Ibid., 24.

63. Stow School Committee, *Annual Report of 1913*, 21.

64. Stow School Committee, *Annual Report of 1915*, 25.

65. Ibid., 8.

66. Francis Warren, *Memoirs*. Unpublished manuscript, 1988.

67. Obituary, *Hudson News Enterprise*, October 1915.

68. Mary Alice Orcutt Henderson, "'Good Morals and Gentle Manners,' Santa Paula Grammar Schools—1869–1897," *Santa Paula Historical Society Newsletter*, 3.

69. Henderson, *The Early Day History of the Santa Clara School* (Santa Paula, California: Santa Paula Historical Society, 1974), 5.

70. Ibid., 4.

71. Personal correspondence with Robert Dudley, 12 June 1992.

72. Henderson, *Santa Clara School*, 5.

73. Political Code of the California State Board of Education, extracted in teachers' *Public School Register*, 1890s.

74. Henderson, *Santa Clara School*, 6.

75. Notice of employment for Gene Bond, signed 26 May 1926. Santa Clara School files.

76. Personal interview with Robert Dudley at the Santa Clara School, 16 March 1992.

77. The Barbara Webster School in Santa Paula was built for Hispanic children in 1927. Personal interview with Mrs. Henderson, 16 March 1992.

78. Edith Esther Redit, "Teachers' Appraisal of Rural School Supervisors' Work in California," *California Department of Education Bulletin* 16 (15 November 1933): v.

79. Ibid., vi.

80. Gulliford, *Country Schools*, 44.

81. "Special Issue on One-Room Schools Part 1. The Advantages," *California School Boards* (November 1977): 6.

82. Ibid., 7.

83. Ibid., 9.

84. Personal interview with Mrs. Ruth Metcalf at the Santa Clara School, 16 March 1992.

8 TWENTIETH-CENTURY URBAN SCHOOLTEACHERS, 1920S–1960S: MARY O'NEILL MULCAHY AND LUCY ARLINE JENSON

Madelyn Holmes

When teachers worked in small rural schools, they were expected to become part of the local community. We might assume that teachers in large urban centers would lead lives distinctly separated from the neighborhoods surrounding their schools. On the contrary, the urban schoolteachers profiled here from both the East and West coasts identified closely with their school communities. When they became principals, their lives became enmeshed with their schools.

"Mrs. Mulcahy knew all the children at the Haggerty School. They and the teachers were in a sense part of her own family."[1] Mary O'Neill Mulcahy served as elementary schoolteacher and head of a K–8 public school in Cambridge, Massachusetts, from 1924 to 1970.

When Lucy Arline Jenson assumed the post of principal at Braddock Drive School in Los Angeles, California, in 1948, "all I found there were five little wooden bungalows surrounded by vegetable fields. We didn't have a school building until 1955, so that the children brought their lunches and sat outside on benches grouped around trees. Schoolwide programs, such as Flag Day celebrations, Mayday dancing, and costumed Halloween parties, took place in the playground."[2] Miss Jenson began her career as an elementary schoolteacher in the Los Angeles public schools in 1938 and retired as school principal in 1974.

The role of teacher and principal in urban neighborhood schools in the mid-twentieth century, however, was not primarily one of community development. Public schoolteachers continued to teach children the three Rs as well as to train them to become moral American citizens. But they did it with a Progressive twist, incorporating elements from the educational philosophy associated with John Dewey and his colleagues. Throughout the United States, beginning in some school systems in the 1920s, teachers learned to work within the progressive school of thought. Public schools reacted variously to progressive ideas, and sometimes the methods adopted for use in the classroom were at variance with the objectives of the philosophy.

Dewey believed that learning through doing, rather than through listening and reading, would teach discipline and social values. "If you have the end in view of forty or fifty children learning certain set lessons, to be recited to a teacher, your discipline must be devoted to securing that result. But if the end in view is the development of a spirit of social co-operation and community life, discipline must grow out of and be relative to such an aim."[3] The Cambridge school system encouraged elementary schoolchildren to exercise self-discipline and social cooperation by establishing in the late 1940s safety patrols and school councils. They learned through doing by constructing supermarkets in the classroom and visiting local fire stations. In Los Angeles schools, groups of children built Indian-style adobe houses, as well as doll houses with furniture modeled from advertisements cut out of popular magazines.

The progressive educational ideas of Jane Addams also were interpreted variously in the classroom. For instance, her conception of how to teach social studies went way beyond the traditional practice of training patriotic American citizens. She wrote in 1908: "It is the business of the school to give to each child the beginnings of a culture so wide and deep and universal that he can interpret his own parents and countrymen by a standard which is world-wide and not provincial."[4] Yet when schools taught social studies, they often presented a narrow version of American culture, the opposite of what Addams had intended. In Cambridge in the 1950s, selling war bonds and pledging allegiance to the flag offered schoolchildren training in American citizenship. In Los Angeles in the 1930s, one of the purposes of social-studies education in primary grades was to "establish proper standards of living with a group of children from indigent non-English speaking families."[5] By the time a schoolchild in Los Angeles reached sixth grade, however, the purpose of social studies had changed. "The general objectives of this grade place the emphasis upon appreciations and the development of a sense of gratitude to our old world ancestors for the heritage they have given us."[6]

Regardless of the progressive teaching methods adopted by the Cambridge or Los Angeles school systems, it was the interpretation adopted by Mary Mulcahy and Lucy Jenson that remained imprinted in the hearts and minds of their students. Nevertheless, teachers and principals did not work in isolation. They were part of a school system, a city, and a larger society. The ways these teachers and principals related to schoolchildren in the mid-twentieth century reflected all these influences.

Mary O'Neill Mulcahy of Cambridge, Massachusetts.

Mary O'Neill Mulcahy was born in 1906, second child of Thomas O'Neill and Rose Tolan.[7] Her older brother Bill was one year her senior and Thomas ("Tip," who would later become speaker of the U.S. House of Representatives) six years younger. Her parents were second-generation Irish, her grandparents having emigrated from County Cork during the potato famine in 1845. They settled in North Cambridge, around present-day Porter Square Station, to be close to the workplace, the brickyards. Her father, too, had started out in the brickyard but had moved out of manual labor into his own contracting business. Elected to the Cambridge City Council in 1900, he was eventually appointed to the politically powerful position of sewer commissioner for the city of Cambridge.

Her father's career was typical of that of many Irish Americans in the

Boston area. The contracting business, along with saloonkeeping and undertaking, offered opportunities for entrepreneurship and a progression into jobs with a modicum of economic independence and prosperity in the nineteenth century. By 1900 the field of local politics had become an Irish-American preserve, as well. Bostonians elected Hugh O'Brien the first Boston mayor of Irish background in the 1880s. Not until the Patrick Collins mayoralty in 1901, followed by those of John Fitzgerald and Jim Curley, did the office of mayor become the domain of the Irish, a pattern upheld until well into the 1960s.[8] Along with the mayoralty came the domination of civil-service positions, such as those of clerk, policeman, fireman, streetcar driver, and the O'Neill family's fields of sewer maintenance and schoolteaching. In the Cambridge school system, Irish Americans composed most of the teaching force by the 1910s; Michael E. Fitzgerald served as superintendent from 1912 to 1945, followed by John M. Tobin, a graduate of Boston College and Suffolk Law School, institutions established as alternatives to Yankee-dominated Harvard University. By 1914 David Walsh captured the governorship of Massachusetts, cementing the transferral of political power in Massachusetts from Yankee Founding Father families to descendants of Irish immigrants.

Mary's father was the parent whose influence was of pivotal importance to her, as well as to her brothers. Their mother died soon after giving birth to Thomas, Jr. (Tip) when Mary was only seven years old. In his autobiography, Tip credits his father for teaching him "four big lessons" for living: "The first lesson was loyalty. The second was to live a clean and honest life. The third was to remember my responsibilities to my fellow man— I am my brother's keeper. The fourth lesson was to remember, always, from whence I came. When people say that I'm like my father, I always take it as a great compliment."[9]

It was Mary's father who was responsible for her life's work as a schoolteacher. She said, "When I graduated from high school in 1922 my father said, 'You're going to normal school with the rest of your crowd.'" She admitted that "at the time I had wanted an office job, but I didn't argue with him." It had not occurred to her to question his plans for her, and she realized herself that "at fifteen I was too young to work as a secretary."

Mary started her schooling in Arlington, where the family lived for a few years before settling permanently in the area near Porter Square in North Cambridge. She was a participant in the Cambridge plan, an experimental enrichment program for elementary schoolchildren that allowed her to complete eighth grade by the age of eleven.

She went on to attend Cambridge High and Latin School from 1918 to 1922. She started in the college-preparatory course, studying French, Latin, algebra, and geometry, but after two years transferred to the commercial course, studying bookkeeping, shorthand, and typing. The school enrolled approximately 2,000 students, 60 percent of whom took the commercial course.

The city of Cambridge had been an early advocate of vocational secondary education. In 1888, the city constructed Cambridge Manual Training School for Boys with funds donated by industrialist Frederick Hastings Rindge. Ten years later the name of the school was changed to Rindge Manual Training School and it became fully integrated into the public-school system, offering courses in carpentry, iron fitting, blacksmithing, engine and boiler care, machine-shop work and electrical machinery. Today, although the original school building has been replaced, the comprehensive high school retains the name Cambridge Rindge and Latin School.

The city of Cambridge, in introducing nonacademic curricula, was responding to the high dropout rates of fourteen-year-olds who were legally able to leave school. In 1899 a school survey revealed that 47 percent of those students who started school "failed to reach even the fifth grade."[10] Not only did the school system provide technical training for boys, but around the turn of the century the English High School had established four-year courses in commercial subjects and in domestic science.

Mary remembered her high-school years as a difficult period in her life. "I had problems with my stepmother; I had problems with motivation for study." Nevertheless, at age fifteen she was a high-school graduate and went on to the State Normal School at Lowell to train to be an elementary schoolteacher, along with many other classmates from Cambridge High. Because there was no dormitory at the State Normal School, she continued to live in Cambridge. She took the train to Lowell, packing a box lunch and returning home in the late afternoon.

Tuition at the school was still free to all residents of Massachusetts who expected to teach in the state's public schools. The curriculum was strictly vocational. Although she was required to take a wide range of courses, the emphasis was "placed not so much on the acquisition of knowledge, as on the development of skill in applying methods of instruction."[11] In both the first and second years, students observed classroom practices and had the opportunity to teach small groups of children. During the second year, student teachers devoted twelve weeks, or one term, to teaching and managing a classroom of elementary schoolchildren in either a rural, suburban, or city school. Mary chose a city school, as she expected to return to Cambridge to teach after graduation.

It was during the two-year teacher-training course that Mary was first introduced to progressive educational methodology. Her course was not academically challenging for her. "I never touched my books," she recalled, but she learned about project work and the activity method of teaching. She remembered that she wrote a school play for a social-science class and built furniture in a Colonial-history course. English courses were in oral and written composition, so that prospective teachers could teach elementary school-children how to express themselves. Similarly, the literature course focused on children's literature, and the mathematics courses listed in the catalog were elementary, arithmetic through decimal fractions and percentages.

The State Normal School at Lowell offered a course for supervisors of music, as well as two- and three-year elementary-school training courses. Mary's memories of her normal-school education contrast in every way with those of Ellen Hyde described in chapter 4. The Lowell school was not established until 1898, the year Miss Hyde retired as principal from Framingham. During those next twenty-five years, many of the higher educational standards and curricula of the nineteenth century were replaced by specifically vocational programs. All the normal schools in Massachusetts taught a basic elementary-school training course, but each one specialized in one particular area of teacher training. Framingham became known for its domestic-science program, whereas Lowell developed its music-education program. It was not until 1932 that Massachusetts normal schools became state teachers' colleges and began to grant bachelor's degrees.

Mary's public schooling was not exceptional for Boston Catholics in the early twentieth century. This less-than-unanimous support for parochial schools in the Boston area may have been a direct consequence of the growth of Irish Catholic influence in the public-school system. As Hasia Diner commented: "The ongoing debate within the Catholic church over the benefits of parochial, as opposed to public, education took on a new dimension when vast numbers of teachers in most urban public schools stemmed from the Irish Catholic communities."[12] Not only did Catholics in Boston run the schools, "they had also succeeded, to a degree at least, in Catholicizing the curriculum."[13] Catholic ideas were especially noticeable in the teaching of character and morality in the 1920s. Whereas Catholic precepts were traditional or conservative, progressive educators encouraged childrens' creative expression and self-discipline. Ironically, what was considered conservative behavior in the 1920s had actually been on the reform agendas of the 1830s:

> The virtues themselves that were to shape the character of the future Bostonian did not differ, if at all, from those preached and practiced

by generations past of Puritans. Indeed, the self-control and self-respect, honor and reliability, duty, loyalty, and above all love of hard work smacked much more of the so-called Protestant ethic than they did of allegedly Catholic and Irish virtues. This suggests that, though the Irish were now dictating policy for the public schools, they had been so thoroughly "Puritanized" by their traumatic stay in Boston that the shift in the balance of power made little real difference in the running of the schools, except perhaps that the descendants of the Puritans had by this time undergone substantial softening and might have preferred a more progressive outlook in the schools. The Catholics, though, took some satisfaction in believing that they had now become the true guardians of that ancient Boston tradition.[14]

When it came time for further education in the O'Neill family, it was not simply a choice between Catholic versus public education. Mary attended a two-year normal school, whereas her brothers attended four-year Catholic colleges. "My father paid for my older brother Bill to attend Holy Cross and Harvard Law School, and he paid for Tom to go to Boston College. I didn't think about going to college. As I said I had wanted to go to work after high school, and it was my father who sent me on to normal school."[15]

Elementary Schoolteacher

Mary's first teaching job was as a substitute assistant teacher at the Putnam School in East Cambridge. When she was graduated in 1924, she submitted an application to the Cambridge school department and then waited for a substitute's job. "I was lucky. I got a steady job as assistant teacher on substitute's pay—$4 a day—for two and a half years. Then my permanent appointment came through at the end of 1926—as a sixth-grade teacher at the Morse School, at an annual salary of $1,150."

She was twenty years old and she recalled vividly those early days of schoolteaching: "I was scared to death. During the first few months I used to stop at the church every afternoon on my way home." She taught fifty-six children, divided into two groups, but she taught them only half the subjects. Another teacher taught math and science; she taught humanities and social studies. "This was departmental work," she explained. "The teachers changed classes. I taught the same subjects to each group." She stood up to teach, walking up and down the seven rows of desks observing the students as they did their exercises. She remembered teaching letter writing to a class that included several rowdy boys. One boy wrote a letter, "'Dear Jack, I'd like to invite you to my funeral,' and another answered, 'Dear

Kenny, nothing would give me more pleasure.' If that was the way they learned, it was all right with me," she commented.

Teaching sixth-grade social studies at the Morse School in the 1920s consisted of following a prescribed curriculum and time schedule, with no small group projects, no filmstrips or radio programs, and limited visual resources. It was a traditional, pre-progressive teaching environment. In a neighboring Boston elementary school, principal Rose A. Corrigan had just developed a course outline for teaching character education in sixth grade. She suggested teaching about Catholic heroes as examples of self-reliance, using Irish history as an example of loyalty to an ideal of nationality, and depicting French missionary kindness to the Indians in Colonial history.[16]

The Morse School was typical of the twenty elementary schools in Cambridge; it was a three-story brick building constructed in 1891. It enrolled four hundred children in kindergarten through eighth grade. John J. Salmon, a graduate of Holy Cross College with a master's degree from Clark University, was master when Mary began. In 1927 the fifteen female teachers at the school were all graduates of normal schools, and half of them had taught in the Cambridge school system for more than twenty years. The younger teachers were similar to Mary in background, Irish Americans born and schooled in Cambridge. When a team of educational consultants surveyed Cambridge schools in 1946, they emphasized the extreme localism, "sad and unreasonable policy of in-breeding," which they documented from the turn of the century.[17] They found that nearly eighty percent of Cambridge schoolteachers had been born in the metropolitan Boston area and more than two-thirds had graduated from Cambridge High and Latin School. They had taught only in the Cambridge schools, and nearly all teachers had been Cambridge residents at the time of appointment. The survey team concluded rather sarcastically: "The evidence is overwhelming that to the resident, or the native belongs the position and that the teachers of Cambridge certainly like to be at home."[18]

Not only did Irish Americans dominate the teaching profession in Cambridge, Massachusetts, but they also were employed in many other American cities with large Irish populations. According to an authority on the lives of Irish-American women, "the attraction of Irish women for schoolteaching grew out of the economic security such work provided. It also drew from the Irish strength in urban politics."[19]

Mary held her job at the Morse School for twenty-six years, through the economic depression of the 1930s and the war years. But she did not have distinct memories of crisis during these decades. When questioned, she did recollect that fifteen percent of her salary had been automatically withheld and contributed to the poor during the depression. The nominal amount of her salary, however, had not been reduced, for the Cambridge School Committee, although decreasing the total school budget, "declined to put the burden of that decrease upon the teachers."[20] She remembered paying for school supplies out of her own pocket, but she also mentioned that she bought her first car in 1933, a used Ford for $350. She recalled that many teachers, including herself, had bought clothing, shoes, and boots for children who could not afford them. The school provided free milk for those whose families could not pay for it.

When she reflected on the overall impact of the depression years on her life as a schoolteacher, however, she found at least one positive effect: "Children benefited in music education," she noted. "Since there were so many musicians out of work, the Works Progress Administration formed orchestras and gave wonderful concerts. They also demonstrated their instruments to the children and taught something about the composers."

Mary's experiences as a Cambridge elementary schoolteacher during the economic depression conformed in large measure with a contemporary assessment of teaching during the 1930s. The authors emphasized that on the whole teaching practices remained unchanged. They contended that "in a time of frightening changes, many people wanted public schools to preach the familiar verities and to keep potentially restive youth in line."[21]

In 1936, Mary's brother Tip was elected to the Massachusetts state legislature. In his autobiography he mentions one educational issue that especially concerned him. "During my first term in the legislature, the only rough spot came over a piece of controversial legislation known as the teachers' oath bill."[22] O'Neill opposed a bill requiring schoolteachers in Massachusetts to take an oath "to support the Constitution of the United States and the Constitution of the Commonwealth of Massachusetts." He thought it was "an insult" to teachers. On the other hand, his sister Mary who was a schoolteacher does not have a strong memory of the oath bill. As for herself, she had "no negative reaction." She said that she "never was a politician." When her brother became speaker of the Massachusetts legislature in 1948, he asked her to be his secretary. "He wanted someone he could trust," she told me. But she refused to take the job because, as she admitted, "I was not street smart. I trusted everyone and always have and that is not good politics."

The loyalty bill, however, was not a matter for politicians alone. Mary worked in a school environment in the 1930s about which Superintendent of Schools Michael E. Fitzgerald said, "There is no problem of disloyalty and no un-Americanism in the schools of Cambridge." In his 1935 school report he wrote:

> In these days when agitators are taking advantage of our economic distress to advance theories opposed to the fundamental tenets of Democracy, the problem of Americanization is all important and basic. Not by force, nor by intimidation, does Cambridge attempt to inculcate Americanism. To the foreign-born and the underprivileged, Cambridge, through her schools, extends a welcoming and helping hand. . . . But Americanism is not to be desired for our foreign-born citizens only. American liberties and institutions are less threatened by alien influences than endangered by the indifferentism of those Americans who have ceased to value their American heritage, the liberties and institutions of Democracy. We are doing less than our duty, unless we impart to all school children a knowledge of American institutions, a pride in the American tradition. To that end we are cooperating to the fullest extent with the educational projects and exercises of our patriotic organizations.[23]

Mary recalled that during the war years teaching social studies took on a new urgency. "The subject became more alive, as war news from Europe and Asia made far-away countries become more realistic." She also remembered discussing the causes of the war with her classes.

The war affected her nonschool life, perhaps more directly than had the economic depression. "With rationing of meat, sugar and butter and gas shortages, travel was limited," she noted. In the 1930s, Mary had taken several trips during school vacations. During the war, she took a training course to become an area warden, checked on lights on blackout nights, and rolled bandages with the Red Cross.

After World War II a survey was commissioned by the school committee of the city of Cambridge and carried out by a distinguished team of national educational experts led by professor Alfred Simpson of Harvard University's Graduate School of Education. The 1946 survey found fault with almost everything it observed. According to the team, the curriculum in elementary schools lacked an underlying educational philosophy. They criticized drab-looking classrooms for being too quiet. Classroom teachers overemphasized textbook learning, according to the survey, and their teaching suffered as well from a scarcity of maps and audiovisual aids. The experts asserted that in Cambridge "the philosophy seemingly guiding these elementary schools is reminiscent of what was typical in the city elementary school of 25 to 30 years ago."[24] In other words, Cambridge elementary schools made no use of progressive methods, such as problem solving, the creative use of free time, activity curricula, and the project method.

The survey team strongly urged the Cambridge school system to introduce practices that would encourage childrens' self-discipline and creativity. It suggested small-group activities, building on children's familiar knowledge, creating a balance between mental and manual learning, and developing differentiated curricula for individual needs. The teaching of science was singled out; "the greatest neglect today is probably elementary science."[25] The survey team recommended that "the primary function of science in daily living should receive much more attention."[26] The teaching of science should include much more than nature-study programs.

As a result of the survey, the Cambridge school system encouraged further education of the teaching staff. The school department established a program of in-service training and instituted a system of pegging salary increments to credits accumulated in additional study. Mary had been taking courses at various colleges for many years, and after attending summer and after-school courses, she finally earned a bachelor of science degree from Boston University in 1950. She went on to receive a master's degree in 1952, writing a thesis on the benefits of travel to schoolteachers.

Another result of the school survey was to base promotion within the Cambridge school system on competitive examination. In 1950 women schoolteachers were permitted to take the exam for schoolmaster, the name formerly used in Cambridge to denote a principal of a K–8 elementary school. Mary had not intended to take the exam, but her friends had encouraged her. She not only passed but came in third. Still, she did not immediately get an appointment as master, in spite of the fact that there was an opening. Her colleagues advised her to ask Tip for help. Her brother, as the speaker of the Massachusetts legislature, was one of the most influential politicians in the commonwealth. He had helped to secure countless jobs for constituents during the depression, ranging from legislative assistant to snow plower. Certainly he would be able to influence John Tobin, superintendent of the Cambridge schools. But Mary refused: "I did not like the idea of asking my brother for help. I felt that it was unfair for me to be overlooked and pushed for justice myself."

Elementary-School Master

In 1953 at the age of forty-six Mary was appointed master of the Haggerty School, becoming the only female master in the Cambridge school system. There were a few female principals who served in elementary schools with grades kindergarten through sixth, but no one else administered a K–8 school. She remained the only female master until the 1960s.

Cambridge elementary schools by 1953 had assumed a new postwar appearance, incorporating the most accessible recommendations from the 1946 school survey. Schools made extensive use of audiovisual materials such as film strips and radio; students were encouraged to assume responsibility in the government of their schools through participation in safety patrols, homeroom committees, and school councils. Classroom curricula included more activities, such as visits to the fire station, art projects, and construction of classroom supermarkets. Schools expanded student-testing programs, introduced public-relations techniques for communicating between home and school, and promoted school spirit through competitive sports for boys and cheerleading for elementary-school girls. Although several high budget improvements, such as new school buildings and school libraries, were not yet in place, lower-priced investments such as installation of fluorescent lighting, new desks, and classroom maps and globes had been made.

Even though Cambridge elementary schools may have looked more progressive in 1953 than they did when Mary started teaching in the 1920s, nevertheless underneath the veneer lay many traditional attitudes, decidedly unprogressive. Homework, for instance, according to the school report of 1951, "serves as the best link between home and school. It gives parents a realistic notion of what their children's school activities are . . . as well as the opportunity of fulfilling their very important parental duty of overseeing and co-operating in their children's education."[27] That commentary was extracted by School Superintendent John Tobin from an article written by the Reverend Charles F. Donovan, dean of the school of education at Boston College. "Parental duty of overseeing" was the very antithesis of progressivist thought, which stressed child creativity, generational and cultural respect, and an entirely different conception of sharing between home and school. Mr. Tobin's interpretation, on the other hand, emphasized the continued need for adult authority:

> Adults are cognizant of the necessity for recognition of duly constituted authority. Children have an even greater need of the proper kind of authority. At no time should they be subject to an authority based upon fear. . . . When the child recognizes the affection and love of the teacher, when he respects her greater wisdom and knowledge, when he realizes the justice, fairness, and honesty shown by her in handling daily situations, then we can expect to see the growth in self-control and group action for which every educator is striving.[28]

Perhaps most sharply in contrast to the progressive ideas of Jane Addams, who advocated the teaching of a broad, multicultural outlook, were the narrow concepts of training American citizens. Beginning his annual report of 1951, Mr. Tobin quoted from a National Education Association article of 1941 calling "schools the training ground of democratic citizenship. . . . The schoolhouse, like the flag, is a symbol of the democratic way of life."[29] He illustrated in his annual reports how Cambridge schools went about "making sound American citizens" by featuring a photograph of students pledging allegiance to the flag in 1950 and a photograph of students selling war bonds in 1952 with the caption "Justly Proud of its Defense Bonds Record." As a sixth-grade teacher at the Morse School, Miss Mary R. O'Neill participated fully in these activities. But she had also introduced into her social-studies lessons Jane Addams's larger vision of American culture. In 1948 she led her class in a Wednesday morning radio program. The show, called a "Visit to a Classroom," featured weekly programs from the Cambridge schools. On 27 October Miss O'Neill's class presented a program entitled "Americans All," exemplifying democratic human relations.[30]

In 1953, the year Mary took up her new post as schoolmaster, Mr. Tobin discussed character education, stressing in particular the teaching of "individual behavior that is promptly and consistently honest."[31] Photographs illustrated the school report of 1953. One, of a young girl standing at an ironing board, with the caption "She will soon find her Prince Charming," epitomized the mid-1950s attitude on the role of women in American society. In this environment, Mary O'Neill paved new paths for herself and for women in the Cambridge public schools.

The Haggerty School, which she entered as master, was a ten-room brick school building constructed in 1915. Although the school was nearly forty years old, it had been spruced up with new shower baths, a new chain-link fence, and movable desks for the fifth- and eighth-grade classrooms. It enrolled slightly more than two hundred students in classes from kindergarten through eighth grade. Located in the western part of the city in the vicinity of Fresh Pond, the neighborhood it served included a public-housing project where Italian and Irish families predominated.

When Mary became master, the school employed only one male teacher among a staff of nine. During her first year at Haggerty she taught the seventh grade as well as attending to school administration. She was the only master in Cambridge required to teach a class, she emphasized during our interview. Afterward, she functioned solely as master but never with paid secretarial assistance. "Because I was a woman, I was supposed to be able to do my own secretarial work. Even when I was transferred to a much larger school, I still was not given a secretary." As master, her salary advanced with her responsibilities. She earned 65 percent more than an elementary school-teacher and served on several citywide curriculum committees.

Mary had started teaching when women were discouraged from combining marriage with a career. In fact, in most school systems in the 1920s, 1930s, and even into the 1940s, married women were not allowed to teach school. By 1957, when Mary married, the rules had finally changed. Her husband, William H. Mulcahy, was a man whom she had known for many years. "We had played golf together and were in the same circle of friends." Their marriage lasted almost twenty-five years, until his death in 1980. He had been an accountant before World War II, but after returning from the war he taught history at Maldane Catholic High School and at Cardinal Cushing College; he wrote a novel, *Fair Blows the Wind,* about an Irish immigrant to the United States. After they married the couple continued to live in the O'Neill house in North Cambridge, where Mary still lives today.

As master of the Haggerty School, Mary established a good working relationship with both teachers and parents. She instituted weekly teachers' meetings, "informal coffees which were not common in the 1950s." She never had the authority to hire substitute or regular teachers; that was done by the school committee and the superintendent of schools. Her job was to administer the staff.

An atmosphere of warmth and friendliness pervaded the school, extending to the students as well as to the teachers. According to Margaret Reis, who taught there from 1958 to 1968, "Mrs. Mulcahy knew all the children at Haggerty. They were in a sense part of her own family."[32] Richard Kelley, who taught seventh grade at the Haggerty School from 1954 to 1966, still recollects his first year at the school. "It was my first teaching job and Mary helped me out, encouraging me to develop rapport with the kids."[33] He worked with Mary for many years, moving with her to the Thorndike School in East Cambridge in the late 1960s. He is still there, as assistant principal at what is now called the Kennedy School.

Margaret Reis also remembered how Mary helped her to improve her capacities as a teacher. "I grew to think of her as a mentor. When I started teaching second and third grade, I was already thirty-one years old, but this was my first teaching job. Mary gave me many helpful criticisms and we went to meetings together." She specifically recalled attending workshops on new math and science teaching. Catherine Synnott, who came to teach at the Haggerty School in 1963 and is still there today, mentioned an example of Mary's administrative tact. "She would often come into the classroom to observe opening daily exercises. I cannot sing. One day, after observing these exercises, Mary came back into the classroom and presented me with a pitch pipe."[34]

Outside her school Mary Mulcahy continued to be an anomaly, as the sole female master in the Cambridge schools. During her tenure at Haggerty School from 1953 to 1965, the school system in Cambridge changed enormously. The Soviet Union's launching of Sputnik in 1957 set off a national competition with the Russians in science and math education. Not only were new elementary schools constructed with the latest in educational equipment, but there was also an increased emphasis on student-testing programs, sports education, individual psychological awareness, special education for the disabled, and provision for the gifted student. Cambridge elementary schools introduced French language instruction in 1959, and in 1963 instituted a new systemwide science curriculum that stressed physical sciences. Mary participated in a citywide committee to revise the elementary arithmetic program in 1957. In 1960 she was involved in workshops for curriculum enrichment in the regular classroom, and each year she took part in the orientation programs for beginning teachers.

By the mid-1960s, the school system in which Mary had participated for more than forty years was facing revolutionary changes, along with most urban school systems in the United States. As educational historian David Tyack contends: "When muckrakers and sober scientists made it increasingly clear that the educational establishment was not fulfilling newly raised expectations, anger and disillusionment erupted, optimism gave way to doubt or despair, and many Americans came to question both the ideology and the institutions of public education."[35]

In 1963 the city of Cambridge established a citizens' committee on Negro history, and racial imbalance in the schools became a topic of community controversy. The relationship between Cambridge schools and the community grew tense. By 1966 the proportion of foreign schoolchildren who could not speak English had risen markedly.

In 1965, Mary was transferred to another elementary school because the Haggerty School was losing its seventh and eighth grades. She was appointed master of the Thorndike School in East Cambridge. In July 1969, however, her husband reached sixty-five and was forced to retire. "So, after a year of my working and his retirement, we decided that I should retire also." She retired in June 1970 at the age of sixty-three.

In the 1990s, although the city of Cambridge and its school population have altered since Mary Mulcahy retired, many of the teachers from her era remain. Mary Quinn fondly remembers the atmosphere among the staff at Haggerty in the early 1960s. She recalls that teachers would go out with Mary to a restaurant, and the children would go home for lunch. Whereas today, "children and teachers bring sandwiches and we take turns supervising."[36] Her colleague at Haggerty, Catherine Synnott, added, "The teacher was more respected by students and parents in those days."[37] She went on, "Yes, we have more equipment today and the readers are more realistic, but we spent more time teaching reading in those days, and the parents used to listen to their kids read at home." She also remembered that "there were not as many special teachers in the 1960s. At that time a music teacher would visit maybe once every six weeks to teach singing, but we taught everything else. Whereas today a special teacher comes in for art, physical education, science." Perhaps the teacher in the 1990s has less opportunity to make a difference in a child's life. After all, the teacher shares her job with computers, specialists, and video programs.

Today, more than half of the schoolchildren in the Cambridge public schools are minority students.[38] At Haggerty both student and teacher populations are ethnically mixed, and in 1986 teachers instituted Spanish language instruction in every school grade. This elementary school is not uniquely diversified, for Cambridge schools introduced the much-praised Cambridge Controlled Choice School Desegregation Plan in 1980. Parents now choose among thirteen elementary schools, so that the neighborhood school of Mary Mulcahy's tenure is part of educational history.

Los Angeles Teacher, Lucy Arline Jenson

Lucy Arline Jenson's career as a public schoolteacher and principal in Los Angeles, California, from 1938 to 1974 conformed in large measure to the experiences of Mary O'Neill Mulcahy in Cambridge, Massachusetts. She taught for several years in a large, inner-city grade school before becoming principal of a neighborhood elementary school in 1948.

Lucy Jenson was born in Salt Lake City in July 1917 and moved with her mother to Los Angeles in 1918.[39] Her parents divorced when she was two years old, and Lucy continued to live with her mother until her death in 1975. The city in which she arrived as an infant was already the tenth most populous in the country, and between 1920 and 1930 the population of Los Angeles more than doubled. By 1930, 1,238,048 people called L.A. their home, and the city, including incorporated communities, was the fifth largest in the United States.

Newcomers flocked to Los Angeles in the 1920s, many responding to vigorous promotional campaigns about healthful climate, outdoor living, get-rich-quick opportunities, and bountiful fruits and vegetables. A majority of the immigrants came from the Midwestern states of Illinois, Missouri,

Lucy Arline Jenson of Los Angeles, California.

Ohio, and Iowa, but substantial numbers came as well from New York and Pennsylvania. During the interwar years, minority populations also increased dramatically. "In the years from 1920 to 1930, Mexican immigrants constituted the dominant element in the great migratory labor pool in California . . . and constituted 7 percent of the population of Los Angeles in 1925."[40] Other growing minorities included blacks, Jews, and Japanese.[41]

With the number of inhabitants expanding rapidly, the number of children attending Los Angeles public schools mushroomed. From a school population of 90,609 students in 1920, the total had nearly tripled to 263,301 by March 1936. A school census listed eighteen language or racial groups, including English, Spanish, Jewish, Negro, Japanese, Italian, and German.[42]

The teaching force in the mid-1930s consisted of more than 10,000 teachers, predominantly women in elementary schools and a majority of women in high schools.[43] Women schoolteachers also made history in Los Angeles during the interwar years. Mrs. Susan M. Dorsey served as superintendent of schools of the Los Angeles public school system from 1920 to 1928. She was the second woman in the United States to serve in that capacity, following in the footsteps of Ella Flagg Young, who had been superintendent of schools in Chicago from 1909 to 1915. Dr. Ethel Percy Andrus, better known as the founding president of the American Association of Retired Persons, was principal of Abraham Lincoln High School in East Los Angeles from 1916 to 1944, one of the first women in the country to administer a metropolitan high school.

During the 1920s, Lucy Jenson attended six different elementary schools in Los Angeles because she and her mother moved frequently. Nonetheless, she did stay for several years at Alexandria Demonstration School, located on Oakwood Avenue near Beverly Boulevard at Normandie Avenue. That public elementary school had been one of the city's earliest progressive schools, established to train future principals in the new teaching methods of cooperative learning and activity programs.

Lucy's family, originating in Utah, were all members of the Church of Jesus Christ of Latter Day Saints (Mormons). She was baptized into the church after her tenth birthday, but did not attend church regularly until she was fifteen years old and attended irregularly during her university and working years.

She went on to high school in 1930, graduating from Los Angeles High in 1934, and then entered the University of California at Los Angeles (UCLA). Teaching had not been her lifelong ambition, but she was a bookworm and liked children. She said, "I had not planned to go to college, but the counselors at LA High encouraged me to take the college preparatory course. My mother suggested that I study education." Lucy had accepted the suggestion because she knew that she had to earn a living and realized that there would always be a need for teachers.

In the 1930s UCLA trained the future teachers of Los Angeles. Lucy Jenson completed the four-year course with a bachelor's degree in elementary–junior-high education in 1938. She majored in social studies, and only in the third year did the education courses, school visiting, and teacher training begin. During her last year at UCLA she taught third grade at a city school and sixth grade at the University Elementary School, operated by Corinne Seeds. That school was "a progressive school in the extreme," according to Miss Jenson. The curriculum was fully integrated, which meant that all subjects, including spelling, reading, composition, geography, and science, were taught together. They did projects and emphasized handwork. According to educational historian Geraldine Clifford, "Seeds' brand of progressive education . . . remained influential in California's public schools even up through Sputnik."[44]

When Lucy Jenson managed her own classroom and later several elementary schools, she rejected many of the elements of progressive schooling to which she had been exposed both as a child at the Demonstration school in the 1920s and as a teacher-in-training in the 1930s. She contended that these methods "lost sight of the basic things you must teach children in elementary school." Along with project work and activity curricula, she believed that "children need some old-fashioned drill, especially in arithmetic. Some children also benefited from drill in spelling," she maintained.

Elementary Schoolteacher

After graduation from UCLA, she took the examination for entrance into the Los Angeles City School District. In 1938 there was a dearth of teaching jobs, however, and she was able to find employment only as a substitute teacher at $6.75 per day, or $135 per month. Eventually she advanced to a position as long-term substitute teacher earning $168 per month, approximately $1600 per school year.

The system that Lucy Jenson entered upon graduation from UCLA was a large, growing, and future-oriented school system. Vierling Kersey, superintendent of schools in 1937, described the educational environment as being "as informal as living has come to be. Schools are places where natural, free expression is so developed, directed, enriched, and encouraged under the guidance of the teacher that every talent and interest of each child has opportunity for expression and improvement. . . . The modern school radiates a happy atmosphere."[45]

One progressive concept that Los Angeles schools supported enthusiastically was the provision of special classrooms for atypical children. In the 1930s, special classes served five types of children: "1. children who are gifted with superior intellectual ability; 2. those who are mentally defective; 3. those who though not sub-normal are seriously retarded academically; 4. those who are under par physically as to need special class handling; 5. those virtually normal children who have reading difficulty so marked that they have been popularly called non-readers."[46] Contemporary administrators espoused these special classes because they offered educators an opportunity to experiment and to provide individualized training not customarily given in a regular class. In such classes teachers could modify teaching methods, adding enriched or specialized curricular materials.

Another emphasis of the Los Angeles school system in the 1930s was an effort to "coordinate in-school and out-of-school learning activities and experiences of children."[47] One out-of-school activity that caused particular concern was viewing motion pictures. In 1934 the school department issued a report, suggesting ways "to correct possible harmful effects from indiscriminate movie attendance."[48] The report recommended that movies based on classic literature be included in the curriculum. Furthermore, it suggested imaginative methods to study movies, such as borrowing sets from studios, offering lessons in photography, creating offscreen plays in class, and visiting movie studios.

As a classroom elementary schoolteacher Lucy Jenson was especially interested in teaching social studies. In the 1930s, when she embarked on her career, the California Department of Education had recently revamped its guide to teachers and issued in 1932 a "Suggested Course of Study in the Social Studies for Elementary Schools." Miss Helen Heffernan, chief of the division of elementary education, headed a committee composed of teachers from the northern counties of California who compiled "a flexible guide which can be adapted by the teachers to the variety of abilities and interests represented in every classroom."[49] State curricular guides were central to elementary schoolteaching; therefore an examination of that curriculum guide helps to clarify how progressive education was then interpreted. Even though teachers were free to utilize the guide in a manner suited to their own teaching programs, what Miss Heffernan and her committee developed in the 1930s laid the foundation for social-studies education in California for several decades.

The 240-page guidebook consisted of an introduction and outlines of study units for the primary grades, fourth, fifth, sixth, seventh, and eighth grades. For each unit, the guide listed aims, approaches, content, activities, and bibliographies. We will focus attention on three of the curricula: those for the primary grades, the fourth grade, and the sixth grade.

In the primary grades the suggested subjects for study were the home, the farm, and community life. The guide began by stating the purpose of teaching social studies in primary grades. "The school of today is active rather than passive. It is a place for children to work rather than listen. The progressive school belongs to the child. It provides an environment planned to develop individual responsibility and to widen social horizons."[50] Following closely upon John Dewey's philosophy, the guide justified starting the curriculum with a study of the home. "The home is the child's first environment. School life should grow gradually out of home life. The familiar activities of the home should be enriched and continued in the first years of school. The larger experiences of community and social life must be built upon the intimate acquaintance the child has with the family as an organized social group."[51]

As the guide continues, describing aims, approaches, and the content of the home-study unit, it becomes evident that one of the unwritten purposes for the curriculum was to teach cultural adaptation, or Americanization. The outline of the contents included a discussion of three types of homes: primitive, pioneer, and modern. But the intended "outcomes of the unit" would be "the development of right personal and social habits . . . and the establishment of right attitudes toward home life."[52] In other words, children were to be taught that a variety of homes existed. Yet they were to learn that there was one type of home more "right" than the others.

In a description of the activity associated with this unit of study, the aim of Americanization was spelled out. "Doll house activity was started by the teacher for the purpose of establishing proper standards of living with a group of children from indigent non-English speaking families. The homes had little furniture and the children had only a vague idea of what an attractive home should be."[53] When children working as a group constructed a doll house, however, they could learn about a real American home. "Pictures cut from the advertising sections of popular magazines and hung about the walls aided the children in thinking of all the uses of the rooms and gave them ideas as to what furniture was needed in each room. These pictures were mounted on tag board and the name of the room indicated by the picture printed beneath."[54]

By the time a child reached fourth grade, the curriculum had broadened to a study of "Our California Home." This five-unit curriculum consisted of a study of water, the first white men, Indians, the gold rush, and

California today. In contrast to nineteenth-century geography and history lessons, this progressive guide suggested countless ways for children to learn by doing, using construction projects, drama, imaginary trips, and map making. It also encouraged the teacher to experiment with a variety of nonbook educational materials such as songs, motion pictures, newspaper articles, and excursions. Nonetheless, the stated aims for the semester's work conformed to traditional goals of teaching children to use reference books and maps, appreciate the responsibilities of citizenship, learn the geography of the state, and increase their vocabularies.

By the time the guide reached the sixth grade, the aims for education in social studies had changed. In the sixth grade the topic for study was world history. The course aimed "to develop a knowledge of and an appreciation for the inheritance given us by our old world ancestors; to give an understanding of the interrelationship between geographical environment and the life of peoples; to increase skill and interest in using maps, globes, and reference material; to develop a perception of the lapse of time; and to develop a background for an appreciation of the relationship between the old world and the new at the present time."[55]

In the case of every country or civilization presented for study, the guide stressed positive aspects of that society. For example, in presenting Japanese society it pointed out that "the Japanese love of the beautiful is reflected in their lives and customs. Some phase of art seems to be reflected in everything they make."[56] The emphasis in a study of Near-East history was on "the contributions of Babylonia, Palestine and Phoenicia."[57] The topic sentence for the Babylonians in the course outline read: "The Babylonians made great progress in civilization while the other people were fighting."[58] Regardless of how progressive the teaching of world history became in the 1930s, nonetheless it did not encompass studies of sub-Saharan Africa or Latin America.

During the five years Lucy Jenson spent as a substitute teacher, she started working part-time on a master of science degree in education at the University of Southern California (USC). She chose USC because she and her mother were living near the campus at the time, and she decided to further her education "upon the advice of a wise principal." She earned her master's degree in 1943, submitting a thesis on "activities supplemental to the curriculum in the elementary school." She immediately took the examination for probationary teacher, a level one step above that of substitute.

She passed the exam and was placed as a probationary teacher at the Sheridan Street School in Boyle Heights in East Los Angeles. That school, instituted in 1890, was one of the oldest and one of the largest in the L.A.

school district. When she entered Sheridan in 1943, the principal, Mrs. Jeanette Schwab, administered a teaching staff of twenty for a student population of approximately 750 children. In the 1920s the school had enrolled more than one thousand children, mostly Jewish first-generation Americans of humble means. By the 1940s the neighborhood was still predominantly Jewish, but Miss Jenson remembered a middle-class environment consisting for the most part of the children of European refugees. "There were also a considerable number of Spanish-speaking Jewish children from families who had emigrated first to Latin America," she recalled. In the 1990s the school enrolls eighteen hundred mainly poor children, 99.9 percent of whom are Hispanic. Jewish families have moved out of Boyle Heights, and Spanish-speaking immigrants now flock to the area "as a point of entry into the United States," principal Joan Mezori affirms.[59]

The four years that Lucy Jenson spent at Sheridan Street School were decisive for her career. The principal encouraged her, offering her on-the-job training in testing and measurement of children. She advised her to earn an administration credential, advice that Lucy Jenson accepted. Therefore, while working as a probationary teacher she also attended classes on weekends, nights, and summers at USC. When her classroom was taken over for gas and sugar rationing during World War II, she taught her class on the stage in the school auditorium. Later, the principal assigned her as experimental office teacher. That position evolved into the job of vice principal as elementary schools enrolled larger numbers of children.

In the classroom Lucy Jenson taught almost every grade and confirmed her own attitudes about teaching methodology. "I believed in a good balance between practical work and academic studies." Once during a geography lesson to sixth graders, the whole class groaned when she asked them to take out their geography books. But she maintained that a good teacher could make any subject interesting. "If the teacher obviously likes the subject, the feeling communicates to the children," she asserted.

In the 1940s the elementary curriculum in California included nineteen subjects. "I enjoyed nearly all subjects, especially geography, history, reading, and art, and my classes soon learned to enjoy them." She remembered that the students at Sheridan were unusually talkative, which enlivened the classroom. The PTA was active and the school was the center of the community. She did not live in Boyle Heights but was involved in many school activities, even physical education.

School Principal

"In the spring of 1947, just before I received my administration credential,

179

the Los Angeles City School District gave the first examination for principal since the depression. About ninety teachers took the exam. I was the youngest, and placed number 27 of the 30 who were on the final list." In February 1948, thirty-year-old Miss Jenson was appointed to the position of substitute principal at Braddock Drive School. The following September she was promoted to probationary principal, and she remained as principal until February 1968.

School class at Braddock Drive School in Los Angeles, 1950.
Teacher, Mildred Forsythe.

According to statistics gathered in 1951, Miss Jenson was an atypical elementary-school principal in California. The report stated that "the ratio of men to women principals is approximately two to one."[60] The median age of women principals was 47.6 years, and 44 percent were married.[61]

Lucy Jenson's initial acquaintance with Braddock Drive School at 4701 Inglewood Boulevard remains a vivid memory. "I drove to the school the weekend before I was to begin. All I found there were five little wooden bungalows surrounded by vegetable fields. I had difficulty finding the entrance, because there was no school sign in the front for identification." This new elementary school, established to serve a community of small single-family houses in the Culver City section of West Los Angeles, enrolled 265 children in grades kindergarten through sixth. The children were mostly white, with several Japanese and Filipinos and a few children of the Mexican farmers who worked in the surrounding fields.

She began her career as a principal with a staff of seven teachers in five classrooms. "The only permanent teacher was Mary C. Powell, who received the same salary as I," she recalled. Median salaries for elementary-school principals were $5,199 for the 1950–51 school year,[62] whereas median salaries for full-time elementary schoolteachers were $3,637 in 1949–50.[63] Salaries for both teachers and principals, however, increased with years of service. The convergence of salary was a reflection of the differences in age and experience between the two women.

The shortage of classroom space meant that from the outset the school rotated on double-session schedules. She noted that every year she added more teachers to the staff. "At first they were assigned to me from the superintendent of school's office, but within a few years I was permitted to select my own teachers from those who were sent by the district office from the examination list." By the fall of 1949 the teaching staff had increased to thirteen, with two custodians and a clerk in addition to Miss Jenson, principal. Only one teacher was male, but several of the women were married. During the Depression, women teachers who married had been required to quit their jobs. Statistics for the school year 1946–47 reveal that 94 percent of elementary schoolteachers in California were women, of whom 54 percent were married.[64]

Lucy Jenson's responsibilities at Braddock Drive in the early years were focused on acquiring supplies, establishing physical facilities, and maintenance. She emphasized the fact that "we didn't have a school building until 1955." Children brought packed lunches to school every day and ate outside on benches grouped around trees. The cafeteria was added in 1955 as part of the building program. Because there was no auditorium, all schoolwide programs took place in the playground. Flag day on June 14, Mayday dancing, and costumed Halloween parties were all held outdoors.

As principal, Lucy Jenson believed in "a cooperative effort between teachers and principal." At the beginning she convened weekly staff meetings after school, but as time went on she realized that once-a-month meetings were sufficient. "I set the standards for the school—for instance I did not allow corporal punishment. I believed in preventive discipline." She also administered the student-testing program until she could train a teacher to replace her. The staff had to correct all the tests, both intelligence and achievement tests, as had been required since testing began in the Los Angeles city schools.

Teachers were left largely to their own resources in the classroom. The city school board laid down the curriculum requirements for each grade. The state assigned the textbooks. It was up to the teacher to cover the material in the best way she could. There were a few subject supervisors, who were expected to help teachers when requested from the district offices. "I visited rather casually," she affirmed, "and kept a loose rein."

The curriculum consisted of twelve subjects: reading, language, handwriting, spelling, arithmetic, geography, history, science, music, art, practical arts, and physical education. On a report card issued four times a year schoolchildren were evaluated in these academic subjects as well as in "qualities of citizenship." The latter included effort, accomplishment, obedience, dependability, promptness, cooperation, courtesy, enthusiasm, habits of thrift, and habits of good health.

The school had few extras for use in the classroom. "We had flags, maps, and a small collection of records," and teachers shared a projector, screen, and a record player. Lucy Jenson established the school library. At its peak, in the 1960s, Braddock Drive School enrolled 1,652 pupils.

The playground, with hopscotch and tether ball, was a good size; Lucy Jenson had made sure before she left in 1968 that that would remain intact. Trees planted in the early 1950s had grown up, and the well kept grounds had brought honors to Braddock Drive School. For five years it has won the school beautification award, granted by the Los Angeles Unified School System. Several teachers who had served under Miss Jenson were still there in 1992. Mrs. Arline Currie came to teach third grade in 1961; now she is an enrichment specialist teaching computer workshops.[65] She remembered Miss Jenson's tenure as principal, mentioning in particular how she had encouraged teachers to maintain "one beauty spot in the classroom." She pointed with pride to the school garden, which Lucy Jenson had created.

As of 1992, the student body was 77 percent Hispanic. Dr. John Manken, principal, administered a student body of 750 with 38 teachers, 32 aides, and 27 additional personnel. Children still ate lunch outside, but lunches were provided free of charge. The school receives "chapter 1" supplemental funds, because of the poverty status of the student population.

After leaving Braddock Drive School in February 1968, Lucy Jenson was assigned to Short Avenue School. She explained that "school policy in Los Angeles changed at that time, and all the principals who had been at their schools for ten years or more were shifted to different ones." She stayed at Short Avenue only two years. "It was another huge school with a vice-principal and I became really very weary there. After Braddock, it was no fun to work there." She was transferred to a smaller school, Ninety-Eighth Street School, where she remained until 27 June 1974, when she retired.

Lucy Arline Jenson spent nearly four decades of her life as a schoolteacher and principal in Los Angeles public schools. She had interpreted the progressive ideas embodied in the system in her own manner. She had embraced the concept of student testing and had received specialized training in the testing and measurement of children. For the teaching of social studies she had responded enthusiastically to new methods and new curricular resources. She was at home in the outdoor lifestyle of California, and made use of nature to beautify the school environment.

Conclusion

The two women schoolteachers profiled here worked in dramatically differing school systems, one on the East Coast and one on the West. The underlying philosophies of education and applied teaching methods as expressed in school practices in Cambridge and in Los Angeles adhere to our stereotypes of Massachusetts and California societies.

Within these societies and urban school systems, these two women succeeded in their careers. Each taught for many years before advancing to an administrative position in elementary schools. In both the classroom and the principal's office, Mrs. Mulcahy and Miss Jenson worked out individual modes of action. Each woman fit into her respective school system. But each managed in her own way, accepting and rejecting some elements and molding them into her style.

Mary O'Neill started her career in unprogressive Cambridge schools in the 1920s. As an Irish-American Catholic she was born into the dominant ethnic community. She personally identified with this community throughout her career, incorporating traditional Catholic concepts into her teaching style. She injected her own personality into her teaching as well. When she taught letter writing to sixth graders, she allowed rowdy boys to have a bit of fun in the classroom by drafting invitations to funerals. Her approach to teaching social studies in the virulently Cold War environment in the late 1940s was to emphasize population diversity in her radio program "Americans All."

Similarly in the 1950s and 1960s when Mary Mulcahy headed her own public school, she adopted Cambridge progressivism in her own way. She made changes gradually, establishing a school science fair and slowly introducing nonbook resources. At the same time she maintained a strong interest in patriotic morning exercises and started a book fair. Although she maintained a familylike atmosphere in the school, nonetheless teachers were respected by both students and master.

In Los Angeles, Lucy Jenson entered into a consciously progressive school system in the 1930s. In an atmosphere permeated with child self-expression, she insisted on the need for some disciplined instruction in the basics. As a classroom teacher, she continued to drill her students on multiplication tables and spelling lists. When she became principal and was faced with limited curricular resources, she chose to establish a school library as a high priority.

Yet, Miss Jenson was able to succeed in a multicultural, informal environment because she adapted to and reveled in new challenges. She created her own definition of progressive educator: tolerant, unassuming, enterprising. When she taught at an elementary school with mostly Jewish children, parents presumed that she was Jewish. She administered her elementary school in a spirit of cooperation between teachers and principal, encouraging individual resourcefulness in the classroom. As principal, when she discovered that her new school had no building, she made best use of the playground.

Both Mary Mulcahy and Lucy Jenson created congenial and pleasant school atmospheres in urban neighborhoods. Mrs. Mulcahy's school was traditional, Massachusetts style; Miss Jenson's school was future-oriented, California style.

NOTES

1. Personal interview on 7 December 1989 with Margaret Reis (Mrs. Charles McCormick), who was a schoolteacher at Haggerty School when Mary Mulcahy was master.

2. Personal interview with Lucy A. Jenson, 18 March 1992.

3. John Dewey, *The School and Society* (Chicago: University of Chicago Press, 1899), 16–17.

4. Jane Addams, *Jane Addams on Education*, ed. Ellen C. Lagemann (New York: Teachers College Press, 1985), 138.

5. "Suggested Course of Study in the Social Studies for Elementary Schools," *Bulletin of the California Department of Education* 13 (1 July 1932): part 3, 17.

6. Ibid., 123.

7. Personal interview with Mary Mulcahy, 5 December 1988.

8. Joseph P. O'Grady, *How the Irish became Americans* (New York: Twayne Publishers, 1973), 106.

9. Thomas P. O'Neill with William Novak, *Man of the House* (New York: Random House, 1987), 12–13.

10. Marvin Lazerson, *Origins of the Urban School: Public Education in Massachusetts, 1870–1915* (Cambridge, Mass.: Harvard University Press, 1971), 140.

11. *Catalog of State Normal School, Lowell, 1922–23*, 14.

12. Hasia R. Diner, *Erin's Daughters in America: Irish Immigrant Women in the Nineteenth Century* (Baltimore: Johns Hopkins University Press, 1983), 97.

13. James W. Sanders, "Catholics and the School Question in Boston: The Cardinal O'Connell Years," in *Catholic Boston: Studies in Religion and Community, 1870–1970*, ed. Robert E. Sullivan and James M. O'Toole (Boston: Roman Catholic Archbishop of Boston, 1985), 154.

14. Ibid.

15. Quotations by Mary Mulcahy from personal interview with author.

16. Ibid., 153.

17. Alfred D. Simpson, *Report to the School Committee of the Survey of the Cambridge, Massachusetts Public Schools, 1947,* 328.

18. Ibid.

19. Diner, *Erin's Daughters,* 96.

20. Cambridge School Committee, *Annual Report of 1935,* 5.

21. David Tyack, Robert Lowe, and Elisabeth Hansot, *Public Schools in Hard Times: The Great Depression and Recent Years* (Cambridge, Mass.: Harvard University Press, 1984), 191.

22. O'Neill, *Man of the House,* 46.

23. Cambridge School Committee, *Annual Report of 1935,* 6.

24. Simpson, *Survey,* 7.

25. Ibid., 33.

26. Ibid., 20.

27. Cambridge School Committee, *Annual Report of 1951,* 5.

28. Cambridge School Committee, *Annual Report of 1947,* 15.

29. Cambridge School Committee, *Annual Report of 1951,* 4.

30. Cambridge School Committee, *Annual Report of 1948,* 22.

31. Cambridge School Committee, *Annual Report of 1953,* 5.

32. Personal interview with Margaret Reis, 7 December 1989.

33. Personal interview with Richard Kelley, 1 December 1989.

34. Personal interview with Catherine Synnott, 30 November 1989.

35. David B. Tyack, *The One Best System: A History of American Urban Education* (Cambridge, Mass.: Harvard University Press, 1974), 270.

36. Personal interview with Mary Quinn, 30 November 1989.

37. Personal interview with Catherine Synnott, 30 November 1989.

38. Cambridge School Department, *General Information Fact Sheet* (Cambridge, Mass.: Public Information Office, November 1990).

39. Personal interview with Lucy Arline Jenson, 18 March 1992.

40. Carey McWilliams, *Southern California: An Island on the Land* (Salt Lake City: Peregrine Smith Books, 1983), 316.

41. According to McWilliams, there were 18,738 blacks in 1920 and 75,209 blacks in 1940. Ibid., 324. In Southern California, predominantly in Los Angeles County, the number of Japanese rose from 25,597 in 1920 to 44,554 in 1940. Ibid., 321. According to estimates of the Jewish population of Los Angeles, there were 20,000 in 1917, 130,000 in 1941, 260,000 in 1948, and 509,000 in 1967. Max Vorspan and Lloyd P. Gartner, *History of the Jews of Los Angeles* (Philadelphia: Jewish Publications Society of America, 1970), 287.

42. Vierling Kersey, *Your Children And Their Schools* (Los Angeles: School Department, 1937), 29.

43. Ibid., 24.

44. Geraldine Joncich Clifford, "Man/Woman/Teacher: Gender, Family and Career in American Educational History," in *American Teachers, Histories of a Profession at Work,* ed. Donald R. Warren (New York: Macmillan, 1989), 298.

45. Kersey, *Your Children,* 9.

46. Psychology and Educational Research Division, "Special Classes in Elementary Schools," *Fourth Yearbook* (Los Angeles: City School District, 1931), 67.

47. Kersey, *Your Children,* 11.

48. "The Motion Picture and its Relation to Education," *Bulletin of the California Department of Education* (1934): 11.

49. "Suggested Course of Study in the Social Studies for Elementary Schools," *Bulletin of the California Department of Education* 13 (1 July 1932): part 3, preface.

50. Ibid., 11.

51. Ibid.

52. Ibid., 16.

53. Ibid., 17.

54. Ibid.

55. Ibid., 123.

56. Ibid., 145.

57. Ibid., 124.

58. Ibid.

59. Personal interview with Joan Mezori, March 1992.

60. Lloyd Bevans, "The Elementary School Principalship in California," *Bulletin of the California Department of Education* (May 1953): 7.

61. Ibid., 8.

62. "Elementary Education in California at Midcentury," *Bulletin of the California Department of Education* (December 1951): 30.

63. James C. Stone, "Elementary Teachers at Work in California," *Bulletin of the California Department of Education* (April 1951): 5.

64. Ibid., 2.

65. Personal interview with Mrs. Arline Currie, March 15, 1992.

TEACHING IN SEGREGATED SCHOOLS
IN THE SOUTH

The history of public schoolteachers in the southern region of the United States is in many ways similar to that of New England, the Midwest, and the West Coast. Although some parts of the South were colonized early, conditions were sufficiently different from those in the North that the public-education system developed more slowly. While district and town schools were possible in New England where the population was more concentrated, the more widely dispersed families in the South found it more practical to follow the English practice of hiring tutors for the household. Clearly, that was a solution open only to the well-to-do, while those who were not affluent were dependent on churches, philanthropists, and an apprenticeship system.[1]

Early in the nineteenth century separate private seminaries for boys and for girls became popular, as they did in the North, but they persisted longer in the southern states. In the antebellum years, schools provided by public funds were stigmatized as institutions created for families who could not afford to educate their children themselves, and the association with services for the poor persisted during the early Reconstruction years, slowing the participation of white students in the public-school system. For African Americans in much of the South, education was illegal until the end of the Civil War.

When public schools were mandated after the war, the culture of the South favored the establishment of segregated schools at a time when separate but equal education, still largely untested, seemed possible of achievement to both African Americans and whites. Segregation was not exclusively a Southern practice. Some cities in Northern states which had long educated African Americans did so in segregated schools. The determining factor was often the number of blacks living in the district, area, or city.[2] Indeed, that is still a major factor in de facto segregation today, forty years after the U.S.

Supreme Court decided in *Brown v. Board of Education* (1954) to outlaw official policies of segregation.

The two women whose narratives appear in this section were drawn from systems segregated by law. Marion P. Shadd, an African American, was a teacher, principal, and administrator in the "colored" school system of Washington, D.C., from 1877 to 1926. Cora Kelly started teaching in schools for white children in Alexandria, Virginia, in 1888 and retired in 1943. For more than three decades their teaching careers overlapped, allowing a vantage point from which to compare the lives and educational practices of teachers in segregated public schools during this period.

Each of these teachers succeeded in her profession and was honored after her death by her community. In the 1950s, the city of Washington, D.C., dedicated the Marion P. Shadd School, and the city of Alexandria named a new elementary school for Cora Kelly. These two public schoolteachers were respected by their communities because each successfully embodied the beliefs and personal attributes her society valued. Both Miss Shadd and Mrs. Kelly taught the curricula prescribed by their communities using practices their societies respected. Yet these women lived very different lives and achieved different degrees of success.

Cora Kelly received neither postsecondary education nor professional teacher training before starting out as a third-grade teacher in 1888 at an annual salary of $250. Marion Shadd, who had received a normal-school education, began as an eighth-grade teacher at a salary of $900 in 1877. Both the grade assignments and the salaries reflected policies based on educational qualifications that were widespread in the nineteenth century. Mrs. Kelly's experience mirrored that of teachers in New England in earlier decades who had fewer opportunities for education or teacher training and who began by teaching the youngest children at the lowest possible salaries. While Miss Shadd seems to have fared well relative to Mrs. Kelly, black teachers in the Washington public schools were not compensated as well as white teachers.

Mrs. Kelly retired as assistant principal of an elementary school, and when she died in 1953 at the age of eighty-five, only ten years after her retirement, the mayor of Alexandria in mourning her death noted that the "entire city expresses its deepest regret. . . . Mrs. Kelly was loved and admired by the community during the half century she taught here."[3]

With Marion Shadd, we continue to trace the careers of women who graduated from the first public normal school in Massachusetts. Although Miss Shadd was not the only woman of color to study at the normal school, her narrative is particularly instructive because she was educated in the segregated schools of Washington, D.C., during the early Reconstruction years, and she returned there to play an active role in the development of the public-school system for African American children. As a high-school graduate and a graduate of the four-year program at Framingham Normal School, Marion Shadd was unusually well educated for a woman of her time, irrespective of color, since only about 1 percent of young women of 15 to 18 years of age were attending colleges or advanced seminaries in 1872.[4] Her excellent qualifications were reflected in her salary, her teaching assignments, and her promotions, which eventually culminated in her appointment as assistant superintendent of schools. Reading her exemplary record, one wonders whether it would have taken nearly fifty years had she been a man.

When Marion Shadd retired from the school system in 1926, she was praised in the board of education report for "efficiency, dignity, fidelity and integrity."[5] During the years from 1877 to 1926, Miss Shadd embodied the values that the African American community worked to impart into the public-school system. She played an important role in the creation of public schools for students of color in the District of Columbia, where the curriculum was as similar as possible to that taught in the schools for white children. As a teacher and supervisor she sought to promote excellent teaching practices despite perennial problems with overcrowding and substandard facilities. Moreover, she addressed the added challenge of providing schooling for those whose education had been deferred for lack of opportunity. She, like other leaders in the black community, understood that high quality in education was as important as access to schools.

The contrasting profiles of Cora Kelly and Marion Shadd provide an opportunity to examine the realities of segregated schooling in the South before the Brown decision. Mrs. Kelly's community honored her because she taught the curriculum it desired using the disciplinary methods Alexandrian parents expected. Her fifteen-inch paddle was well known to three generations of students, and her social-studies lessons reinforced traditional, pro-Confederate attitudes. Miss Shadd represented the educated African American who could serve as an efficient educator and role model for children of color. Both operated within the particular constraints imposed by the segregated systems of their communities.

NOTES

1. Thomas Woody, *A History of Women's Education in the United States*, vol. 2 (New York: Octagon Books, 1966), 268.

2. Linda M. Perkins, "The History of Blacks in Teaching," in D. Warren, ed. *American Teachers: Histories of a Profession at Work* (New York: Macmillan, 1989), 349.

3. *Alexandria Gazette*, 10 November 1953.

4. Woody, *Women's Education*, 396.

5. *Annual Report of the Board of Education of the District of Columbia* (1926–27), 27.

9 AN AFRICAN AMERICAN TEACHER IN WASHINGTON, D.C.: MARION P. SHADD (1856–1943)

Beverly J. Weiss

Marion P. Shadd, circa 1920.

The segregated school system of the nation's capital is a particularly dramatic setting for the life story of an African American teacher, one who was born to a family of free blacks and who was educated in the North to be a teacher. This is the story of Marion Purnell Shadd. She studied for four years at the Framingham Normal School, graduating from the advanced course, which comprised high-school and post–high-school studies. In 1877 Marion Shadd went to Washington, D.C., to teach. For almost fifty years she played a significant role in the District's evolving public-school system, rising to the position of assistant superintendent of schools, the first woman to hold this position.

Marion Shadd's story is particularly engaging for a number of reasons. To begin with, it is seldom noted that there were students of color at the first public normal school established in Lexington in 1839, although Marion was neither the first nor the last. Massachusetts Secretary of Education Horace Mann and Cyrus Peirce, principal of the Lexington Normal School, shared the philosophy that the school should be open to black women, and that philosophy continued to guide admissions to the Normal School throughout the nineteenth century, as the school moved from Lexington to West Newton to Framingham. Although documentation exists for several women of color who graduated from the Normal School in the early years, it has been difficult to ascertain the number of black students who attended the Normal School. Very little information was recorded at registration, especially in the early years, and certainly not race or ethnicity. Moreover, alumnae files and publications that might provide clues contain records only for graduates. We know from other documents that students, among them women of color, attended the Normal School for shorter periods of study than that required for graduation, and even a few months of study often qualified young women to teach in some districts.

Marion (or Marian) Shadd's story is instructive also because she was a student in Washington during the Reconstruction years, and she began teaching in 1877, when the public-school system was in the early stages of organization. During her fifty years of service, it grew in size from a system serving about 21,000 children, one-third of whom were black, to a system for about 70,000 children, and the system developed an increasingly complex administrative organization. Many of the issues that emerge from the pages of the board of education reports, including those written by Marion herself, have as much to do with changing views of education and with the problems of a large urban system as they do with segregation. That is not to say that segregation was unimportant, for segregation certainly was largely responsible for crowding, unsanitary conditions, and inadequate funding in the schools for blacks. But the administrators and teachers for the schools established to serve the African American children were dedicated to providing the best possible education as an avenue to equality. That meant keeping the focus on appropriate curricula, the best teaching methods, and the selection and retention of the best teaching staff available, salient issues in all school systems.

To judge by the profile Bettye Collier-Thomas sketched of black women teachers before 1900,[1] Shadd's experience was unusual in that she seems to have had no difficulty in obtaining a teaching position in an urban public institution at a salary consistent with those being paid for the grade level. In Shadd we also have an example of a woman who distinguished herself both as an educator and as a clubwoman who contributed to the development of a community institution, the Young Women's Christian Association (YWCA).

EARLY LIFE

Marion Shadd was born in 1856 or 1857 in Chatham, Ontario, Canada, to a prominent family of free African Americans. Prior to her birth, her parents, Absolom and Eliza Shadd, had lived in Washington, D.C., for some years; Mr. Shadd had owned and operated a prosperous restaurant at Sixth and Pennsylvania Avenue, N.W. Nevertheless, the Shadds decided to sell the business about 1854 and to follow Absolom's brother Abraham to Chatham, where they hoped their three young children could grow up in freedom. Marion, the fourth child, was born in Canada.[2]

In the decade following the 1850 enactment of the Fugitive Slave Law in the United States, the black community in Chatham, Ontario, increased dramatically.[3] Many free blacks, fearing that they would be seized and placed in bondage, emigrated from the United States. Absolom bought two farms so that they would be able to live and support themselves. Since he knew nothing of farming, he brought Osborne Anderson with him from West Chester, Pennsylvania, to work the rich Ontario farmland.[4] The Chatham community included many black doctors, shopkeepers, and other affluent professionals who were able to encourage and employ some of the fugitive slaves arriving "almost daily." Still, conditions were far from ideal, for they encountered segregation and hostility in the new promised land.[5]

Members of the extended Shadd family, especially Abraham and his daughter Mary Ann, were active abolitionists, writing about the evils of slavery and urging slaves to escape and find their way to Canada. In 1858 the John Brown convention was held in Chatham. Thirty-four blacks and twelve whites met with Brown to plan strategies against the slaveholders.[6] When

Brown and his party attacked Harper's Ferry, West Virginia, in 1859, Osborne Anderson from Absolom Shadd's farm was with him. Anderson did escape, however, and he returned to the farm in Chatham.[7]

Thus, Marion Shadd was born into an educated, activist family, in the midst of a segregated but growing, thriving community. Sadly, shortly after her birth, Absolom died. Eliza Shadd and the children remained in Chatham until 1866, when they returned to Washington, D.C. By this time economic conditions in Canada had worsened, while the advent of emancipation gave promise for a new life in the United States. Marion's brother Furman was among the first students enrolled at Howard University in the preparatory course. He received an AB degree in 1875, a master's degree in 1878, and a medical degree in 1881.[8]

It is unclear where Marion, ten years old in 1867, was being educated. Some records state that she was not educated in the Washington public schools, and she may well have attended one of the many private schools operated by blacks or by one of the benevolent societies established by Northern sympathizers. The public schools for African American children were very crowded during this period and for many years afterward. Superintendent of colored schools of Washington and Georgetown, George F.T. Cook wrote that despite several new school buildings "more than five thousand children of school ages are excluded from the schools on account of the insufficiency of accommodation." Those five thousand children represented about half of the school-age population. Cook continued, "Since the circumstances of these children compel them to depend almost wholly upon the public school for whatever education they may receive, this becomes a matter of gravest importance, not only to them, but to the nation."[9] He was emphasizing the fact that the last of the benevolent societies had "terminated its labors here with the school year."[10]

According to the registration book at the Framingham Normal School, Marion attended "Washington High School."[11] The high school was introduced in 1870, when it became evident that students of color who had persisted in the elementary schools needed an expanded program.[12] The school began in the basement of the Fifteenth Street Presbyterian Church with four students, one of whom was John Nalle, later to be Shadd's colleague in the Washington schools. The high school moved to the Sumner Building under Principal Richard T. Greener, the first black graduate of Harvard University,[13] and Marion listed him as her teacher when she registered at the Normal School. Another teacher was Mary J. Patterson, the first black woman to graduate from Oberlin College.[14] In time the school gained a reputation for excellence as the M Street High School, and later as Dunbar High

School. Marion must have been among the first students to study at the new high school.

Two courses of study were offered at the high school, one general and the other classical. The general program covered algebra, geometry, trigonometry, history, botany, natural philosophy, rhetoric, logic, English literature, a choice of German or Latin, as well as a group of practical courses such as navigation and surveying, bookkeeping, astronomy, chemistry, and mensuration. The classical course emphasized Greek and Latin, mathematics through trigonometry, along with history, composition, and natural philosophy.[15] Diplomas were not awarded until 1875.

In 1873, at the age of sixteen, Marion Shadd traveled to Massachusetts and entered the Framingham Normal School. It is interesting to speculate how Marion knew about the Normal School and why she decided to go there. She certainly had other choices. Marion, too, could have enrolled in the normal program at Howard University or at any one of the more than sixty normal schools and eleven colleges in the nation intended for black students by 1871.[16] It also appears that her family could have afforded to send her to Oberlin College, one of the earliest colleges to admit and graduate African Americans.

It is possible that Marion was influenced by other women who had attended the Framingham Normal School. We do know that Mary Miles Bibb, class of 1843, emigrated with her husband to the Chatham, Canada, area in the 1850s and that they both were active and well known in the black community.[17] In fact, the Shadd and Bibb families were aware of each other: Mary Ann Shadd, Marion's cousin, and Henry Bibb, both editors and publishers, had some philosophic differences about long-term plans for the immigrants from the United States.[18]

It is also quite likely that the Shadd family had encountered some of the Massachusetts teachers and philanthropists who had been a part of the Freedmen's Society and other benevolent associations active in the South during the Reconstruction. The Framingham Alumnae records show at least half a dozen graduates living in Washington, D.C., in the 1860s and 1870s, and some were still active in the schools. According to George F.T. Cook, superintendent of the colored schools, "four teachers were furnished and paid by the New England Friends' Association" for the 1871–72 school year,[19] and Sarah Gibbs, Framingham Normal School graduate of 1865, was still teaching in District 1, a school for white children.[20]

EDUCATION AT THE FRAMINGHAM NORMAL SCHOOL

Marion Shadd arrived at the Framingham Normal School in 1873. By that time the Normal School was firmly established under the able leadership of Principal Annie Johnson, the first woman to be appointed as head of a Massachusetts normal school, and she would be succeeded in 1875 by her assistant, Ellen Hyde.[21] According to the State Normal School "Catalogue and Circular," published in 1873,[22] forty weeks comprised the school year, which was divided into two terms, each including a week's vacation. The fall term ran from early September until the end of January, the spring term from the end of February to the middle of July. The course of study included:

> . . . reading (with analysis of sounds and vocal gymnastics), writing, spelling (with derivations and definitions), punctuation, grammar (with analysis of the English language), arithmetic, algebra, geometry, physical and political geography (with map-drawing), physiology, botany, zoology, geology, chemistry, natural philosophy, astronomy, mental and moral philosophy, school laws, theory and art of teaching, civil polity of Massachusetts and the United States, English literature, vocal music and drawing. Constant and careful attention will be given throughout the course to drawing and delineations on the blackboard. . . . The Latin and French languages may be pursued as optional studies, but not to the neglect of the English course. There are general exercises in composition, gymnastics, object lessons, etc.[23]

The length of the regular course was two years, but the catalog offered the possibility that "pupils who had much experience in teaching, and are well-qualified, may complete it in a shorter time." Provision for a longer study period was made also. "Those who, in all probability, would become successful teachers, but who fail for any reason to complete the course in the required time, must, and others who desire it may, take a longer time." In addition there was a second course of two years, the advanced course, for students who aspired to high-school teaching.

Candidates for admission to the Normal School had to be at least sixteen years of age and willing to pledge themselves to remain in the school "at least four consecutive terms." Other requirements were "certificates of good physical, intellectual and moral character, from some responsible person" and an avowed intention to teach in the public schools of Massachusetts after graduation. Each candidate had to pass an admission examination in "reading, spelling, writing, defining, grammar, geography and arithmetic."

Students had some choices for living accommodations. Those who were fortunate enough to come from families living on the railroad line were able to live at home, and they were assisted in obtaining tickets for the term at a cost ranging from $10 from nearby South Framingham to $37 for Fitchburg some thirty miles away. Board with private families in the community was also available for $4.50 to $5.00 per week "exclusive of fuel and lights." The school supervised these arrangements. Marion Shadd availed herself of the boarding house recently built on the school grounds. Room and board were available at a cost "as small as is consistent with the securing of healthful food and general comfort," which in 1873–74 was $70 per term, or $4 per week.

The school was characterized as being "situated on a beautiful eminence, commanding a fine westerly view that embraces a part of the village, and a wide and varied landscape." The resources of the school included a "well-selected library" with textbooks, encyclopedias, dictionaries, and "many other works of reference," all of which were accessible to students free of charge. The school also had "apparatus for the illustration of principles in natural philosophy and chemistry," and a valuable cabinet of minerals and geological specimens. There was a primary school—the model, or practice, school—conducted by the Normal School, where students could observe and would teach during their senior year. There were many churches of all denominations in the community, and students were required to choose one of them for regular attendance.

Tuition at the Normal School was free for those intending to teach in the Massachusetts public schools, although students were admitted who intended to teach in other states or in private schools. Those students, Marion Shadd among them, were required to pay $15 per term. All students were assessed $1.50 per term for "incidental expenses." For students in need of financial aid the state appropriated $1,000, which could be distributed to applicants who had completed at least one term and who furnished the principal with a "compelling reason" for requesting aid. The principal also had a discretionary fund from which loans might be given.

There is little information available about Marion Shadd as a student at the Framingham Normal School. Her name appears regularly on the class list as she moved steadily through the course of study, completing both the regular program and the advanced course. Her name appeared in the school journal when she was elected school librarian.[24] During Marion's last term at the Normal School there were 104 students in the general program, including Catherine H. Slade, another young woman of color from Washington, D.C., who did not graduate but who did return to teach in the Washington schools. There were eleven students, including Marion, in the advanced course, five in Marion's class, and six who were in their third year at the Normal School.

Marion Shadd completed four years of work at the Normal School, studying under two able women administrators, Annie Johnson and Ellen Hyde, who were dedicated to providing an education for women comparable to that available for men. While the theory, art, and practice of teaching were the central mission of the Normal School, both principals held their students to high standards of competency in the subjects they were expected to teach. Considering that Marion Shadd had attended high school as well, she was among the better educated women of her day.

EDUCATION FOR BLACKS IN WASHINGTON, D.C.

Marion Shadd was graduated from the advanced course in 1877 and returned to Washington, D.C. She was hired on 1 September 1877 to teach in the eighth grade for a yearly salary of $900. She took up her career in a school system still struggling with organization, with finding adequate space for schools, and with wresting sufficient money from the national government to function.[25] The organization of the schools in 1877 is more easily understood in the light of their history.

The land for the District of Columbia originally came from Maryland and Virginia around 1800, states having codes restricting personal freedom for free blacks. Although there were a significant number of free blacks in the District prior to the Civil War, they were "considered extra-legal with respect to public education."[26] The first school law passed in the city of Washington in 1804 specified that schools were to be established for poor youth. Although many blacks certainly would have qualified on that criterion, the social usages of the community made it unnecessary to state that the schools were for whites only.[27] In many states the first public schools were established for low-income families as a way of assisting parents who could not afford an education for their children, and public schools were regarded as a form of welfare. This attitude and practice resulted in the reluctance of those who could afford private education to send their children to public schools. Thus, funding for public education, whether for whites or blacks, was not a popular cause in a number of states outside of New England.

There were, however, as many as fifty-two private day schools opened for blacks between 1807 and 1861, as well as sixteen Sabbath schools and three night schools. Free blacks themselves initiated or organized the majority of the schools, and most of the teachers were blacks as well. Although adults as well as children attended these schools, few schools offered study beyond the elementary level.[28] It should be noted that schools for blacks were tolerated in the District of Columbia at a time when there were laws in the slave-holding states against educating blacks. Nevertheless, the independent and persistent efforts of blacks to educate themselves were met at times by violence, such as the "Snow Riot" of September 1835, when many of the schoolhouses were damaged or destroyed along with furniture and books. One of the targets of the riot was John F. Cook, a former slave who had established a school in 1834. Though forced to leave his school and flee, he returned, continuing the school until his death in 1855. Two of his sons carried on his work until 1867.[29] One of those sons was George F.T. Cook, who, as superintendent of the colored schools for Washington and Georgetown from 1868 to 1900, guided the organization and development of the public schools.

With the advent of the Civil War and the emancipation of blacks, large numbers of refugees flooded the District, so that between 1860 and 1863 the black population increased by about 68 percent. Many of them were illiterate and without any means of support.[30] Military officers appealed to Northern philanthropists for aid for the contrabands, as fugitive slaves were called, while local individuals and organizations, black and white, and the federal government also responded to the needs of the refugees.

The first of the schools was organized under the American Tract Society, which was soon joined by Pennsylvania Freedmen's Relief, National Freedman's Relief, African Civilization, Reformed Presbyterian, Old School Presbyterian, American Missionary, New England Freedmen's Aid, New England Friends, Philadelphia Friends, Free Baptist Mission, Baptist Home Missionary, Bangor Freedmen's Relief, and others. After 1868 all of these organizations withdrew except for the Association of New England Friends, which continued through the close of school in 1872.[31]

In May 1862 a public system of primary schools for blacks living in Washington and Georgetown was authorized by an act of Congress, which also gave citizenship to all blacks living within the District of Columbia. The first public school opened in 1864, but of the 254 schools established over the next ten years, 190 were supported by benevolent societies.[32] These societies selected, dispatched, and supervised the teachers, and for larger schools they appointed principals. Most of the teachers were women, but principals and superintendents were usually men. As one might expect, the schools tended to resemble those in the North with respect to the school calendar, hours of study, and basic curriculum. Dabney estimates that about 36,960 pupils of all ages studied in these schools between 1861 and 1872, and Marion Shadd was probably among them.

The influx of teachers, principals, and superintendents from the North during the Reconstruction determined the organization and form of the schools for blacks and provided a structure and model that persisted in the new public schools. The Northerners left behind them students they had educated and teachers they had trained, as well as new school buildings and books.

Prior to 1874, there had been four separate boards of trustees for Washington, to serve the white children of Washington, the white children of Georgetown, the white and colored children of the county, and the colored children of Washington and Georgetown. Each was administered according to its own set of "rules and usages."[33] In 1874 the four systems were placed under the administration of a single board, and, although the separations remained, the organization and administration of each system became similar. The board of trustees report for 1877, however, makes it clear that reorganization was still taking place and that roles were being defined. The total school age population in 1870 (6–17 years of age) in the sixty-four-square-mile area of the District of Columbia was 31,671, of whom approximately one-third were listed as "colored." Public-school enrollment was approximately 21,000 pupils.[34]

In addition to the two superintendents, there were supervising principals, principals, teachers, and assistant teachers, about 430 in all. Men were employed as supervising principals and as assistant teachers in the boys' schools, usually the upper grades. The remaining teachers were women. Salaries were based on grade level, beginning at $400–500 annually for the first grade and reaching $800–900 for the eighth grade. Principals at the elementary level were paid $900–1,000, principals in the boys' schools $1,550–1,650. The superintendent for the white schools earned $2,700, the superintendent for the "colored" $2,250.[35] Generally, teachers in the "colored" schools were paid less.

Teacher Marion Shadd

Marion Shadd returned to Washington and took up her teaching career on 1 September 1877. She was assigned to teach the eighth grade at the John F. Cook School on O Street between 4th and 5th streets Northwest. The School was housed in a new three-story brick building, the replacement for the original John F. Cook School, which had been built in 1871 and destroyed by fire in January of 1877. The school building was named "in honor of the late Reverend John F. Cook, who was so well and favorably known in this city as a successful educator of youth, and for his untiring energy and zeal in the elevation of his race."[36]

The new school building was overcrowded, even as it opened in September of 1877. Superintendent George F.T. Cook reported that, in addition to the ten classrooms, a small room of 81 cubic feet with no ventilation except for windows was also being used, as a classroom for sixty children. "Its unfitness for its present use is apparent," he said, "and the sooner it is abandoned the better it will be for the health of its occupants."[37] Sixty children was considered the normal class size for one teacher, but Cook makes it clear that they were all too often crowded into inadequate space. Nevertheless, based on the local census of 1878, he estimated that the "colored-school" population was 10,387, for whom there were but 5,483 seats in the schools.

Despite the crowded conditions, Cook maintained that the course of instruction in his division's schools was similar to that of other cities, and in comparison "shows very fair advantage." He tried to keep the delicate balance between retaining the African American children in school at least through the elementary years and gradually raising the standards. During Miss Shadd's first year of service the practice of examining each child individually to determine his or her attainments was introduced in an effort to find the "true position of the pupil." This examination and the teacher's recommendation were considered in placing the child for the next year. Considering the size of the classes, that must have been a difficult task for the teachers, and especially for a new teacher trained in the North where classes in the Practice School were more likely to have been thirty than sixty.

Whatever the difficulties of teaching in Washington in 1877, they did not include a lack of direction. School hours were 9 a.m. to 3 p.m. with a fifteen-minute recess at 10:30 and an hour at noon, although the youngest children might be dismissed at 2 p.m. at the discretion of the teacher and the principal. Detention was permitted when necessary for discipline or to make up "neglected" lessons, but not for more than one hour. The holidays were Thanksgiving, the week including Christmas and New Year's Day, and Washington's birthday.

Opening exercises were mandated, as was their content: "reading by the teacher, without note or comment, a portion of the Bible; repeating the Lord's prayer; at the option of the teacher, appropriate singing by the pupils." More significant matters were mandated as well: "The following course of study, text-books, books of reference, etc., are prescribed, and no other text-books shall be used in the schools, and none shall be used in any grade for which it has not been designated."[38] The eighth-year program Miss Shadd was expected to teach was outlined as follows:

Reading: Franklin Sixth Reader

Spelling: Words from Reader, Spelling Exercise Book, Word Analysis.

Written Arithmetic: Duodecimals, ratio, simple proportion, compound proportion, rule of three, double rule of three, discount, banking, equation of payments, assessing taxes, custom-house business, currency, allegation, involution, evolution, extraction of square root, extraction of cube root, arithmetical progression, geometrical progression, mensuration, gauging, metric system, method of dividing and finding true remainder when divisor is composite number, entire practical arithmetic. Selected examples from University and other arithmetics to be given.

Mental Arithmetic: Intellectual arithmetic finished and reviewed. Mental questions given by teacher without time for special preparation by pupils.

Language: Common school grammar finished. Composition continuing.

Geography: Complete course reviewed. Map drawing reviewed.

History: Campbell's U.S. History, Constitution of the U.S.

Writing: Copy-Book Number 5 in girls' schools and 4 1/2 in boys'. Duplicate for exercise book.

Physiology: Structure and function of human body and essentials of hygiene. Hotze's First Lessons in Physiology.

Algebra: Definitions, signs, fundamental operations, formulas, factoring, greatest common denominator, least common denominator, fractions, equations of first degree, Davies' Elementary Algebra through article 117.

Drawing: Free hand, model and object. Teachers Manual of Free-hand Drawing in Intermediate School.

Music: Review previous course. National Music Charts, Third Series.

Intermediate Music Reader and other exercises as required by Director.[39]

Consider, if you will, the implications of the rules and the curriculum as they were set forth. First, it says a great deal about how much the students were expected to have learned by the time they reached the eighth grade. Small wonder that so few reached that level, considering the crowded school conditions and the fact that some children were not able to start their education at the appropriate age. There was also the issue of the likelihood of African Americans finding employment that would justify the struggle to attain that level of education. For young women particularly, teaching offered such an opportunity.

Second, the curriculum gives an indication of the proficiency expected in the teacher, although the detailed prescription of books and topics may reflect a lack of confidence that teachers would be able to select texts and appropriate materials. Marion Shadd, with four years of education at the Framingham Normal School, probably had no difficulty with the range of subjects she was required to teach. She may have had sixty students in her classroom, as this was considered a "school" and the appropriate responsibility for one teacher. There were, altogether, three classes of eighth graders in the District, and the students in each were probably drawn from a wide area.

Superintendent Cook's reports over the next decade provide the backdrop of conditions, issues, and conflicts against which Marion Shadd taught with apparent success. For example, in his report of the 1879–80 school year, Cook characterized the space situation as "far from satisfactory." There were, he said, twenty more schools (a class of up to sixty children) than school rooms, so that first- and second-grade children had to share the same classroom, one attending in the morning and the other in the afternoon. He was concerned, also, about the enrollment of male students in the high school. With each school year male enrollment decreased until they constituted but 20 percent of the high-school student body.

But Cook raised an even more troublesome issue. A new law had been proposed relating to the distribution of educational funds. He noted that "the establishment and present existence of separate schools for Colored children in the District of Columbia are due to a prevailing local sentiment adverse to the admission of this class to common schools." He went on to say that the Act of 1864 had mandated that funds raised in Washington and Georgetown be allocated to the school districts proportionate to the number of school children of 6–17 years of age. That distribution, he said, "is equitable and just, since losing sight of the complexion of the child and merely recognizing humanity, it takes the child as the unit and gives equally to all." The new law would put the money into a common fund where its distribution would no longer be mandatory and proportional but arbitrary, with "no positive assurance of equitable division." He strongly opposed the repeal of the distribution law unless it was accompanied by the abolition of separate schools on the basis of color.[40]

An examination of the reports published and summarized for the 1889–90 school year did not show appreciable differences between the white and colored schools with respect to class size. Per-pupil expenditures, however, were 19 percent higher for white than for black pupils.[41] Superintendent Cook described crowded, unsanitary conditions over the entire decade that were not reflected in Superintendent Wilson's reports or those of his successor, Superintendent Powell, for the white schools. For example, Cook's report for the 1885–86 school year states that there were eight schools in which children were taught in basements that were dark and damp, with improper heating, ventilation, and lighting.

The school population increased steadily year by year, showing a 40 percent increase during the decade 1877–87, but the ratio between the white and colored pupils remained constant because access was limited for children of color and attendance was still not mandatory. There was a difference, however, in that the white population tended to stay in school through the eight grades while the "colored" enrollment decreased with each grade. The board commented that in the large industrial cities of the North, enrollments generally were more similar to the "colored" pattern in Washington because industries created "have and have not populations," whereas income in Washington was more evenly distributed.[42] They did not appear to apply that line of reasoning to the differences between their own segregated populations. The board was pleased that public schools had come to be more widely accepted as appropriate schooling even for those families affluent enough to afford private schools.

One casualty of the increasing size and complexity of the school system was the detailed reporting of school activities and teacher placement. It does appear, however, that Marion Shadd remained at the John F. Cook School, and in 1887 she became its principal. In tributes to her after her death, Miss Shadd was credited with instituting in-service programs for teachers, but more specific evidence is lacking. We do know that the new principal was charged with putting a revised course of study into effect, one that was certainly closer to the instruction she had received at the Framingham Normal School than the rules and practice in effect when she had first taken up her duties. The language work was to focus on proper day-to-day usage, and the reading instruction was to take advantage of current materials "hektographed" (duplicated) in quantity for the class. Arithmetic instruction was to be based more on "training with objects, especially in the lower grades," with more independent work and emphasis on underlying principles. There was to be more collateral reading in geography and history, making use of developing school libraries. New courses were being introduced in industrial arts, cooking, and sewing, and instruction in physical culture was a new goal.[43]

Although the number of children of color enrolled in the schools had increased every year, Cook continued to remind the board yearly that only about two-thirds of the estimated population were in school. In his report for the 1891–92 school year, he began to argue for compulsory school attendance, pointing out that the burden of illiteracy falls on the community no less than on the individual. Vice and crime, he said, "so prevalent in this community . . . largely arise from the want of timely and proper training of the young."[44] Moreover, thousands of children four and five years old were "neglected by force of poverty and other adverse circumstances." For these children, in their most formative years, Cook recommended that kindergartens be established. Meanwhile, the crowded and unhealthful conditions of the schools had not been alleviated, and Cook urged new school buildings to relieve the situation.

PRINCIPAL MARION SHADD

In 1892, Marion Shadd was appointed principal of the Abraham Lincoln School, one of the school buildings erected in 1871 near the Capitol grounds. It was a three-story brick building, with ten schoolrooms and an assembly hall on the third floor, one of the "good" buildings, according to Superintendent Cook. The ventilation was poor, however, and the basement floors, wood laid on bare ground, were decaying and odorous. That was to be her school home and her responsibility for the next sixteen years, years that brought the establishment of kindergartens, including one at Lincoln School, the advent of free textbooks, and the Evening Star Fund to assist families with food, fuel, and clothing.

Although conditions remained crowded, both superintendents were intent on improving instruction in the schools. Cook lauded the "positive trend . . . toward the teaching of the principles underlying the subject. . . . [I]t is more and more recognized that the greater value lies not in the acquisition of knowledge, but in the mental power and mastery gained through the means of acquisition."[45] He stressed also the close connection with the "outside world" and "a preparation for life." The following year, a long section of Powell's report explained the system of instruction he advocated, and it was endorsed strongly by the board of trustees.

Although Powell's philosophy was hardly new, it did reflect the tenets of the kindergarten movement and the movement led by Francis W. Parker at the Chicago Normal School. The "new" learning, Powell said, begins with the senses and "takes advantage of the child's aptitude and interest in things about him and in the exercise of his senses. . . . From things known and familiar and of interest, it goes on to things unknown and unfamiliar, and carries along the same interest, and needs no whip or spur or reward or punishment." Learning proceeds from the concrete to the abstract as children perceive the purpose of reading and writing. The teacher takes the role of guide rather than that of driver, and since all children can learn in this way, there will be no "dunces." The challenge, however, is for teachers to become leaders capable of giving sound instruction.[46]

It is easy to believe that this was familiar ground to Marion Shadd. The pioneers of the Framingham Normal School had been readers of Froebel and advocates of learning by experience. Each generation of educators seems to work the themes anew to fit the time and circumstances, but the basic melody of reform remains the same and the reaction is just as predictable. By the 1900–01 school year, both Powell and Cook, after many years of working together, had retired, and the new superintendent, A.T. Stuart, was reinstituting drill in spelling, penmanship, arithmetic, grammar, and geography, as well as a return to textbook instruction. There had been, he said, too much attention to "nature or science studies" and that had "interfered with success in primary training in the schools."[47]

Meanwhile, the supervising principal in Shadd's division, E.W. Brown, had suggested that all of the teachers in each building meet at the end of each day in the principal's office to outline a plan of lessons for the next day. Shadd also organized monthly meetings, and the theme chosen for the 1898–99 school year was "Truancy: Its Causes and Cure." The first meeting, dealing with parental duty, was presented by Miss Shadd, and the teachers were to follow with discussions of other aspects of the problem.[48]

The twentieth century was ushered in not only by new administrative officers but also by a reorganization of the administration. The board of trustees became the board of education and the members were no longer designated as representatives from a particular division of the District, although the schools were still assigned to divisions. The original four systems had gradually expanded into thirteen divisions, Divisions 1–9 for white children under Assistant Superintendent Ida Gilbert Myers, and Divisions 10–

13 for children of color under Assistant Superintendent Winfield S. Montgomery. There was one superintendent of schools, A.T. Stuart. The work of the board of education was distributed among committees, and the board of education report consisted of the reports from the various committees, such as the Committee on Teachers and Janitors and the Committee on Industrial Education and Special Instruction. The enrollment was approaching 48,000, nearly half students of color, and the teachers numbered more than 1,000.[49]

Members of the board of education for the District of Columbia had included prominent members of the black community since 1891, when Marion's brother, Furman Shadd, a distinguished medical doctor by that time, was appointed. He served until 1896, as did Mary Church Terrell (1894–98), an activist for women's suffrage as well as for civil rights, and Mrs. Bettie Francis (1898–1905), wife of physician John R. Francis and one of the founders, along with Marion Shadd, of the Phyllis Wheatley Young Women's Christian Association. Mrs. Terrell subsequently served a second term on the board of education beginning in 1905.

Superintendent Stuart's report to the board of education for 1901–02 covered a number of other significant developments. Congress, he announced, had for the past two years appropriated funds for new schoolhouses, and should this generosity persist, it should be possible to eliminate half-day classes despite the rapid growth of the school-age population. Apparently attention was paid to the needs of the schools during this period because, by the 1906–07 school year, a compulsory education law had been passed and attendance officers had been appointed. The school enrollment was "unprecedented." The law covered ages 8–14, but school administrators were already urging that it be expanded to require school attendance from 6–16 years of age.[50]

THE SUPERVISING PRINCIPAL

In the 1907–08 board of education report, Marion Shadd was listed as the supervising principal for the Eleventh Division, although the appointment date to that post was listed as 1 July 1908 in other documents. She was responsible for thirteen schools with names that evoked a sense of history and the long struggle toward freedom—Brightwood, Blanche K. Bruce, Bunker Hill Road, John F. Cook, Fort Slocum, Henry Garnet, William Lloyd Garrison, John M. Langston, Military Road, Lucretia Mott, Orphans Home, James W. Patterson, and John F. Slater.

The reports of special directors reveal the direction in which the schools had expanded—domestic science, music, physical training, school gardens, and kindergartens, to mention a few. The first of Marion Shadd's reports as a supervising principal was written for the 1909–10 school report. One of her concerns was the "overage pupils" who were now in the primary grades, the combined result of the years of failure to provide sufficient space for all the children and the more recent laws making school attendance compulsory. In that year, new classrooms were opened so that the older children might have a separate classroom.[51]

Miss Shadd set up monthly in-service conferences for the teachers of grades five to eight. She selected readings from texts on school management, arithmetic, composition, and physics and distributed them to the teachers. Teachers were asked to identify the particular topics in which they "felt the weakest." Other teachers were asked to demonstrate their methods of presentation, and the demonstrations were used as the basis for the discussion. When it was discovered that physics presented a challenge for several, Marion arranged for a physics teacher to come to the group and demonstrate apparatus and lessons they would be able to use in their classrooms.

Miss Shadd also visited the classrooms in schools under her supervision, and she reported that she had made 960 such visits during the school year—more than twenty a week. She concluded her report: "In the division there has been nothing throughout the year to disturb the harmony, which is absolutely necessary if the best good of the child is to be attained."[52]

In the report for the 1910–11 school year, Miss Shadd noted that the enrollment had increased and a new kindergarten had been added in an annex to the John F. Cook School. She expressed concern for the "clever child." "Much has been done for the atypical child and the incorrigible child but little for the clever child," she said, and she asked the teachers to look for the bright child who could do more. Thirty-one children were identified, and she reported that twenty-nine of them completed the work of two semesters in one with this special attention from the teachers.[53]

As school enrollment increased so did the levels and numbers of administrators. By 1914 there was an Office of the Superintendent presided over by Superintendent of the Public Schools Ernest L. Thurston. The administrative staff included the assistant superintendent for the white schools, Stephen E. Kramer, and the assistant superintendent for the "colored" schools, Roscoe Conkling Bruce, son of Senator Blanche Kelso Bruce. The supervising principals for divisions 1–9 reported to Kramer, 10–13 to Bruce. Marion Shadd was designated to write the report for the "colored" divisions for the 1914–15 school year, a chore now shared among the supervisors.

Miss Shadd's report reflected the changes in curriculum, teaching methods, and "vocational ideas" urged by the new administration and prepared by committees "representing the teaching body." First, she discussed the curriculum under the "new course of study." In arithmetic, the new textbooks were written to suit the mental development and vocabulary of the child. "[T]he making of problems by the child along the lines of his experiences, and the elimination of nonessential subjects, are considered vital improvements by the teachers." The curriculum in history began in the early grades with life in the home and neighborhood and progressed to "our life as a Nation." Emphasis on time periods gave way to topics such as social and economic conditions of the nation, including comparisons with French and English history. Poems and fiction were used throughout to stimulate the interest of both children and teachers. Miss Shadd was less specific about the course in English, except to say that it had received the general approval of the teachers because of the "general and specific suggestions for the teaching of composition in each grade." The introduction of technical grammar was postponed until the seventh and eighth grades. The supervisors, Miss Shadd said, were "unanimous in the opinion that the greatest improvement in teaching this year has been in the subject of composition."[54]

Marion Shadd's discussion of teaching and teaching methods gives the reader a glimpse of the work done by the supervising principals. They observed regularly in the classrooms of their divisions and then met monthly to discuss what they had seen and what needed to be done. For the 1914–15 school year they recommended new books and suggested changes in the graded courses that "compelled teachers who have been in the service many years to start afresh. New outside material and devices have been brought into the classroom, and as a result we have had invigorated teaching." Children were also being taken to the public library, many government buildings, the Zoological Park, the National Museum, and other places of interest connected to their studies.[55] Although Marion does not mention the fact, such visits were complicated by the requirements of segregation even at those public sites.

The Lucretia Mott School, under Miss Shadd's supervision, introduced motion pictures with the permission of the board of education. At a cost of $400, raised by the teachers, they installed an "Edison motion-picture machine" to present educational films, not only for their own students but for children from other schools as well. Carefully wording her report, Miss Shadd said that their short experience with "the application of the motion picture to the classroom work confirms the position held by David Snedden, Commissioner of Massachusetts." She went on to quote two paragraphs from his 1914 address to the National Education Association predicting that "the motion picture is destined to be an educational agency of first-rate importance."[56]

In the section of her report dealing with vocational ideas, Miss Shadd seemed to switch from the language of the group to say that she felt that sewing, cooking, and carpentry, even in the early grades, furnished "an immense quantity of concrete material for the number and language work in the classroom—concrete material within the comprehension and interest of the child."[57] She apparently advocated expanding that part of the curriculum, which was limited then to sewing in the third to sixth grades and carpentry and cooking in the seventh and eighth grades.

Finally, Marion Shadd tackled the topic of "Improvement of Teachers in the Service." Curriculum changes, better preparation of teachers for service, and an excellent service record "are not sufficient" to meet the demands of an ever-changing society. Teacher improvement, she said, must be continuous, and how can the school system encourage teachers to renew their efficiency? She concluded, "This matter is a constant source of anxiety and perplexity to the supervisor."[58] Readers may not find these trends or her comments significantly different from those being discussed today.

Over the next few years some new services and issues were addressed in the board of education reports. Physicians, dentists, and nurses were added to the staff to initiate a medical inspection service. Superintendent Thurston spoke of a new law, the "so-called social center bill" in the 1915–16 board of education report that would allow broader use of the schools for community activities, such as civic meetings, recreational playground use, and supplementary educational services. The bill had been urged, he said, by Miss Margaret Wilson, the president's daughter. He noted that teachers could not be required to give extra service to make these resources available, a nod to the growing influence of teacher organizations. By the next year mothers' clubs, the Parent/Teachers Association, and other community agencies were using the school buildings. Military drill and physical training were also being offered on the school grounds.

Shadd did not again write a section for the board of education report until 1918–19, and by that time effects of the World War had been felt on both school personnel and supplies. The influenza epidemic forced the closing of schools for the entire month of October 1918, and when school reopened in November it was discovered that there was "a large shrinkage in the attendance of children over 14 years of age." Investigations showed that the schools had closed during a period of particularly high cost of living coupled with a special drive by the government to recruit young workers for defense-related work. A "back to school drive" was initiated that successfully brought in more than 100 children, although some parents had been pleased to have their children working and were not eager to have them return to school.[59]

Health generally had become a major concern, and the Health Association had launched a survey of the growth and physical condition of ten-year-old children. A "modern health crusade" was launched in the elementary schools, in which children were instructed in health practices like tooth-brushing and hand-washing, and a card was sent home with them for parents to sign when the "chores" had been completed. Miss Shadd thought this helped to instill health habits and was also a factor in "establishing a close relation between the home and school."[60]

Shadd noted that the "condition of world affairs" had provided "an abundance of material for special work in geography and history." Teachers were urged to use current events whenever possible, and the children collected pictures and articles to make booklets, especially about events in their own city. Those booklets also became an occasion to write about the special contributions of the "Negro in the War," and by extension to negroes in other wars.[61] This was an early effort by the schools to engender pride in the children's heritage, other than the naming of some schools for black activists and educators.

Little more was heard from or about Marion Shadd until 1924. It is worth noting, however, that the impetus given health issues by the finding that so many young men were not sufficiently fit to serve in the armed forces continued to have an impact on school programs. Children with tuberculosis were segregated in an "open air class" where food for hot lunches was supplied by the Anti-Tuberculosis Society. A second classroom was designated for anemic children who were ill-nourished and ailing but not tubercular. The schools had taken on the task of delivering food and health services to children in need.[62]

THE ASSISTANT SUPERINTENDENT

The report of the board of education for 1924–25 described another reorganization of the administrative staff. On 18 December 1924 a new position was created for "one colored first assistant superintendent" who would be in charge of "all employees, class and schools in which colored children are taught. . . . This is the first time in the history of public education in America that a person of color has occupied such a position in a public school system." At the same time, Marion Shadd was promoted to the rank of assistant superintendent in charge of elementary schools, the first woman promoted to this position. Miss Shadd was also appointed chief examiner for the Board of Examiners for the Colored Schools, a newly created post.[63] She had been serving on the board of examiners and had been elected its secretary prior to this appointment. The board of examiners was charged with conducting examinations to qualify candidates for teaching, so it was an extremely influential and powerful position.

There were no more reports written by Miss Shadd and no documents to show us what she thought of the position she had attained. We are told in the board of education report for 1926–27 that she had chosen to retire, effective 1 September 1926. Retiring in the same month was John C. Nalle, a long-time colleague of Miss Shadd's and supervising principal since 1902, and the two were honored together. The superintendent called them the two "most experienced and faithful school officials of divisions 10–13." Their work, he said, had been characterized by "efficiency, dignity, fidelity and integrity."

> The splendid school organization in divisions 10–13, the fine esprit de corps among our education employees, the successful careers of thousands of former students and graduates of the public schools of Washington are after all the best evidence of the manner in which these two faithful and efficient public servants have discharged their duties.[64]

Lifetime habits of intellectual activity, work, and service to others are not easily set aside at retirement. Marion Shadd remained active in the Booklovers Club throughout the 1930s, frequently serving as hostess, regularly presenting talks with titles such as "Introduction to Russian Literature," "Japan's Economic Difficulties," "Contribution to Art by People of Color," and "African Civilizations."[65] She also continued her work, begun many years before, with the Young Women's Christian Association.

THE YOUNG WOMEN'S CHRISTIAN ASSOCIATION

In April 1905, Marion Shadd was one of a group of women, members of the Booklovers Club (a literary club organized in 1893), who met at the Berean Baptist Church to consider organizing a YWCA. The roster of women who participated in the Booklovers Club and in the organization of the YWCA included a network of prominent black families active in the social, educational, and political movements of the early twentieth century in Washington and in the nation. The call for the meeting was instigated by Mrs. Rosetta E. Lawson, founder with her husband, Dr. Jesse Lawson, of the Bible Educational Association, later renamed Frelinghuysen University. Mrs. Bettie G. Francis, formerly a member of the Washington, D.C., Board of Education and wife of Dr. John R. Francis, a physician and surgeon, was elected president. Miss Marion Shadd was named treasurer, a post she continued to hold for more than twenty-five years. Mrs. Lawson served as chairman of the executive committee, and her board included Mrs. Mary Church

Terrell. Another prominent member of the Booklovers present at the organization meeting was Mrs. B.K. Bruce, a schoolteacher and the widow of Blanche Kelso Bruce, "the first black to serve a full term in the United States Senate (1875–81)."[66] By the end of the year Mrs. Anna J. Cooper, author and teacher, graduate of Oberlin with a doctorate from the Sorbonne, had become a life member.[67]

In 1930, Marion Shadd chaired a committee to prepare a history of the twenty-five years of the YWCA. It is difficult to say whether she wrote the history itself. It seems likely that she may have, since she was retired by that time and she had been the treasurer throughout the period. Mrs. Annie E. Cromwell, another of the founders, was also a member of the committee; but the only acknowledgments were to Mrs. L.N. Calloway, the business secretary who had been hired about 1921 as a desk clerk, for collecting data, and to Miss Bertha McNeill, teacher at the Dunbar High School, for reading and criticizing the manuscript. In any case, the account shows clearly the mission of the YWCA, the long-time commitment of its founders, and its expanding role in the black community.

The central mission of the YWCA was to provide better lodging for girls and women who came to Washington to work; to that end, they rented two rooms in the old Miner Institution Building. In one of her early reports, President Bettie G. Francis gave voice to their philosophy: "Undesirable lodging places for working girls is one of the great social evils in the life of young colored working women. It can not then but be considered obligatory on the part of every woman of comfortable home and means to give of her time and of her means toward carrying this work, the aim of which is to help this branch of social service."[68]

Mrs. Francis called their work "practical Christianity." They provided for church services and prayer meetings, and rejoiced when those who had benefited from their practical services embraced their faith as well. But they do not seem to have made their services contingent upon a religious commitment. It was a "Christian home" they offered, to shelter and protect "needy young colored women, as well as a place of congenial abode for the poor working girl."[69] Fitzpatrick and Goodwin refer to the "bleak years of segregation at the turn of the century."[70] People of color were confined and constrained in traditional neighborhoods, and efforts of the well-off and better-educated African Americans to assist others less fortunate to find work and housing were vital, not only to the black community but also to the city of Washington. As an administrator in the public schools, Marion Shadd was well aware of the importance of their work with families, and as a member of the affluent, socially prominent group, she knew how to draw on the strengths and resources of her peers.

Over the years, the services offered by the YWCA were varied. In the early days they seem to have taken on needs as they saw them. For example, they mention caring for a family of five children while the parents were ill; Mrs. M.E. Holland, the Sunday school teacher, took responsibility for "five small boys arrested for some minor offense"; and they collected clothing and other donations such as soap, matches, and furniture.[71] Nor did they neglect the need for recreation. Between 1905 and 1907, three hundred mothers and children were taken on day outings to Mount Vernon and other sites on the Potomac. Later, as their resources and numbers grew, they acquired more commodious quarters and the capacity to offer a greater range of services, including a cafeteria, club rooms and recreational facilities. Gradually, a paid staff was acquired, although the "volunteers" continued to supervise and manage the programs.

The advent of World War I disorganized families and brought an influx of girls and women into Washington, some without food and shelter, and many trying to reach destinations in the North with no means of transportation. The YWCA responded by organizing a traveler's aid committee and joining forces with men from the YMCA to meet the trains at Union Station at "all hours of the day and night." Space at the YWCA proved inadequate to the demand for temporary housing, and the officers decided to approach the War Work Council and the national YWCA for assistance in building a new facility. Impressed by the work of the YWCA, the War Work Council granted an appropriation to construct a "demonstration building in Washington for colored work."[72]

When the building was finished in 1920, it afforded offices, club rooms, a gymnasium, showers, a cafeteria, forty-three single bedrooms and one double room. Its bronze dedicatory plaque was inscribed "To the glory of God, in service for our young women, this building is dedicated in the year of our Lord MCMXX." The new building was given the name "Phillis Wheatley" in honor of a woman who was brought to Boston in 1761 as a slave and who gained her freedom on the death of her owners. Her first poem, published in 1770, made her a celebrity and a symbol of black achievement.[73] In 1923 the National YWCA finally agreed to change the articles of incorporation to read "Phillis Wheatley Young Women's Christian Association," omitting the word *colored*.[74] The new building also represented a large financial and managerial responsibility, but once more the organization proved equal to the task of raising funds and hiring a staff to carry out the programs. Generally measured and objective in language, this section of the history ends on an exuberant note: "And so succeeded the experiment in Washington—that demonstration of the ability of the colored woman to manage and finance the work!"[75]

This account of the YWCA says little directly about Marion Shadd, but it is evident that she had been a constant and consistent participant. For example, YWCA reports for individual years contain detailed financial reports by Marion Shadd. One reason for supposing that Shadd did in fact write the history is that so little is said of her beyond listing her name on various committees or as a donor or participant in an activity. Of the "finance department" the history says that finances are not the important work of the association, but does acknowledge that the important work has depended on the ability of the association to raise the finances. Two persons were responsible for the finances from the beginning of the association in 1905 to the report of 1930; they were Miss E.F.G. Merritt and Miss Marion Shadd.[76] As chairman of the finance committee, Miss Merritt had the responsibility of planning the fund raising. Miss Shadd as treasurer was responsible for managing the finances and accounting for them, professional skills she exercised daily as an administrator in the public schools.

So Marion Shadd's work with the YWCA began in 1905 when she was still a principal and continued through her years as a supervising principal and assistant superintendent, and well into her retirement. She must have known that Mary Swift Lamson from the first class at the Lexington Normal School was one of the founders of the Boston YWCA, and it is very likely that she had met Mrs. Lamson during her days in Framingham. Perhaps it was enough that she knew of the conditions of the poor in Washington. She brought her skills and resources not only to her profession, but also to the work of the YWCA to do what she could to alleviate the ills she saw. Well connected to the elite black community, Marion Shadd might have, but did not, allow herself to be sheltered from either the struggles of blacks or of women. When she died on 6 March 1943, she left a farewell gift of $1,000 to the Phillis Wheatley YWCA, and $5,000 to be used for scholarships to women graduates of the Armstrong High School.

The Marion Shadd School

There is a footnote to the story of Marion Shadd and her influence in the Washington, D.C., school system. In 1956 a new school was built at 56th and East Capitol streets, S.E., and named for Marion P. Shadd. The biographical directory of the public schools of the District of Columbia contains an entry for Miss Shadd, tracing her career as a teacher and as an administrator. It says in part: "Miss Shadd, a lady of highest character traits and possessed of brilliant intelligence, was deeply devoted to the cause of public education in the city of Washington. Possessed of high ideals, she stimulated all those who came under her wise guidance and leadership to contribute their very best for the education of young children."

The Shadd School serves about six hundred children, from prekindergarten to sixth grade, all of whom were African Americans in April 1992. The school was segregated by design in Miss Shadd's day, and population trends and housing patterns keep it so today. Reading and math are considered crucial subjects, and the children understand that there are skills to be learned at each grade level. Cooperative learning is fostered in the classroom, and a peer coaching program encourages children to keep up their grades, have a positive attitude, and help others. Teachers, too, work in teams, and the school schedule is arranged so that they can plan together and collaborate in teaching. Volunteers from the community, about fifteen each day, participate with the teachers and children. The children's recitations convey a sense of community, responsibility for self and for others that does not end with the school day. Programs include a Junior Citizens Corps, whose members declare themselves willing to help anyone who needs help; an after-school study program in which three teachers offer extra help in reading and math four days a week; basketball for fifth-grade boys; school-crossing guards; and Girl Scouts.

A picture of Marion Shadd hangs in a prominent place in the hallway and every person who works at the Shadd School receives a short biography of Marion Shadd. We are "very much carrying on what she started," says the principal.[77]

Teachers do make a difference, by their day-to-day encouragement and the goals they set for the children in their care, by their attention to the challenges the children face outside the protective walls of the school, and by the pride they have in the children's accomplishments. These characteristics were palpable in the classroom and in the principal's office. They and the children respect the legacy of Miss Marion Purnell Shadd, who had shared their city and who had worked throughout her life to create a school and a system where children would receive an education worthy of a free people.

NOTES

1. Bettye Collier-Thomas, "The Impact of Black Women in Education: An Historical Overview," *Journal of Negro Education* 51 (1982): 173–80.

2. I am deeply indebted to Mrs. Brenda Edmonds Wallace, who discussed the history of the Shadd family, of which she is a member, with me at length on several occasions. She also copied and sent me both unpublished family documents and published articles from which I have drawn the facts about Marion Shadd's immediate family.

3. Gwendolyn Robinson and John W. Robinson, *Seek the Truth: A Story of*

Chatham's Black Community (Chatham, Ontario: Privately printed, 1989), 3.

4. Unpublished family document courtesy of Mrs. Wallace.

5. Robinson and Robinson, *Seek the Truth,* 3.

6. Colin A. Thomson, "Doc Shadd," *Saskatchewan History* (1977): 44.

7. Unpublished family document, courtesy of Mrs. Wallace.

8. Henry S. Robinson, "Furman Jeremiah Shadd, MD: 1852–1908," *Journal of the National Medical Association* 72 (1980): 151.

9. George F.T. Cook, "Annual Report of the Superintendent of the Colored Schools of Washington and Georgetown," *Twenty-fifth Annual Report of the Board of Trustees of Washington, D.C. (1871–72),* 12.

10. Ibid., 28.

11. *Register of the State Normal School,* "Entrance and Graduation Register," Framingham State College Archives.

12. Lillian G. Dabney, *History of Schools for Negroes in the District of Columbia, 1807–1947* (Washington, D.C.: Catholic University of America Press, 1949), 248.

13. Sandra Fitzpatrick and Maria R. Goodwin, *The Guide to Black Washington* (New York: Hippocrene Books, 1990), 89.

14. Ibid.; see also Barbara Solomon, *In the Company of Educated Women* (New Haven: Yale University Press, 1985), 76; Mary J. Patterson was listed in the 1871–72 board of trustees report as a teacher in the preparatory high school at a salary of $900, and Richard T. Greener as the principal.

15. *Annual Report of the Board of Trustees (1871–72),* 117.

16. Robert C. Morris, *Reading, 'Riting, and Reconstruction: The Education of Freedmen in the South 1861–1870* (Chicago: University of Chicago Press, 1981), 160.

17. Afua Cooper, "The Search for Mary Bibb, Black Woman Teacher in Nineteenth-Century Canada West," *Ontario History* 83 (1991): 39–54.

18. Thomson, "Doc Shadd," 42.

19. Cook, "Superintendent's Report," 27.

20. *Annual Report of the Board of Trustees (1871–72),* 72.

21. Beverly J. Weiss, "Growth and Outreach," in *Pioneers in Education: A History of Framingham State College* (Framingham: Privately printed, 1989), 15–30.

22. "Catalogue and Circular of the State Normal School at Framingham, Massachusetts for the Term Ending January 22, 1874," Framingham State College Archives.

23. Ibid., 10.

24. Handwritten journals of the day-to-day activities at the Normal School were maintained from the earliest days of the school. Some of these have survived in the archives of the Framingham State College Alumni.

25. Both Marion Shadd and Catherine Slade appeared on the list of teachers in the *Annual Report of the Board of Trustees (1877–78).* Slade was hired to teach the second grade at a salary of $400 despite the fact that she had not been able to pass the course at Framingham Normal School.

26. Dabney, *History of Schools for Negroes,* 243.

27. Ibid., 244.

28. Ibid.

29. George F. T. Cook, "Report of the Superintendent for the Colored Schools," *Annual Report of the Board of Trustees (1891–92),* 177.

30. Dabney, *History of Schools for Negroes,* 245.

31. Cook, "Superintendent's Report," 179. This section of Cook's report was entitled "A Retrospect," and in it he traced the history of schools for colored children in Washington and Georgetown, specifically naming the men and women, black and white, who organized schools and who had taught in them since 1807.

32. Dabney, *History of Schools for Negroes,* 245.

33. *Annual Report of the Board of Trustees (1876–77)*.

34. Ibid.

35. Ibid.

36. *Annual Report of the Board of Trustees (1871–72)*, 9.

37. *Annual Report of the Board of Trustees (1877–78)*, 221.

38. Ibid., 320.

39. Ibid.

40. Cook, *Annual Report of the Board of Trustees (1879–80)*.

41. *Annual Report of the Board of Trustees (1889–90)*, 20.

42. *Annual Report of the Board of Trustees (1886–87)*.

43. Cook, *Annual Report of the Board of Trustees (1887–88)*.

44. Cook, *Annual Report of the Board of Trustees (1891–92)*, 160.

45. Cook, *Annual Report of the Board of Trustees (1895–96)*, 153.

46. Powell, *Annual Report of the Board of Trustees (1896–97)*, 11–13.

47. A.T. Stuart, *Annual Report of the Board of Education (1901–02)*, 66.

48. *Annual Report of the Board of Trustees (1898–99)*.

49. *Annual Report of the Board of Education (1901–02)*.

50. *Annual Report of the Board of Education (1906–07)*.

51. Marion P. Shadd, *Annual Report of the Board of Education (1909–10)*, 218.

52. Ibid., 219.

53. Shadd, *Annual Report of the Board of Education (1910–11)*.

54. Shadd, *Annual Report of the Board of Education (1914–15)*, 255.

55. Ibid., 255.

56. Ibid., 256.

57. Ibid., 256.

58. Ibid., 257.

59. Shadd, *Annual Report of the Board of Education (1918–19)*, 258.

60. Ibid., 259.

61. Ibid.

62. Earnest L. Thurston, *Annual Report of the Board of Education (1919–20)*, 194.

63. *Annual Report of the Board of Education (1924–25)*, 84.

64. *Annual Report of the Board of Education (1926–27)*, 27.

65. Vertical files, Washingtoniana Room, Martin Luther King Library.

66. Fitzpatrick and Goodwin, *Black Washington*, 165.

67. "A History of the Phillis Wheatley Young Women's Christian Association, 1905–1930." Furnished by Elizabeth Norris of the National Board of the Young Women's Christian Association, New York, New York.

68. Bettie G. Francis, "The Colored Young Women's Christian Association, Third and Fourth Years Report, May, 1907 to 1909," 4. Library of Congress.

69. Ibid.

70. Fitzpatrick and Goodwin, *Black Washington*, 243.

71. "A History of the Phillis Wheatley YWCA," 5.

72. Ibid., 8; see also Martha McAdoo, "Phyllis Wheatley Y.W.C.A. Passes a Milestone," *Woman's Press*, Washington, D.C., May 1925. According to the YWCA history, Mrs. Martha Allan McAdoo had been the general secretary of the YWCA in Chicago, and on 15 April 1921 she was appointed general secretary in Washington, D.C. By 1921, the YWCA had 3,155 members and a paid staff of six in addition to Mrs. McAdoo.

73. Fitzpatrick and Goodwin, *Black Washington*, 168.

74. "A History of the Phillis Wheatley YWCA," 12.

75. Ibid., 11.

76. Ibid., 18.

77. I wish to thank Mrs. A. Benay Glymph, principal of the Shadd School, for her time and her courtesy. She generously shared with me the information she had about Miss Shadd, including the contact with Mrs. Brenda Edmonds Wallace, and she allowed me to photograph the portrait of Miss Shadd, the only picture of her I have seen.

10 A White Teacher in Alexandria, Virginia: Cora Kelly (1868–1953)

Madelyn Holmes

Cora Kelly, painted by Ina Connaway.

In 1779 Thomas Jefferson submitted a bill to the legislature in the state of Virginia proposing a "whole scheme of education . . . teaching all the children of the State reading, writing, and common arithmetic."[1] Jefferson's proposals never became law, however, and public school education in the South trailed behind that of the North by approximately forty years. In Alexandria, Virginia, it was not until 1871, after the adoption of the state's Underwood Constitution of 1869, that the city instituted a system of public schools. And when it did, Alexandria's newly established elementary schools were divided by sex and by race.

The historic port city of Alexandria, founded by Scottish merchant John Alexander in 1749, is located on the west bank of the Potomac River directly across from the District of Columbia. The town's history is closely associated with George Washington, who lived in adjacent Mount Vernon. The town was ceded to the nation's capital from 1791 to 1847. Reintegrated into the state of Virginia in 1847, it was occupied by Union forces during the Civil War. Even though its prosperity as a seaport was thwarted by the coming of the railways, by 1940 the city's population had reached 33,523.

Prior to 1871, educational facilities in Alexandria were limited and predominantly privately operated. The only public free school for white children in existence was the Alexandria Academy, endowed by George Washington in 1785 for the "education of orphans and other poor children."[2] For African Americans the Freedmen's Bureau had established the Jacobs Free School in 1864, and by 1869 there were two "colored school houses" in Alexandria built by the Freedmen's Bureau.[3]

From 1871 through the early years of the twentieth century, two schools for African Americans and two schools for white children coexisted: Washington School for white boys, Lee School for white girls, Snowden School for "colored" boys, and Hallowell School for "colored" girls.[4]

By the early 1900s white boys were given an option to study high-school subjects in a ninth and tenth grade at the Washington School. All other schools continued to operate eight grades only. By 1908 a separate high school for grades eight through ten enrolled thirty-one white boys.[5]

Alexandria was not acting alone in extending public-school education, for the state of Virginia during the beginning of the twentieth century experienced what has been described as an "educational renaissance."[6] Responding to the results of a citizens' crusade in behalf of public education called the May Campaign, the state enacted among other reforms the Mann High School Act in 1906. That law provided funds to local communities for the establishment of new high schools.[7]

Efforts were soon made to institute high-school education for white girls in Alexandria. By 1911 the first Alexandria High School, a four-year coeducational institution for white students, was established. At the same time, African American children in Alexandria were not able to receive any public schooling beyond the eighth grade. The only high schools available for them were located in Washington, D.C., and countless youths commuted there to further their education. Not until 1936 was a high school for African Americans constructed in Alexandria.

Only during the late 1950s, and because of pressure from the federal government, did a system of racially integrated public schools in Alexandria begin to develop. As elsewhere throughout Virginia, the public-school administration did not immediately take action to comply with the 1954 Supreme Court decision (*Brown v. Board of Education*) that banned segregated schools. According to Patrick Welsh, an Alexandrian high-school English teacher, the seeds of desegregation were sown in 1959. "Negro students could apply to the school superintendent in writing to attend a white school in their neighborhood. However, an 'ability' test was required and had to be sent to a board in Virginia for approval before admittance could be granted."[8] Nevertheless, in February 1959 "five Negro students enrolled in all-white Ramsay Elementary School," as did two children in both the Ficklin School and at Hammond High School.[9] By the fall of 1964 all sectors of the public-school system of the city of Alexandria had been integrated.[10]

WHITE WOMEN SCHOOLTEACHERS

Traditionally, the education of white children in Virginia—as throughout the South—had been a family concern. The wealthy had hired tutors and the middle class utilized the extensive system of private schools and academies. When the state instituted public schools in the 1870s, the reaction of its citizens was similar to the response in Massachusetts in the 1830s. Local schools were established, but the teachers were untrained and the level of education was rudimentary. Working conditions, curricular materials, the attitudes of school superintendents and school boards, and even the personal histories of the women who taught in these schools agreed in large measure with the description of the first generation of women teachers presented in chapter 2.

Throughout the South, "the increasing interest in education coincided with the need of large numbers of women to find paid employment," according to Professor Anne Firor Scott.[11] "Significant social change" took place in the lives of southern women after the Civil War. Not only did the abolition of slavery and the destruction of the plantation system affect southern women, but "the war had created a generation of women without men."[12] Large numbers of women, therefore, had to earn a living.

"Schoolteaching had always been a respectable thing to do, and now it was the first thought of many upper-class women who needed to earn money."[13]

In Alexandria, Virginia, the public-school system offered employment to a considerable number of women. The vast majority were local women who had received no teacher training. From the beginning, women taught and acted as principal at the schools for girls. The superintendent of schools frequently discussed the problem of meager pay for teachers, stating forthrightly in 1888 that "our best teachers must serve eight years before they get the salary paid to a policeman."[14] In 1895, the average annual salary paid to white males was $1,000, and to "colored" males $533. In comparison, white women earned on average $405 per year and "colored" women $375.[15]

Not all of the first generation of teachers were successful and deserving of praise. The superintendent of schools, however, writing in the city's annual reports, included lengthy obituaries of at least two long-serving Alexandrian schoolteachers. The teaching careers of Miss Virginia E. Clarkson and Mrs. Virginia Baggott provide portraits of two early Southern public schoolteachers.

Virginia Clarkson, who died in 1888, was a native Alexandrian. Although "she had not enjoyed many advantages of education," she started teaching poor children before the Civil War.[16] She opened her own private school in 1861, but when public schools were established in 1871 she started teaching at Washington School, the school for white boys. In 1872 she became vice-principal of the Lee School, the school for white girls, and from 1878 until her death in 1888 she held the post of principal there.

> She served faithfully, always at her post, always at work, despite the ever increasing pain of the malady which affected her. When she became unable to walk to her schoolroom, she made arrangements to ride there, and such was her punctuality that never but once . . . did she fail to be present fifteen minutes before the hour, as the rule requires, thus setting a worthy example to her pupils and fellow teachers. Miss Clarkson was a lady of strong will and great power of command, and her government, though kind, was rigid. She preserved excellent order in the building under her charge, and though she was feared yet she was loved by her pupils. She was not a lady of prepossessing exterior or engaging manners, but she concealed under an appearance of sternness, a real kindness which few possess and which extended even to the brute creature, and she manifested her charity by leaving a large portion of the means her careful habits had enabled

her to lay up, for the poor, the sick, and the aged.[17]

Mrs. Virginia Baggott, born in 1820, taught school in her native city for a third of a century. Many of her third-grade students from the Lee School attended her funeral in 1894 at St. Mary's Catholic Church. She had married a farmer, John T. Baggott, before the Civil War and was widowed at the age of fifty in 1871. She taught second and third grades at both Washington and Lee schools, and when she died at the age of seventy-four the school board erected a memorial to her.

"She was connected with the public schools of Alexandria from a period shortly after their establishment, and her capacity, zeal and fidelity materially aided in the carrying on of the great work. . . . The teachers and pupils of the school paid their last tribute to her memory and that her fidelity, industry, skill and patience may remain for the emulation of those who come after her, the board directs this tribute be entered upon its records."[18]

This chapter will describe the following generation of public schoolteachers, those who took their place in an already well-established, segregated school system. It will focus on the career of Cora Webster Kelly, who taught in schools for white children in Alexandria from 1888 to 1943. Even though the city in 1888 was "a rather sleepy, segregated southern community,"[19] the public schools enrolled 1,669 students, of whom 983 were white.[20]

Mrs. Cora Lee Webster Kelly

Cora Lee Webster, who was born in Alexandria in 1868, taught in the city's public schools for fifty-five years. Two years after her death in 1953, the city "honored the late beloved teacher" by naming a new elementary school the Cora Kelly School.[21] Her extraordinary longevity as well as her intimate association with public-school education allows us a vantage point from which to view segregated schoolteaching in the South.

Her father was James F. Webster, city policeman and captain of the Alexandria police force for many years. Her mother, Elizabeth, who never learned to read or write, "kept house" according to the enumeration in the 1870 census. Both of Cora's parents were born in Virginia; the only nineteenth-century immigrant was her father's foreign-born mother. Cora was the third-born child. Her elder brother William became a bricklayer, and she lived in the 1950s with a sister named Catharine.

Cora Webster attended two private schools in Alexandria: St. Mary's Academy and Mount Vernon Institute. St. Mary's, a Catholic school for female students, was established by the Sisters of the Holy Cross in 1869.

When Cora was a student there in the 1870s the school was located at 211 North Fairfax Street. According to Alexandrian lore, the school building had been constructed in 1749 with historic bricks, whose origin had been traced to ballast from a 1600s sailing vessel. Formerly, the school building had been used for a Quaker school, but during the Civil War it had been turned into a hospital. The Catholic church bought the building "with the money that the hospital's patients had left with a priest at St. Mary's parish and that had never been reclaimed."[22] St. Mary's Academy remained small during Cora's tenure, with six sisters as teachers and ninety female students in elementary and secondary grades.

Because Cora Webster graduated from Mount Vernon Institute, we can assume that she attended St. Mary's Academy for her early schooling only. Mount Vernon Institute for young ladies was a private school operated on South Washington Street by Miss Mary A. Roach in the late nineteenth century. There is no extant record of the school's curriculum, but presumably Miss Webster received no explicit teacher training there.

Even though Cora Webster did not acquire professional training before beginning her long career as a teacher, there did exist in Virginia at that time two state normal schools, one for white women and one for "colored persons." In 1883, Virginia Normal and Collegiate Institute for Colored Persons, the state's first public-teacher training institution, was established in Petersburg. The following year the State Female Normal School for white women opened in Farmville.

During the summer of 1888 at the outset of Miss Webster's tenure as teacher at the Washington School, Alexandria hosted a Peabody Normal Institute.[23] It is highly likely that she attended. Held for three weeks and financed by the Peabody Education Fund, it attracted 260 people from Virginia and five other states. They heard distinguished educators and professors lecture on pedagogy, Chaucer and the beginnings of English grammar, physiology, hygiene, and calisthenics. Richard L. Carne, superintendent of schools in Alexandria and organizer of the normal institute, reported that Virginia's superintendent of public instruction had also addressed the meeting. In Carne's report, he notes that during one of the organized excursions to Washington, the group of teachers "were specially received by the President of the United States."[24]

In addition to hosting the Peabody Normal Institute, Mr. Carne regularly conducted teachers' institutes, holding separate meetings "on one Saturday of each month for white and for colored teachers, at which various subjects relative to teaching have been discussed."[25] The principal of Washington School, Theodore H. Ficklin, A.M., assisted him in the instruction of arithmetic and grammar. During Cora Kelly's long tenure as a public-school teacher she also attended summer normal institutes in Charlottesville, Virginia, and in Knoxville, Tennessee.

Miss Cora Lee Webster began teaching third grade at Washington School in 1888, at a starting salary of $250. That school served as Alexandria's sole public school for white boys, enrolling a total of 576 students in grades one through eight. The school employed ten teachers, eight of whom were women. The school was headed by a male principal, who also taught seventh and eighth grades, and another man taught the sixth grade. Miss Webster taught fifty-two boys whose average age was ten. From her first year, she earned a reputation as a strict disciplinarian. She reported using corporal punishment on sixty-two occasions, primarily for misconduct but also for truancy and tardiness.[26]

In January 1889 the pupils of Washington School ceremoniously moved into a new building that School Superintendent Carne described enthusiastically: "The new house has fully answered our expectations as to its usefulness. It has eight large rooms, each seating fifty boys, with broad aisles and ceilings 13 and 14 feet high, wide halls and stair cases, and the best system of heating and ventilation known—the Smead-Ruttan."[27]

Sometime during the first decade of the twentieth century the name of Miss Cora Lee Webster, as teacher at the Washington School, disappeared from school records in Alexandria and in its place the name Mrs. Cora L. Kelly appeared. In the 1907 *City Directory* William P.H. Kelley, pipe fitter, is listed as residing at 408 Wilkes Street in addition to James F. Webster, Cora's father. In the 1915 *City Directory,* however, only Mrs. Cora L. Kelly and her father are listed at that address. From then on she was known as Mrs. Kelly, although her students continued to call her "Miss Kelly." No further record of her marriage or husband has been discovered.

Although it is known that Cora Webster taught third and fourth grades at Washington School, it is difficult to determine the nature of what she taught to her students. The annual reports written by the city superintendent of public schools give some idea. In 1908, School Superintendent Kosciusko Kemper listed textbooks that the state board of education and the city school board had adopted for use in primary- and grammar-school classes.

For teaching reading, two series of readers were mentioned: *Stepping Stones to Literature* and *Graded Classics Readers.* The first series of readers emphasized children's interests, and in line with progressive attitudes included imaginative stories, poetry, and selections to encourage classroom conversation. In the preface to *A Third Reader,* the authors suggest that the teacher read the "best poems" to the children. Furthermore, "every lesson suggests topics for outside reading, for study, and for conversation. The story of "The Flax" for instance, leads directly to conversation about fabrics."[28] In the *Fourth Reader*, children are introduced to mythology. The authors inform the teacher that they are stressing "myth and wonder—those subjects which appeal to the child's imagination and carry him out of his limited environment into a larger world."[29]

The other reading series, *Graded Classics,* was published in 1901 by the B.F. Johnson Company in Richmond, Virginia. The reading selections in that series, compiled by Margaret Winifred Haliburton and Frank Turner Novell, included a number of Southern stories as well as a number of Biblical references. The Southern bias is especially pronounced in *The Fourth Reader,* with several selections set during the Civil War. The authors describe the story "Two Little Confederates" by Thomas Nelson Page as "an interesting book for children . . . full of stirring incidents."[30]

For the study of geography, *Frye's First Course in Geography* by Alexis Everett Frye was listed. This geography textbook, published in 1906, stressed the learning of "leading facts" especially about commerce and the United States. In sections entitled "Helps," the author provides questions for the pupils to answer "not in the words of the book but in their own language."[31] The chapter on Races of Men teaches children that black people in middle Africa and many of the red men in South America are savages. The author never actually defines the word *savage.* He seems, however, to exclude the "many Negroes (who) have been carried to lands where white people live. These black people have learned to live as the white people do."[32] His description of the white race concludes: "The white people have the best schools in the world."[33]

The state Board of Public Instruction required that all state public schools teach the history of Virginia. Mary Tucker Magill wrote a textbook in 1873 that was adopted by the state for use in fourth and fifth grades. When Miss Webster began teaching third grade in 1888, Magill's *History of Virginia* had been adopted for use in the city of Alexandria. Magill started out describing Virginia's history from the year 1492 and ended in 1859 with John Brown's raid. She justified her termination date in the following way: "This was the commencement of a series of events which constitute a new era in the history of Virginia, too new to be described with that spirit of calmness and impartiality which should ever characterize the historian."[34] In 1890 the publisher encouraged her to enlarge the history text, and she added "Virginia's part in the great struggle between the States." So that at the beginning of the twentieth century, children in Cora Kelly's classes were learning about the history of Virginia from 1492 to 1865. Everything that happened after the Civil War was too contemporary to teach in a public school classroom. Similarly, Mary Magill's *Stories from Virginia History,* published in 1897, ended with ten stories about generals in the Civil War. The concluding story in the book was based on a personal reminiscence about a Confederate soldier's heroic raid on a Northern encampment.

Magill explicitly stated in the preface to her history book that she had included profiles of heroes for young Virginians to emulate. She hoped that the student "may strive to imitate the many worthy examples held up before him in its pages."[35] In addition to military heroes from the Revolutionary War and the Civil War, she praised Hiawatha, Pocahontas, Patrick Henry, Nathaniel Bacon, George Washington, John Randolph, Marquis de Lafayette, Thomas Jefferson, and James Monroe. Magill's *History of Virginia* reinforces a strictly Southern view of history. She graphically describes the scalping practices of the Indians, the condemnatory character of John Brown, and she romanticizes the plantation system of antebellum Virginia.

Mrs. Kelly continued to teach young boys at the Washington School throughout World War I. One of her students, Robert Howard, a retired food broker in Alexandria, remembered her vividly.[36] He was born in 1908 and started school, as was customary, at the age of six. Mrs. Kelly was his third-grade teacher in 1916. "I remember that she was especially thorough. She carried a long ruler and if a student misspelled the capital of a state, she would smack him on the hand." He did not recall getting smacked himself, but geography lessons were what he associated especially with Mrs. Kelly.

When a new coeducational elementary school was built in the early 1920s Mrs. Kelly transferred to Jefferson School, where she taught seventh grade. Her beginning salary in that position was $1,250 for the 1923–24 school year. Mrs. Kelly remained at Jefferson School until her retirement in 1943. Many local inhabitants of Alexandria remember Mrs. Kelly as their "strict teacher." William Smith, who was her student in 1936, contends that she was tough but a "fair person" and "a great teacher."[37] He described how she taught English grammar, geography, and history. "She was of the old school and required memorization. She wrote on the blackboard what you had to learn, and we learned it." Her discipline was legendary. Many students not only "stood in awe of her," he recalled, but were "scared to death of her." Her thinking belonged to the past as well, for as Mr. Smith emphasized she was thoroughly "pro-Confederate." According to Hilda Pullman, Mrs. Kelly's niece, "she also taught her pupils how to be good citizens and to live a good religious and moral life."[38]

Local Alexandrians, many of whom grew up to be judges, attorneys, and politicians, remembered being disciplined by Mrs. Kelly. In her obituary, she was quoted as having stated that "I had a 15-inch paddle and I never hesitated to use it."[39]

She taught an entire generation of students during her twenty years at Jefferson School. During the heart of the economic depression in 1933, she saw her salary fall to $1,200, but in 1936 she was promoted to assistant principal with a salary of $1,400. When she retired from the school system at the age of seventy-five in June 1943, her salary had reached $1,700.

During her ten years in retirement, Mrs. Kelly continued to live in Alexandria and maintained a strong interest in education. In 1952 she appeared on a Washington, D.C., television program entitled "Schools of Long Ago," and she taught "children in the neighborhood almost up to her last day."[40] She never forgot her "boys," as she referred to her former students. A few days before her death, "she got up out of her sick bed and went to the polls to vote for her boys—Armistead Boothe and Leroy Bendheim."[41]

She died at the age of eighty-five on 9 November 1953. A funeral Mass was held at St. Mary's Catholic Church and the headline of her obituary in the local newspaper read "Mrs. Cora Kelly, City Teacher, Dies; Alexandria Mourns Her Passing."[42]

On 15 December 1955 a newly constructed elementary school in northeastern Alexandria was dedicated and named for Cora Kelly. The original school building had twenty-three classrooms and an auditorium and accommodated 725 pupils. In 1959, when Alexandria's public schools began the embittered process of desegregation, the white Cora Kelly School served 553 students. In the mid-1960s, the population around the school began to change, becoming primarily African American. When a policy of busing was instituted in Alexandria to enforce elementary-school desegregation, Cora Kelly School was paired with a white school in the northwest section of the city. In 1984, the school board "approved an elementary redistricting plan that dissolved two pairings. . . . Cora Kelly was made a modified neighborhood school with a magnet component that offered computer science and laboratory science instruction."[43]

NOTES

1. Quoted in *Thomas Jefferson and Education in a Republic*, ed. Charles Flinn Arrowood (New York: McGraw Hill, 1930; repr. 1971), 83.

2. "Alexandria Academy," *William and Mary Quarterly* 1, series 2 (1921): 58.

3. "Schools," Vertical files, Lloyd House, Alexandria Public Library, Alexandria, Virginia.

4. John D. Macoll, ed. *Alexandria A Towne in Transition, 1800–1900* (Alexandria, Va.: Alexandria Bicentennial Commission, 1977), 109.

5. Alexandria Superintendent of Public Schools, *Annual Report of 1908–09*, 11.

6. J. L. Blair Buck, *The Development of Public Schools in Virginia 1607–1952* (Richmond: Commonwealth of Virginia State Board of Education, 1952), 121.

7. Raymond H. Pulley, *Old Virginia Restored: An Interpretation of the Progressive Impulse 1870–1930* (Charlottesville: University Press of Virginia, 1968), 142.

8. Patrick Welsh, *Tales Out of School* (New York: Viking Penguin, 1986), 95.

9. *Washington Post,* 11 February 1959.

10. *Memories of Parker-Gray School 1920–1965* (Alexandria: Privately printed, 1965), 11.

11. Ann Firor Scott, *The Southern Lady from Pedestal to Politics 1830–1930* (Chicago: University of Chicago Press, 1970), 111.

12. Ibid., 106.

13. Ibid., 111.

14. Alexandria Superintendent of Public Schools, *Annual Report of 1887–8,* 10.

15. Alexandria Superintendent of Public Schools, *Annual Report of 1894–95,* 92.

16. Alexandria Superintendent of Public Schools, *Annual Report of 1887–8,* 4–5.

17. Ibid.

18. Alexandria Superintendent of Public Schools, *Annual Report of 1893–94,* 106.

19. Welsh, *Tales,* 8.

20. Alexandria Superintendent of Public Schools, *Annual Report of 1889–90,* 4.

21. Jean Moore Rhodes, "Cora Kelly School Dedication Honors Late Beloved Teacher," *Alexandria Gazette,* 16 December 1955.

22. Patricia King, "Academy Has Vivid History," *Alexandria Gazette,* 1 March 1969.

23. George Peabody of Danvers, Massachusetts supported a wide range of educational forums throughout the South. For a description of the Peabody Educational Fund in Virginia, see Buck, *The Development of Public Schools in Virginia,* 86–87.

24. Alexandria Superintendent of Public Schools, *Annual Report of 1887–8,* 6.

25. Ibid., 5.

26. Alexandria Superintendent of Public Schools, *Annual Report of 1888–9,* 17.

27. Ibid., 7.

28. Sarah Louise Arnold and Charles B. Gilbert, *Stepping Stones to Literature, A Third Reader* (Boston: Silver, Burdett and Company, 1897), v.

29. Arnold and Gilbert, *Stepping Stones to Literature, Fourth Reader,* 5.

30. Margaret Winifred Haliburton and Frank Turner Novell, *Graded Classics, The Fourth Reader* (Richmond: B.F. Johnson, 1901), 298.

31. Alexis Everett Frye, *Frye's First Course in Geography* (Boston: Ginn, 1906), preface.

32. Ibid., 32.

33. Ibid., 36.

34. Mary Tucker Magill, *History of Virginia* (Lynchburg, Va.: J. P. Bell, 1882), 257.

35. Ibid., vi.

36. Personal interview with Robert Howard, Alexandria, March 1993.

37. Telephone interview with William Smith, Alexandria, April 1993.

38. *Alexandria Gazette,* 16 December 1955.

39. Quoted in obituary, *Alexandria Gazette,* 10 November 1953.

40. Ibid.

41. *Alexandria Gazette,* 16 December 1955.

42. *Alexandria Gazette,* 10 November 1953.

43. "History of Cora Kelly Magnet School" (Alexandria: Cora Kelly School publication), 2.

11 CONCLUSION: IN PRAISE OF TEACHERS, PAST AND PRESENT

From its inception in the United States, public education, or organized education for the masses, has meant both opportunity for women and the occasion for their economic exploitation. It created opportunity in that education became more available to women, and more jobs opened to them outside the home. On the other hand the proliferation of public schools led to exploitation of women, because the jobs generally had low status and low salaries, and women's entry into teaching was often predicated on the fact that they could be hired at lower wages than men. With each advance in extending educational services to more children, such as mandating school attendance, came an increased demand for teachers. That often meant at least a temporary reduction in professional requirements and a concomitant reduction in status and salaries.

As women began to take on teaching positions, there were those who believed that they were superior teachers; the records are replete with statements that schools fared better under the direction of women than under men, especially in matters of discipline and order. Women were promoted to positions as principals when the school population made that step necessary and feasible, but advancement to superintendencies was not common. In fact, until late in the nineteenth century school superintendents were often influential men with little or no school experience.

Just as teaching provided one of the first occupations outside the home for New England women, teaching became one of the first options for educated blacks, who also embraced the opportunity, as women had done, with missionary zeal for the cause and for their own personal advancement. Women teachers of color faced all of the same career and salary disparities as their white sisters, and, in addition, the burden that black teachers were regularly paid even less than white teachers. They also faced the problem of increased demand leading to lowered qualifications for teachers along with lowered status and salaries. Both compulsory school attendance and black communities' preference for teachers of color created a demand with the same undesirable result.

Schoolteaching in the twentieth century offered opportunities to American women whose families had immigrated to the United States from Europe. Public schools provided education and training to children of immigrants. If a young woman succeeded in school, she could hope to step into self-supporting employment as a teacher and thereby achieve status in American society and in her community.

The biographical sketches of women teachers and principals in this book cover a time span from the early nineteenth century to the latter half of the twentieth century, and range geographically from Massachusetts to California, from Michigan to Virginia and Kentucky, and across the Midwest. Our research has convinced us that broad-stroke, composite descriptions of teachers have obscured both the strengths women have brought and continue to bring to the teaching profession, and the nature of societal problems for which they often have borne the onus, however unrealistic that may have been.

Against the backdrop of ever-present discrimination, prejudice, low expectations, and limited opportunities for education and employment, the women profiled in this book, and countless millions like them, lived lives that were, as Ellen Hyde said, "grand." They seem not to have wasted time fretting about the constraints, but rather to have seized the opportunities for "autonomy and advancement" and the responsibilities that were open to them.[1] In the process, they made not only satisfying lives for themselves, but also opened new opportunities for their students and others simply by doing what they did very well. Some, for example Ellen Hyde and Lelia Patridge, worked quite consciously to effect change in teaching or in the preparation of teachers. Many more made their impact every day in the classroom simply by demonstrating regard for their students, their skill in teaching, and their love of learning.

Throughout the book we have been mindful that women public schoolteachers have functioned as part of a public school establishment. Many have taught successfully, even brilliantly, but they taught a curriculum stipulated by the society of which they were a part. In order to understand more fully the impact of women teachers on American society, therefore, we have included descriptions of subjects and teaching practices, recognizing that a schoolteacher not only creates social relationships with children but also transmits her society's values to the following generation.

During the decades before the Civil War, public schoolteachers using textbooks steeped in Protestant moral traditions that espoused an ethnocentric vision of the world created proud young citizens of the new nation. After the 1860s when public schools were established throughout the Southern, Midwestern and Western United States, schoolteachers taught a more inclusive nationalism using teaching materials that emphasized values appropriate to an emerging industrial society. By the beginning of the twentieth century, progressive ideas associated with John Dewey began to permeate public schools, emphasizing child-centered curricula more attuned to the psychological development of the child. Nonetheless, regional differences continued to influence the way teachers related to their students. In the segregated schools of the South, Caucasian public schoolteachers reinforced pro-Confederate attitudes, and in the West public schoolteachers embraced informality and encouraged free expression. During the decades following World War II, concepts of progressive education were adopted in one form or another throughout the United States, with public schoolteachers blending their communities' with their own interpretations.

There has been a recurrent debate in American society about the goals of education. Some people have seen schooling as a unifying and cohesive force that prepares students, particularly those from minority and ethnic groups, to fit into or accommodate to the existing social and political system. Others emphasize the role of schooling in preparing informed citizens who can participate effectively in democratic and political institutions to bring about necessary changes. Communities, school boards, and educational hierarchies who prescribe curriculum and textbooks strongly influence the extent to which these goals are emphasized, but the teacher in the classroom chooses as well. She communicates her choices through the relationships she establishes with her students and the ways in which she creates opportunities for making comparisons, engaging in critical thinking, and articulating a reasoned position.

Whereas curricula in public schools have undergone extensive changes over the past century and a half, the elements regarded by reformers as necessary for good teaching have remained essentially unchanged over the years. Although the words used to describe the "new" education (and it is always regarded as new) reflect the time and place, the emphasis has continued to be on reasoning over rote learning; investigation and discovery over memorization; cooperative, peer learning; discipline and achievement based on the joy of learning; learning that begins with common everyday experiences; and child study as the teacher's best guide to effective practice. Moreover, throughout the decades spanned by these narratives, there have always been teachers who, through training or their own intuitive processes, have taught in a manner consistent with these ideas; seldom, if ever, have reformers or historians recognized such teachers.

This book devotes considerable attention to the development of the first normal school in the United States, because the concepts of pedagogy formulated there and disseminated through the careers of its graduates have influenced the course of public education throughout the country. As the first secretary of the Massachusetts Board of Education, Horace Mann became the dynamo and the evangelist for public schools, and the normal schools were the centerpiece of the plan.

The selection of Cyrus Peirce as principal of the Normal School in Lexington set that school on a course that led toward the recognition of teaching as a profession. What made Peirce and the school he administered outstanding was his determination to teach both in the Normal School and in the Model School by principles based on an understanding of "the nature of children, of youthful developments." He "aimed to make better teachers . . . who would teach more philosophically, more in harmony with the natural development of the young mind, with a truer regard to the order and connection in which the different branches of knowledge should be presented to it. . . ."[2] In the language of today's education literature, Peirce might have said that he wanted teaching to be more reflective, to be based on studies of child and cognitive development, and that he wanted teachers better educated in the content areas they teach so they can see the connections among subjects and with the children's knowledge.

Peirce transmitted to those early graduates ideals of service to society, a philosophy of education characterized by active, self-directed, cooperative learning, and a sense of efficacy. The narratives about Electa Lincoln Walton and Ellen Hyde describe the continuity in the philosophy and practice at the Normal School over the rest of the century; Catherine Tilden Avery, Lelia Patridge, and Marion Shadd are examples of women who carried the philosophy and the teaching skills to other states. The normal-school graduates who appear in these pages were remarkable women, and there have been many others who made special contributions to teaching and to women's history.

WOMEN TEACHERS TODAY

The first normal school, which opened in Lexington in 1839, is today Framingham State College, a liberal arts college serving approximately three thousand students with twenty-five majors. There are still education majors, and they study in the Child Development Laboratory with Professor Jeanne Canelli, who was graduated from the college in 1970. The laboratory resembles the practice school of one hundred years ago in that Jeanne serves as the teacher for the class of four-year-olds as well as for the college students, who observe and teach under her supervision. As was true in the days of Ellen Hyde, students entering the laboratory find a bright, attractive room filled with the pleasant babble of children at their work. Everywhere there are pictures, objects, and books that connect the children to the familiar world of home and neighborhood and lead them into an exploration of new territory.

For the college students as well as the children in the laboratory school Jeanne emphasizes investigation and discovery, reasoning about observations, cooperation with peers, and recognizing the inherent motivation and pleasure in learning. Her classroom is integrated with respect to the curriculum content and the cultural mix of children who attend. More recently, children with physical challenges have been included in the class. As part of an innovative project, a multidisciplinary team of specialists works with all of the children in the classroom setting.

Jeanne Canelli is but one of the many competent, dedicated teachers today who, like teachers of the past, demonstrate their skill in teaching and their love of learning every day in the classroom. They open new opportunities for others simply by doing their work very well.

Since 1986, schools throughout the United States and abroad have been named for Christa Corrigan McAuliffe, the Teacher in Space and a 1970 graduate of Framingham State College. Christa McAuliffe, a social-studies teacher, died in the *Challenger* space shuttle tragedy, along with six other members of the crew, on a mission designed to focus public attention on educational issues and the role of teachers. In the wake of the tragedy, memorials to the astronauts were established, many in the form of scholarships and programs to carry on the goals of the mission. Among these initiatives is the Christa McAuliffe Fellowship Program, a federally funded project that recognizes outstanding classroom teachers and provides fellowships to enhance their work.[3] We can see the themes and issues of the past in their projects, as well as the ways in which excellent teachers are addressing the dilemmas and challenges of today.

These teachers are aware that there are still inequalities in education for a number of different reasons, and some seek to broaden opportunities and alleviate inequities for all students in their communities. Judith Barnes, a fifth-grade teacher in Alabama, prepared for her project by taking graduate courses in physics and astronomy. She has developed interactive science programs for elementary students, using a portable planetarium and other sophisticated electronic equipment, as well as up-to-date books in science, so that she can bring children in the rural areas some of the technological advances in education that otherwise would be unavailable to them. Vivian E. Kean's project in New Jersey is designed to provide elementary-school girls and minority students in mathematics and science with academic enrichment and after-school programs.

Benita Miller in New York, who began as a teacher in Spanish and French, has initiated an English-as-a-Second-Language program in which culture as well as language becomes a shared experience. A high-school English teacher in Montana, Dorothea M. Susag, has been developing a Native American literature curriculum based on her studies at the University of Montana and her visits to Native American communities in the state. The curriculum will focus on the oral tradition and contemporary life of Native American people.

Donna Butler, a music educator in New Hampshire, is dedicated to facilitating the integration of children with special needs into mainstream schools using the resources of the arts curriculum. Becky Goodwin, an elementary-school teacher in Kansas, has designed an environmental laboratory, both indoors and outdoors, with and for the deaf children she teaches.

Elaine Capobianco has taken on the problem of inequality with respect to both race and sex. She is a teacher in the city of Boston and a 1979 graduate of Framingham State College. Her project, "Patchwork of Dreams," was designed as an interdisciplinary experience for her fifth-grade students to study "diverse groups of people on their road to freedom." Quilts were used as the vehicle for the children to begin their year-long study of nineteenth-century women in the textile mills of the North and people of color in bondage on the cotton plantations of the South, and to explore the connections between them. As Mrs. Capobianco began her project she wrote:

> Aside from the knowledge gained, this project will enhance the students' self-esteem by allowing them a different perspective of history, one that they will develop independently as researchers viewing history through their own eyes. They will enhance their critical thinking skills and sharpen their abilities to find and process information. The students will take pride in their own discoveries. If children discover something new by themselves, they own it forever.[4]

Another continuing theme from the past is that teachers need to be more thoroughly educated both in the subjects they teach and in the art of pedagogy. Many McAuliffe fellows, therefore, use their awards to pay for sabbaticals to attend college, or to prepare workshops and materials for other teachers. Fa'auisa M. Sotoa in American Samoa has used her fellowship for graduate study at the University of Wisconsin so that she will be able to work more effectively with students in the vocational-education program. Vicki Fortson Shirley, a high-school mathematics teacher in Mississippi, is assisting other teachers to increase their skills in mathematics and in using the available technology, such as computers and graphing calculators, in their teaching.

Marilee Donovan, an elementary-school teacher in Idaho, is introducing her colleagues to peer coaching to enhance their skills in teaching science and to provide professional development. Connie Nerby in Wyoming directed her energies toward helping teachers understand new directions in assessing student progress, an increasingly important issue as new instructional techniques are developed.

Teachers are still preparing students for citizenship and for jobs by helping them to learn about their environment and how to communicate effectively. Many teachers today teach reading and writing within the context of a theme or project. Charlotte B. Hughes, a first-grade teacher in Delaware, calls her project "Whole Language with an Environmental Twist"; she builds her curriculum around environmental literature and observations of the natural world. Cynthia Chun, an elementary schoolteacher in California, assists her fourth- and fifth-grade students in producing a monthly television magazine on a local television station. Her goal is to assist them in developing effective communication skills.

These are a few of the women teachers selected as the 1992–93 Christa McAuliffe fellows. They are representative of excellent classroom teachers throughout the United States. Taken together, the projects encompass all of the subjects teachers teach, and there are teachers from every elementary and high-school grade. Some of the projects affect the children directly, and others seek to improve the knowledge and skills of those who teach. They all represent issues and subjects these teachers think are important and can be done better. Their themes are as old as public education; their tools are state-of-the-art.

In this book we have explored the careers and the lives of invisible women with the hope of making them visible; they deserve to be remembered for their many acts of service, great and small. We also think that those who would understand our schools better, as they were in the past and as they are today, with their strengths as well as their shortcomings, may find new insights in the lives and work of those who succeed despite the odds. It seems abundantly clear that excellent teachers do know what is needed to make our schools better, and they continue to work toward that end as good teachers have always done.

Why do excellent, intelligent, skillful teachers who obviously have other career choices choose to stay in the classroom and teach our children year after year? The McAuliffe fellows had no difficulty answering:

Seeing the light bulbs come on in children's faces.

Children are our greatest resource—I know I make a difference.

The motivation to teach comes from the excitement of learning.[5]

Ellen Hyde had it right more than one hundred years ago: "To hear lessons and control restless children six hours a day through thirty-six weeks in the year is wretched drudgery, but to train and develop human minds and characters is the most inspiring work in the world."[6]

NOTES

1. Ann D. Gordon, "Writing the Lives of Women," *NWSA Journal* 2 (1988–89): 223.

2. Arthur O. Norton, *The First Normal School in America: The Journals of Cyrus Peirce and Mary Swift* (Cambridge: Harvard University Press, 1926), 278.

3. The fellowships are directed toward encouraging excellent teachers to continue their education, develop innovative programs for their schools or districts, and, in general, to engage in activities to improve teachers' skills and the quality of the education offered to students. Approximately two million dollars each year has been distributed among the states and territories for this work. From the McAuliffe Program's inception through the 1992–93 school year, 523 teachers from all fifty states, Washington, D.C., American Samoa, Guam, the North Mariana Islands, Palau, Puerto Rico, and the Virgin Islands have received awards. Information courtesy the U.S. Department of Education, Office of Elementary and Secondary Teaching.

4. From material submitted to the Christa Corrigan McAuliffe Center by Elaine Capobianco.

5. At the August 1993 annual conference the question was asked of the McAuliffe fellows, and those were some of the answers. I am indebted to all of the McAuliffe fellows who have shared their work and taught me about teaching in the public schools today.

6. Unpublished material. Framingham State College Alumni Association archives.

12 BIBLIOGRAPHY

Adams, C.F. *The New Departure*. Boston: Estes and Lauriat, 1879.

Addams, Jane. *Jane Addams on Education*. Edited by E.C. Lagemann. New York: Teachers College Press, 1985.

Akers, William J. *Cleveland Schools in the Nineteenth Century*. Cleveland: William Bayne Printing House, 1901.

Annual Reports of the Massachusetts Board of Education.

Armstrong, S.E. *Memories of Old Hampton*. Hampton, Va.: Institute Press, 1909.

Baylor, R.M. *Elizabeth Palmer Peabody, Kindergarten Pioneer*. Philadelphia: University of Pennsylvania Press, 1965.

Bentley, G.R. *A History of the Freedmen's Bureau*. New York: Octagon Books, 1970.

Catalog of the State Normal School at Framingham.

Cheney, Ednah D. *Memoirs of Lucretia Crocker and Abby W. May*. Boston: Massachusetts School Suffrage Association, 1893.

Childs, Ethel B. *History of Stow*. Stow, Mass.: Stow Historical Society, 1983.

Clancy, Paul, and Shirley Elder. *Tip A Biography of Thomas P. O'Neill Speaker of the House*. New York: Macmillan, 1980.

Clifford, Geraldine C. "Man/Woman/Teacher: Gender, Family, and Career in American Educational History." In *American Teachers: Histories of a Profession at Work*. Edited by Donald R. Warren. New York: Macmillan, 1989.

Collier-Thomas, Bettye. "The Impact of Black Women in Education: An Historical Overview." *Journal of Negro Education* 51 (1982): 173–180.

Collins, Catherine, and Douglas Frantz. *Teachers Talking Out of School*. Boston: Little, Brown, 1993.

Cooper, Afua. "The Search for Mary Bibb, Black Woman Teacher in Nineteenth Century Canada West." *Ontario History* 83 (1991): 39–54.

Cremin, Lawrence A. *American Education, The Metropolitan Experience, 1876–1980*. New York: Harper & Row, 1988.

———. *Popular Education and Its Discontents*. New York: Harper & Row, 1990.

Cuban, Larry. "Persistence of Reform in American Schools." In *American Teachers: Histories of a Profession at Work*. Edited by D. Warren. New York: Macmillan, 1989.

Custis, John T. *The Public Schools of Pennsylvania*. Philadelphia: Burk & McFetridge Co., 1897.

Cyr, Ellen M. *The Children's Second Reader*. Boston: Ginn and Co., 1894.

Dabney, Lillian G. *The History of Schools for Negroes in the District of Columbia, 1807–1947*. Washington, D.C.: Catholic University of America Press, 1949.

Dewey, John. *The School and Society*. Chicago: University of Chicago Press, 1899.

Dexter, Edwin G. *A History of Education in the United States*. New York: Macmillan, 1919.

Diner, Hasia R. *Erin's Daughters in America: Irish Immigrant Women in the Nineteenth Century*. Baltimore: Johns Hopkins University Press, 1983.

Du Bois, W.E.B. *The Education of Black People: Ten Critiques, 1906–1960*. Amherst: University of Massachusetts Press, 1973.

Federation of Women's Clubs. *From the Past to the Future: A History of the Massachusetts State Federation of Women's Clubs 1893–1988*. Canaan, N.H.: Phoenix Publications, 1988.

Finkelstein, Barbara J. *Governing the Young: Teacher Behavior in Popular Primary Schools in Nineteenth-Century United States*. London: Falmer Press, 1989.

First State Normal School in America: The State Teachers College at Framingham, Massachusetts. Framingham, Mass.: Alumnae Association of Framingham State College, 1959.

Fishbane, R.B. "The Shallow Boast of Cheapness: Public School Teaching As a Profession in Philadelphia 1865–1890." *Pennsylvania Magazine of History and Biography* 108 (1979): 70.

Fitch, George W., and George W. Colton. *Colton and Fitch's Modern School Geography*. New York: Ivison, Phinney, Blakeman, 1864.

Fitzpatrick, Sandra, and Maria R. Goodwin. *The Guide to Black Washington*. New York: Hippocrene Books, 1990.

Forten, Charlotte L. *The Journal of Charlotte Forten: A Free Negro in the Slave Era*. Edited by Ray A. Billington. New York: W.W. Norton, 1981.

Foster, M. "Constancy, Connectedness, and Constraints in the Lives of African-American Teachers." *NWSA Journal* 3 (1991): 233–261.

Fuller, Wayne E. *The Old Country School*. Chicago: University of Chicago Press, 1982.

Glenn, Charles L., Jr. *The Myth of the Common School*. Amherst, Mass.: University of Massachusetts Press, 1988.

Goodrich, Samuel G. *Peter Parley's Method of Telling About Geography*. New York: Collins & Hannay, 1832.

Grimke, Charlotte Forten. "Personal Recollections of Whittier." *New England Magazine* (June 1893): 468–476.

Gulliford, Andrew. *America's Country Schools*. Washington, D.C.: Preservation Press, 1984.

Guyot, Arnold H. *Guyot's Geographical Series. Intermediate Geography*. New York: Charles Scribner, 1869.

Haskins, James. *Ralph Bunche: A Most Reluctant Hero*. New York: Hawthorn Books, 1974.

Henderson, Mary A.O. *The Early Day History of the Santa Clara School*. Santa Paula, Calif.: Santa Paula Historical Society, 1974.

Herbst, Jurgen. *And Sadly Teach: Teacher Education and Professionalism in American Culture*. Madison: University of Wisconsin Press, 1989.

———. "Nineteenth Century Normal Schools in the United States: A Fresh Look." *History of Education* 9 (1980): 219–227.

———. "Beyond the Debate over Revisionism: Three Educational Pasts Writ Large." *History of Education Quarterly* 20 (1980): 131–145.

———. "Teacher Preparation in the Nineteenth Century." In *American Teachers: Histories of a Profession at Work*. Edited by Donald R. Warren. New York: Macmillan, 1989.

Hillard, George S. *A Fourth Class Reader*. Boston: Hickling, Swan and Brewer, 1857.

———, and L.J. Campbell. *Franklin Second Reader*. Boston: Brewer and Tileston, 1875.

Historical Sketches of the Framingham Normal School. Framingham, Mass.: Alumnae Association of Framingham Normal School, 1914.

Hoffman, Nancy. *Woman's "True" Profession: Voices from the History of Teaching*. Old Westbury, N.Y.: Feminist Press, 1981.

Holmes, Madelyn J. "Unsung Heroines: Women Teachers in Salem before the Civil War." *Essex Institute Historical Collections* 122 (1986): 299–310.

Howe, Julia W., ed. *Representative Women of New England*. Boston: New England Historical Publishing Company, 1904.

Ingham, W.A. *Women of Cleveland and Their Work*. Cleveland: W.A. Ingham, 1893.

Kaestle, Carl F., and M.A. Vinovskis. *Education and Social Change in Nineteenth-Century Massachusetts*. New York: Cambridge University Press, 1980.

Katz, Michael B. *Class, Bureaucracy, and the Schools: The Illusion of Educational Change in America*. New York: Praeger, 1975.

————. *Irony of Early School Reform: Educational Innovation in Mid-Nineteenth Century Massachusetts*. Boston: Beacon Press, 1968.

————. *Reconstructing American Education*. Cambridge: Harvard University Press, 1987.

Kaufman, Paula W. *Women Teachers on the Frontier*. New Haven: Yale University Press, 1984.

Kearney, E.W. *Chicago State College: A Centennial Retrospective*. Chicago: Chicago State College, 1969.

Kidder, Tracy. *Among Schoolchildren*. Boston: Houghton Mifflin, 1989.

Lamson, Mary S., ed. *Records of the First Class of the First State Normal School in America*. Boston: Privately printed, 1903.

Lazerson, Marvin. *Origins of the Urban School: Public Education in Massachusetts, 1870–1915*. Cambridge: Harvard University Press, 1971.

McPherson, J.M. *The Abolitionist Legacy: From Reconstruction to the NAACP*. Princeton: Princeton University Press, 1975.

McWilliams, Carey. *Southern California: An Island on the Land*. Salt Lake City: Peregrine Smith Books, 1946. Reprint, 1983.

Mann, Mary P. *Life of Horace Mann*. Boston: Walker, Fuller, 1865.

Memorial of the Quarter-Centennial Celebration of the Establishment of Normal Schools in America. Boston: C.C.P. Moody, 1866.

Messerli, J. *Horace Mann: A Biography*. New York: Alfred A. Knopf, 1972.

Mitchell, S. Augustus. *Mitchell's Primary Geography*. Philadelphia: Thomas, Cowperthwait, 1843.

Morris, Robert C. *Reading, 'Riting, and Reconstruction: The Education of Freedmen in the South, 1861–1870*. Chicago: University of Chicago Press, 1981.

Morse, Jedidiah. *A New System of Geography*. Boston: Richardson & Lord, 1822.

Nelson, Margaret. "Female Schoolteachers as Community Builders." In *The Teacher's Voice*. Edited by R.J. Altenbaugh. London: Falmer Press, 1992.

Norton, Arthur O. *The First State Normal School in America: The Journals of Cyrus Peirce and Mary Swift*. Cambridge: Harvard University Press, 1926.

Notable American Women 1607–1950: A Biographical Dictionary. Cambridge, Mass.: Belknap Press, 1971.

O'Neill, Thomas P., with William Novak. *Man of the House*. New York: Random House, 1987.

Patridge, Lelia. *Quincy Methods*. New York and Chicago: E.L.Kellogg, 1891.

————. *Notes of Talks on Teaching*. New York and Chicago: E.L. Kellogg, 1883.

Pelton, C. *Series of Outline Maps*. Philadelphia: C. Pelton, 1850.

Perkins, Linda. "The History of Blacks in Teaching." In *American Teachers: Histories of a Profession at Work*. Edited by D. Warren. New York: Macmillan, 1989.

Pioneers in Education: A History of Framingham State College. Framingham, Mass.: Framingham State College, 1989.

Postman, Neil. *Teaching as a Conserving Activity*. New York: Delacorte Press, 1979.

Raitt, R.L. *Campus on a Hill The Story of Santa Paula High School and a Century of Community Yesterdays*. Santa Paula, Calif.: Mehle Printing, 1988.

Records of the First Class of the First State Normal School in America: Established at Lexington, Massachusetts, 1839. Boston: Privately printed, 1903.

Robinson, Gwendolyn, and John W. Robinson. *Seek the Truth: A Story of Chatham's Black Community*. Chatham, Ontario: Privately printed, 1989.

Ronda, Bruce A., ed. *Letters of Elizabeth Palmer Peabody, American Renaissance Woman.* Middletown, Conn.: Wesleyan University Press, 1984.

Rosenberg, R. *Beyond Separate Spheres: Intellectual Roots of Modern Feminism.* New Haven: Yale University Press, 1982.

Sanders, James W. "Catholics and the School Question in Boston: The Cardinal O'Connell Years." In *Catholic Boston: Studies in Religion and Community, 1870–1970.* Edited by R.E. Sullivan and J.M. O'Toole. Boston: Roman Catholic Archbishop of Boston, 1985.

Scharf, J.T., and T. Westcott. *History of Philadelphia 1609–1884.* Vol. III. Philadelphia: L.H. Everts & Co., 1884.

Schroeder, Fred E.H. "The Little Red Schoolhouse." In *Icons of America.* Edited by R.B. Browne and M. Fishwick. Bowling Green, Ohio: Popular Press, 1978.

Scott, Ann F. *Making the Invisible Women Visible.* Urbana and Chicago: University of Chicago Press, 1984.

———. *The Southern Lady: From Pedestal to Politics 1830–1930.* Chicago and London: University of Chicago Press, 1970.

Shapiro, M.S. *Child's Garden: The Kindergarten Movement from Froebel to Dewey.* University Park: Pennsylvania State University Press, 1983.

Shepard, Mary L. *Ships on the Sea.* Boston: Privately printed, 1894.

Shor, Ira. *Empowering Education Critical Teaching for Social Change.* Chicago: University of Chicago Press, 1992.

Smith, D.H. *The Bureau of Education: Its History, Activities and Organization.* Baltimore: Johns Hopkins University Press, 1923.

Smith, Page. *Daughters of the Promised Land.* Boston: Little, Brown, 1970.

Smith, Roswell C. *Smith's First Book in Geography.* Portland, Me.: Sanborn & Carter, 1846.

Solomon, Barbara M. *In the Company of Educated Women: A History of Women and Higher Education in America.* New Haven: Yale University Press, 1985.

State Normal School Framingham, Massachusetts Catalogue of Teachers and Alumnae 1839–1900. Boston: Wright & Potter Printing, 1900.

Stern, Madeline P. *We the Women: Career Firsts of Nineteenth Century America.* New York: Schulte, 1963.

Swan, William D. *The Primary School Reader. Part Second.* Philadelphia: Cowperthwait, Desilver and Butler, 1844.

Tharp, Louise H. *The Peabody Sisters of Salem.* Boston: Little, Brown and Company, 1950. Reprint, 1988.

Thomson, Colin A. "Doc Shadd." *Saskatchewan History* 30 (1977): 44.

Troen, S.K. *The Public and the Schools: Shaping the St. Louis System, 1838–1920.* Columbia: University of Missouri Press, 1975.

Tyack, David. *The One Best System: A History of American Urban Education.* Cambridge: Harvard University Press, 1974.

———, R. Lowe, and E. Hansot. *Public Schools in Hard Times: The Great Depression and Recent Years.* Cambridge: Harvard University Press, 1984.

Van Tassel, David D., ed. *The Encyclopedia of Cleveland History.* Bloomington: Indiana University Press, 1987.

Warren, Donald R. *To Enforce Education: A History of the Founding Years of the United States Office of Education.* Detroit: Wayne State University Press, 1974.

———, ed. *American Teachers: Histories of a Profession at Work.* New York: Macmillan, 1989.

Weiss, Beverly J. "Growth and Outreach." In *Pioneers in Education: A History of Framingham State College.* Framingham, Mass.: Framingham State College, 1989.

Westbrook, R.B. *John Dewey and American Democracy.* Ithaca, N.Y.: Cornell University Press, 1991.

White, Theodore H. *In Search of History: A Personal Expedition.* New York: Harper & Row, 1978.

Wickersham, J.P. *A History of Education in Pennsylvania*. New York: Arno Press and New York Times, 1969.

Woodwell, R.H. *John Greenleaf Whittier: A Biography*. Haverhill, Mass.: Trustees of the J.G. Whittier Homestead, 1985.

Woody, Thomas. *A History of Women's Education in the United States*. New York: Science Press, 1929. Reprint. New York: Octagon Books, 1966.

Wright, Conrad. *The Beginnings of Unitarianism in America*. Hamden, Conn.: Archon Books, 1976.

INDEX

Madelyn Jamison Holmes (left) and Beverly J. Weiss

Madelyn Jamison Holmes is a women's historian and author of *Forgotten Migrants: Foreign Workers in Switzerland before World War I* and articles in *Women's Studies International Forum, The Christian Science Monitor,* United Nations, National Geographic Society, and National Park Service publications. She also has written local history booklets about Salem, Massachusetts and the Woodley Park neighborhood of Washington, D.C. She has taught at Harvard College, Christ's and Trinity Hall Colleges at Cambridge University, George Washington University and the Smithsonian Institution. She is a graduate of Radcliffe College with a Ph.D. from the University of East Anglia in England.

Beverly J. Weiss is a developmental psychologist and educator; Professor Emerita and former director of the Christa Corrigan McAuliffe Center at Framingham State College; Mellon Fellow (1980–81) at Wellesley College Center for Research on Women. She taught at Rutgers University Newark, Harvard Graduate School of Education, and at Boston University where she earned her doctorate. She was editor and co-author of *Pioneers in Education* and has written numerous articles about nineteenth-century women teachers. Weiss has presented papers at conferences of the Massachusetts Psychological Association, Eastern Psychological Association, National Women's Studies Association, Association for Women in Psychology, and the History of Education Society.